W9-CKP-644

A WOMAN'S BOOK OF
NETWORK MARKETING

dream BIG!

BOOST YOUR INCOME NOW • IT'S EASY TO GET STARTED AND SUCCEED • ACHIEVE FINANCIAL INDEPENDENCE WHILE WORKING FROM HOME • LEARN FROM ASTONISHING SUCCESS STORIES OF WOMEN NETWORK MARKETING MILLIONAIRES

CYNTHIA STEWART-COPIER

Adams Media Corporation
Holbrook, Massachusetts

Copyright ©2000, Cynthia Stewart-Copier. All rights reserved.
This book, or parts thereof, may not be reproduced in any form
without permission from the publisher; exceptions are made for
brief excerpts used in published reviews.

Published by
Adams Media Corporation
260 Center Street, Holbrook, MA 02343. U.S.A

ISBN: 1-58062-267-4

Printed in the United States of America.

J I H G F E D C B A

Library of Congress Cataloging-in-Publication Data
Stewart-Copier, Cynthia.
Dream big / Cynthia Stewart-Copier.
      p.   cm.
Includes index.
ISBN 1-58062-267-4
1. Business networks. 2. Women--Social networks. 3. Businesswomen. I. Title.
HD69.S8 S734   2000
650.1'082--dc21   99-089983

This publication is designed to provide accurate and authoritative information with
regard to the subject matter covered. It is sold with the understanding that the publisher is not engaged in rendering legal, accounting, or other professional advice. If
legal advice or other expert assistance is required, the services of a competent professional person should be sought.
      — From a *Declaration of Principles* jointly adopted by a Committee of the
American Bar Association and a Committee of Publishers and Associations

Cover photo ©Larry Williams/Masterfile.

You may reach the author by e-mail at *cynthiacopier@hotmail.com*
or *www.dreambignow.com*

This book is available at quantity discounts for bulk purchases.
For information, call 1-800-872-5627.

Visit our exciting small business Web site: www.businesstown.com

Dedication

To my loving husband and precious children who continue to
encourage me to dream big! And to all the dreamers who
had the courage to chase their dreams.

CONTENTS

SECTION ONE
WHY IT WORKS
WHAT MAKES NETWORKING GREAT

SECTION TWO
HOW IT WORKS
SEVEN STEPS TO SUCCESS

SECTION THREE
WORKING IT
HOW TO MAKE IT WORK FOR YOU

SECTION FOUR
WOMEN OF INFLUENCE
SUCCESS STORIES OF WOMEN AT THE TOP

DREAM BIG

BY RENE REID YARNELL

As we turn the corner of a new millennium, we are seeing significant changes in the way we as women are approaching our lives. More and more are becoming fed up with the inequalities and insecurities of working for someone else. Similarly, many of us who have tried starting our own conventional businesses are just as tired of the headaches and the personal drain to their lives. Millions of women are finding a better way and we are doing it from home.

When Cynthia Stewart-Copier asked me to write a Foreword for her book, as I read through her chapters, I was struck by two similarities between us: our personal climb out of devastating ruin and the synchronicity of our thought processes about women. As she describes experiencing the loss of nearly everything dear to her in life—her business, her finances, her home, and ultimately her husband—I identified so deeply that I felt immediately drawn to support her in this book project. A similar situation had recently happened to me. At the same time, it was encouraging to discover that we both, through our respective writings, are currently pointing to the fact that dramatic opportunities are available to women today as we search for ways to improve both our personal and professional lives.

The number of female-owned businesses has grown at nearly twice the national average since 1987 according to the National Foundation for Women Business Owners (NFWBO). The eight million businesses owned by women are generating about $2.3 trillion in revenue, a 236 percent jump since 1987. What is interesting, but not surprising, is that female-owned businesses are more likely to remain in operation than the average firm. This certainly is, in no small part, a reflection of that aspect of the female psyche that builds on nurturing relationships. The Small Business Administration reports that nearly three-fourths of firms launched by women in 1991 were still operating three years later, as compared to the two-thirds survival rate of all companies.

Perhaps one reason for this growth of female-owned businesses is that studies show that women are more likely to take greater risks. Why shouldn't we? We have less to lose. If we try and fail, we pick ourselves up, shake off the dust, and try again. Each failure brings us that much closer to a victory.

But now, having tried it all, we are leading the migration homeward bound. The profession that stands apart as most likely to advance women in our search to gain control over our lives is network marketing. Built on strengthening personal relationships—clearly one of women's strongest inbred qualities—this industry is positioning itself to be in the forefront of a new era of professionals who, by choice, want to make a living but also make a life.

As women, we are processing our decisions more carefully, seeking careers without sacrificing our life priorities. We see an increasing number of young women postponing marriage until their professional lives are more firmly established. And this may lead to more solid, well-thought-out, lasting relationships. Mothers are choosing to spend more time with their children, some at a moderate decrease in income, and others are discovering ways to make just as much or more and gain control of their lives.

I am convinced that women who spend more time working from home will contribute in innumerable ways to the progress of our society. They will be better mothers, there when their families need them rather than stuck in gridlock on a freeway. They will reestablish priorities and create lives with a more elevated sense of purpose and fulfillment. With more capital in the hands of responsible entrepreneurs, I expect to see countless people making more money than they ever dreamed. And many of them will use their new-found wealth for altruistic causes.

Women Struggle in the Workplace

Since the advent of the two-paycheck household, this country has had a large, underpaid minority. We are called women. According to a White House task force, women earn just 76 cents for every dollar that men earn. This is an improvement over the 63 cents per dollar women "enjoyed" in 1979, according the US Bureau of Labor Statistics.

Rather than wait for the government to enforce equality, more and more women are deciding to leave their j.o.b.s (journey of the broke) to become entrepreneurs. Many of us gave up on corporate jobs after finding wages stagnant and feminist rhetoric about self-fulfillment empty. Juliet Schor, author of *The Overworked American,* reported that 28 percent of the respondents in a recent survey had made a voluntary change in lifestyle that involved a significant reduction in earnings as they moved to a less stressful job, turned down a promotion, or refused relocation.

More and more mothers are working part-time and they routinely make less an hour than full-time workers doing the same job. I see another new trend: If women can work at home making a significant fraction of the money they made in the secretarial pool, they'd still prefer to be with their kids. Some creative entrepreneurial women are learning they can stay at home with their kids without sacrificing their income.

Even so, the number of women 45 and older employed or looking for work swelled from 14.8 million in 1988 to 20.3 million last year, according to the US Department of Labor. With this increase, it is clear that women as well as men are looking for the solution to financial stability in their lives. This seems to be so whether they are married or single.

"Age plays differently for women than it does for men," says Deborah Chalfie of the American Association of Retired Persons (AARP). "Baby boomers have a much stronger attachment to the workplace than…their grandmothers, so it's likely to become an increasing issue."

The challenge is even greater for women executives who aspire to the top. The typical Chief Executive Officer this year is 56 years old, male, white, and Protestant. In the past, it has proven nearly impossible for a woman to break through the bias in favor of men.

Network marketing presents women with a unique opportunity in business. Free from the confines of glass ceilings, as well as the many political games and the often-biased advancement and pay policies of traditionally male-dominated work environments, women have found that a home business allows them to be at home with their family.

Women as a whole have finally had enough. We are believing in ourselves more and banking on our own abilities. We no longer are willing to miss out on the important phases of our lives. We are no longer willing to be controlled by others. We are no longer willing to give the best of ourselves in order to make someone else wealthy. As women, we are ready to risk all in order to take our stand in the business world. We recognize that we must be involved in the economic contributions to our families. And yet our business decisions are often influenced by where we choose to place our values, recognizing along with Barbra Streisand that "People who need people are the luckiest people in the world." We are gravitating toward entrepreneurial ventures and home-based businesses because the people in our lives count for everything...far more than money.

Network marketing offers a true sense of purpose, unlimited altruistic options, balance, nurturing, and, if we continue to exercise the values that mean so much to us, it can be an industry that exudes fundamental integrity. Whether man or woman, these are qualities that are inherent in the female side of the human psyche.

Read this book with hope. It is not hype. The facts, the stories, the outline of the needed steps to succeed are based on genuine experience. If you are a woman who dares to dream, this book will encourage you to dare to *Dream Big!*

Rene Reid Yarnell
Author of *The New Entrepreneurs*
Co-author of *Your First Year in Network Marketing*

PREFACE

While flying across the country to attend a business conference, I perused a complimentary copy of *Time* magazine. A particular article caught my attention, the caption reading, "For the first time in history, women outnumber men in the work force." That statement struck a nerve in me, not because of my opinions about women in the workplace, but because day after day I talk with women across the country who are tired of the "rat race," frustrated with their salaries, and feel inadequate in their home lives. Many seem to live lives of quiet desperation. This is not to say that women do not want to work—they do—but they typically aren't in a satisfying or profitable situation and they want that to change. Women today work hard, often struggling to balance their careers, family, and finances. Many women ask themselves, "Is it really worth it? Is this all there is?"

Today women are searching. Searching for a way out of the endless spiral of debt, the helpless feeling of modern corporate life, and the anti-family structure of the 9 to 5 job. Women are searching for a path to financial independence. Many of these women, if offered the opportunity, could find that path with network marketing.

But many of these same women are skeptical. Perhaps they think, like I once did, that network marketing was only about selling products or doing home parties. These same women, if given the right information, would understand that network marketing could give them the financial independence and time freedom they are searching for. Many of these women, if given the facts about the opportunity that awaits them through network marketing, would take that chance.

But how would they begin? Certainly there are special challenges that face women as they try to develop their own networking business. Where are the stories of women with lives just like theirs who took a chance on network marketing and made their dreams come true? Where are the stories of the struggling single mom, the married woman with the doubting husband, the professional with no time for herself and her family, or the widow with a small pension?

In the last few years I have built a network marketing business of my own, often under challenging personal circumstances. Starting first with a loving husband and a busy career, I then carried on as a grieving widow with four children at home. I continue to build my business today, offering hope to other women that they too can make their dreams come true. By committing a few hours a week to develop their own business, women will find that they can balance their busy schedules, give a sense of meaning to their lives, develop lasting relationships, bring peace and comfort to their homes, and live a life of security and freedom beyond their wildest dreams, if they will but dare to dream big.

—Cynthia Stewart-Copier

Acknowledgments

As time goes by, the number of people to whom I find myself indebted seems to grow exponentially and I find myself struggling to find a way to say "thank you" when there are so many people who have been such powerful influences in my life, as well as in this project. The names that follow can only be a representative sampling. To those named and unnamed, I extend my heartfelt gratitude for your contribution to making *Dream Big* a success.

First and foremost, I thank my husband, Floris. He is my partner in marriage, business, and in life. Without him I would be lost. To my children, Clinton, Cami, Tyler, and Rebecca, for giving me a huge reason to dream big, and a special thanks to my daughter, Rachel, for holding us all together through the past few months.

Jennifer Basye Sander for encouraging me to stretch beyond my comfort zone. Sheree Bykofsky, my agent, for her continual support and belief in my dream. Adams Media Corporation, especially Jere Calmes, my editor, and Dawn Thompson for their vision and determination to help this book become a success. Josephine Gross, Director of Circulation, Network Marketing Lifestyles, for her contribution and support of this book.

My deepest thanks and appreciation go to my dearest friends, Don and Ruth Storms, for their wisdom and inspiration. To my eternal friends, Leo and Amy Grant, for their continued faith and support and to Jan and Gretchen Graf, for teaching me lessons of life. Jamie Miller and Laura Lewis for showing me that miracles do happen. Marty Mieszkowski, for his willingness to give to others and change lives, especially mine.

A special thanks to each of the women who generously and graciously gave their time to share their stories and secrets of success. And to all of the women who have built their own network marketing business, created wealth, and dared to dream big!

INTRODUCTION

I have traveled the world over for the past thirty years. I have been in the company of heads of state and presidents of countries and Fortune 500 executives. You are about to be introduced to what I feel is a best kept secret. This book is a message to you, woman to woman. In the following pages you will find an option most of us have never considered or perhaps never knew existed. What if I were to tell you that there is a way that each of us can have a positive effect on our culture and society while simultaneously generating income for ourselves and our families?

Network marketing can pave a new superhighway to success and wealth. You will find it to be a level playing field for those with and without money and without a formal education. The key to success in this industry is belief in yourself and your choice of companies. Determination and drive are also important. Network marketing is the only playing field, I might add, where women and men can earn the same income dollar for dollar. Nurturing is at the very core of network marketing, and this is second nature to us as women.

Women are moving up in the business world. They now fill eleven percent of senior executive positions in the Fortune 500 arena, and in a new study of two hundred Internet companies, it was found women are in two percent of the board seats. What was it I was saying about a level playing field? Not in that ballpark. Many of these women are leaving their jobs in order to have and raise families. Why not have it all? In this industry you do not need thirty years of experience. In fact, you do not even need to be thirty years old. Some additional good news is that you can even be over fifty when you begin and become a successful businesswoman. I am living proof. I started my network marketing career by accident at age fifty, and at fifty-three I have become one of the leading income earners in my company—an income that rivals the Fortune 500 group's. Interested? Keep reading. Would you like to take charge of your life and your future? If not now, when? I challenge you not to be stuck in the old way of thinking and working.

With our volatile economy, both women and men need versatility, not expertise or pedigrees. We all need to learn to be generalists. If you think you are in need of particular credentials or training, think again. Debby Hopkins, of Boeing, lacked an MBA and experience in the aircraft industry; however, she was able to join the company and implement change where there had been resistance to it in the past. You will find successful people in business where you find people comfortable with alternative methods of action and rapid decision-making skills. If you are flexible, adaptable, and open to new ideas, the door to success will open. I feel this applies more to the industry of Network marketing than it does to any other industry.

One thing that has helped the leading women succeed is a certain comfort with ambiguity and a faith in serendipity. Why shouldn't you and I put these philosophies into practice in the industry of Network marketing? I encourage you to release any sense of limitation and to rise to your vision of your successful self. Women have great people skills, and it is time we make good use of them. While some of us may be reluctant to employ problem-solving skills in our personal and professional lives, embracing it will enable us to conquer many issues. Developing long-term relationships is another key to Network marketing. Some still think the industry of Network marketing has a questionable reputation, but by the time you have finished this book, you may begin to see options that you had not seen before. I am enjoying being part of the evolution of the industry's changing reputation.

In this business you can be teacher, cheerleader, and CEO all in the same day, while continuing your role of wife and mother. You can be the role model for others by living the example of a woman who can balance her personal and professional lives with a responsible career choice. To combine work and family, you should examine this unconventional way of earning. Statistics show that women who work outside of the home work an average of twenty-one hours per week more than their male counterparts.

It is time to look for the career that fosters a balanced lifestyle without a glass ceiling and without limited income potential. In so doing, it is important to consider trends such as the baby boomers that have driven the economic wave of the past and are continuing to do so. Remember to choose a company with great care. Make sure you know the mission statement and vision of the company of your choice.

I have found, as perhaps you have, that we know not what tomorrow brings. We must plan our future now. As women we have the advantage of having plenty of choices. Let's make the right one.

Which one of us will be the next to win the Nobel Peace Prize? Will one or two of us reshape history? Find a cure for one of the degenerative diseases? Please join me in the belief that millions of us can do something great daily and join forces to find a way to have balance in our daily lives. Are your dreams realized? Are your needs met in the workplace and at home? Is your future secure?

Together we have the ability to make the difference for ourselves and others . . . this level playing field could be the way to make your dreams a reality. Read this book, share the vision, and dare to dream.

—Susan E. Waitley

SECTION ONE

Why It Works:
What Makes
Networking Great

CHAPTER ONE

ANY WOMAN CAN!

Women Can!

What you are about to read can change your life. "Oh sure," you say. "I've heard that before." Probably many times, but in this case you're going to be pleasantly surprised because this information will change the way you think—about yourself, your life, your finances, your goals, your future—about everything that touches your life. You will get facts, figures, and the latest information from top industry experts. This information can kick you into over-drive, just as it did many other successful women in network marketing. You'll read their stories as they share their challenges, hopes, obstacles, and victories. One thing is for sure—any woman can succeed in network marketing. You've come a long way—and you've only just begun!

Never before in the history of this country have women had the opportunities they have today. We have come to a crossroad and met the challenges of our past—and won! So why do some women still feel an absence of success? Many women find traditional business is still dominated by men. Is there a financial opportunity where no such barrier exists? Yes, in network marketing there is no gender gap. Any woman can reach the highest levels of success in this type of business. More than 16 million Americans are doing some kind of entrepreneurial activity from their homes, and experts predict that number to double in the next decade. As great as network marketing is today, it is only going to get better. Why not get in now when this is just the tip of the iceberg? You can position yourself today with network marketing to earn top dollars, have a global business, set your own schedule, and live the life of your dreams.

What You Don't Need

Women have the greatest advantage for success in network marketing. And there are many things they *don't* need to succeed in this business. Women don't need a particular education, a huge capital investment, a bank loan, a perfect figure, or the help of a spouse or other male companion. They don't need to live in a certain neighborhood, have a particular color of skin, drive an expensive car, or have experience in business. They don't have to be short or tall, rich or poor, beautiful or skinny, blonde or brunette, because in the business of network marketing, *any woman can!*

Cash Out

Ok, admit it—the pace of life has quickened to a breakneck speed and the ante has been upped. Traditional corporate success demands extraordinary, exhausting effort. Women seem to be saying, "Is this stress really worth the reward?" "Is this life I am living shortening my life?" "Is this *all* there is?"

In the workplace women are filled with a lack of trust—watching uneasily as loyal employees are being laid off when corporations are bought and sold like Monopoly properties. Many women are finding their traditional health coverage and other benefits

---

FOUR GREAT REASONS TO BUILD IT

1. Network marketing is a tremendous opportunity to create financial independence. Over 16 million Americans are doing some type of entrepreneurial activity from their homes, and experts predict that number to double in the next decade.
2. Women can set their own hours, adjust their schedules to meet other demands, develop a permanent inheritable income, and create lasting relationships based on mutual trust and respect.
3. Network marketing has no gender gap. Any woman can reach the top levels of success in this business.
4. To succeed in network marketing women don't need a huge capital investment, a perfect figure, particular color of skin, or an expensive car to create a wealthy lifestyle. In network marketing, any woman can!

Yes, there are special challenges facing any woman today who wants to step out of the stereotypical lifestyle and reach for the stars. You will learn that through network marketing women can truly *have it all!* Throughout the pages of this book, you will learn the inside success tips from the top producing female networkers, creative ideas in developing your own network marketing business, and a step-by-step guide to financial independence.

cut back as well. Women today are looking for a way out—way to retreat. Thanks to technology we are able to do just that through network marketing.

Hi-Ho, Hi-Ho, It's Off to Work We Go

What drew people away from home to work in the first place was industry or factories; the workers went to the equipment like slaves to machines. Then, when the Age of Information replaced the Industrial Revolution, the office took the place of the factory. Workers went to work where information processors were: office equipment, management, and huge files of data. The workplace was the repository of information.

With the coming of age of the microchip, however, this is no longer true. Information has been decentralized. The PC, modem, fax, and digital phone have all made information as close as our fingertips and accessible around the world. So why go to the office?

Working It—At Home

It's another beautiful day. You jump out of bed to the squeal of the electronic rooster, put on a suit you don't feel like wearing, grab some breakfast you don't have time to eat, drive your car through the danger zone of the morning commute to a place you don't want to go, and work with people you don't really like. That's your job. Somebody has to do it.

Wait a minute, you say! Let's rewind and try that one again. It's a beautiful day. You wake up to the sun streaming in your window and the smell of coffee brewing. You slowly stretch and gently raise yourself from your pillow. As you grab your favorite pair of jeans and comfy tennis shoes, you think about what to have for breakfast. You walk out on your deck and enjoy the warmth of the sun on your face, then casually stroll into the next room to your home office.

Sound better? Sure it does! That's why more and more women are doing some type of entrepreneurial activity from their homes. Ok, so being your own boss may not just be about wearing whatever you feel like to work, but it is about doing what you want, for yourself. Women who own their own network marketing businesses might have taken some risks, but they are also taking control of their lives.

Time Out!

It's not just that we don't have *enough* time. It's as if time itself has become, well, *faster* than it used to be. There isn't time to stop or take a breath. There is nowhere to run and nowhere to hide. We carry our phones in our briefcase, our pagers in our purse. We even have call-forward/call-waiting features. There is never an excuse to be out of touch. So what's the antidote?

We don't want *more* anything anymore. Women are pleading for fewer choices and ways to make our lives easier. We are trying to edit. Cut back. Pare down. Simplify. Streamline. Women today want achievement without exhaustion. Accomplishment with less stress. We want to buy back time—and that's exactly what network marketing can do for you.

Hello American Dream!

"How would you like to quit your job, become your own boss, and build up enough residual income in a few years to support yourself for the rest of your life?" asked Danielle's sponsor. "I thought network marketing was some sort of pyramid scheme designed to bamboozle the gullible and naïve. Of course, I had to admit that my sponsor seemed normal. He was finishing his last year in medical school when he introduced me to network marketing. I probably wouldn't have even given it a second thought if it weren't for the obvious success my sponsor had attained. It was his credibility that moved me to consider taking a good, hard look at the facts," said Danielle.

Sadly, like Danielle, many people simply don't understand network marketing, nor do they understand how it's changing the way we live, work, and move goods and services around the world. Network marketing is a phenomenal method of doing business that is growing by leaps and bounds, emerging as a powerful force in the new era of global networking. "As a business owner, I could hardly imagine a business with no inventory, no employees to manage, no payroll to meet, and I could take off on a dream vacation for six months and come back making even more money than when I left! This was a business-owners dream," Danielle says.

How It Began

Network marketing is more than just a business. I believe that it provides a future for women where they no longer cower before bosses and bureaucrats but stand tall, take control of their lives, and design their own future. Network marketing (sometimes called multilevel marketing, or MLM) really began over fifty years ago. When Carl Rehnborg invented network marketing—a busi-

> ### FIVE FABULOUS BENEFITS
> 1. Work from your home, an airplane, or an exotic island resort.
> 2. Simplify and streamline your life.
> 3. Develop a business that pays you forever! With network marketing you can develop residual, ongoing income that is inheritable to your family.
> 4. Choose the people with whom you associate.
> 5. Spend your time in a positive and uplifting environment. Unlike the dog-eat-dog environment of corporate America, network marketing provides a motivating and positive environment conducive to success.

ness system designed to make it easy for anyone to succeed—he started a company called California Vitamins, later known as Nutrilite. Ten years later Amway launched the sale of household products. Over the past fifty years, the industry has matured into a legitimate and efficient channel of distribution thanks to Rich DeVos and Jay VanAndel for having the vision to pioneer this industry. Network marketing annual sales are around $20 billion in the United States alone, involving an estimated 8 million people. Network marketing has evolved over the past fifty years from a door-to-door selling business into an efficient way to distribute goods and services, offering a realistic promise of financial freedom to those with goals and visions—to those who *dare to dream big*!

Show Me the Money

"In the beginning I did my homework and found out that not only was network marketing a respected industry, collectively it was responsible for creating more millionaires than any other single industry," said Danielle. "I definitely got started in the beginning for the money. I was working 50-60 hours a week at my business, commuting over 30 miles one way just to open the doors. At the end of the day, I would drag myself out of my car and try to muster up the energy to meet the demands of a busy family. I would often fall into bed at night thinking, "Is this all there is?" Danielle continued. "If I had to work an extra 8 to 10 hours a week for the next few years with the hope that I could replace my income from my traditional business and buy back my life—I was willing! My alternatives were not too appealing. I definitely got in for the money."

What Danielle didn't realize at first were the many other benefits of owning your own network marketing business. What she couldn't see in the beginning were the personal growth, development of management and people skills, personal satisfaction, and long-term rewarding relationships that she would gain as she worked her new business. "Being somewhat successful in a business of my own before network marketing, I suppose I had an attitude in the beginning that slowed my progress—namely I thought I knew it all! It took me a while to understand that network marketing was a different kind of business and I needed to learn and develop skills necessary to build a long-term, profitable business. That is where the personal development part of network marketing really paid off. I learned, through reading books and listening to the suggestions of my upline leaders, how to make changes in myself that enabled me to move ahead, get that leading edge I was looking for," adds Danielle.

In traditional business, owners of companies hire and fire employees, make decisions that affect the lives of their personnel, and always are most concerned with their own bottom line. The business of network marketing does not work that way. You do not employ people; you register or sponsor them to be independent business owners—a volunteer army of sorts. Instead of driving people to meet your expectations and replacing the ones that don't measure up, you are paid for helping others succeed. The big money in network marketing comes when you've helped those that you've sponsored to make money first.

Help Others Get What They Want First

"At first all I cared about was making money and getting *myself* out of the pounding pressure of debt," says Danielle. "After I began to really understand the marketing plan, I realized that as I built my own business, I was really helping others more than myself, and that felt good."

Danielle learned, as many other successful networkers have learned, that long-term residual money in network marketing comes from developing a strong downline organization. In simpler terms, big numbers create big money. By helping her downline make money, Danielle naturally made money for herself. "The more people I

4 MORE BENEFITS
• Personal growth
• Development of management and people skills
• Personal satisfaction
• Long-term rewarding relationships

helped," said Danielle, "the more money I made. It is a great concept. In my other business, I made money by selling merchandise to the public. In my network business, I made money by helping my business partners create a solid income. Seeing their lives change for the better was even more rewarding than the money. I saw women quit their jobs, lose the stressed out look on their faces, and emerge with relationships strengthened and closer family ties. This was priceless to me," she adds.

The Future Is Now

Still not sure? Ok, ask yourself these questions:

Am I truly happy with my current job or profession?

Am I experiencing joy and personal satisfaction related to my career choice?

Am I making all the money I deserve?

Am I growing and moving personally in the direction I feel is important in my life?

Am I spending enough time with my family, friends, or for myself?

Am I in control of my future, my life, or is someone else determining my success?

Do I see my life getting better if I continue on the path I am on?

Am I willing to make some changes in order to have more money, satisfaction, and time?

Most of the women you will read about in this book have asked themselves these same questions—and they didn't like the answers at all! So they took a chance, opened up, took a good look, and made a big step, a step that put them in the direction of success they had never known was possible.

It's not just about money, either. It is about running your own show—calling your own shots. It is about being in charge of your own life and having choices—real ones—not just the ones others tell you are yours to make. It's about sharing dreams and time with the people who matter most in your life—your family and friends.

Now Is the Best Time!

There has *never* been a better time than now to take a chance on network marketing. Network marketing has evolved over the years into a respected way of making money in today's economy and a powerful way of doing business in today's market. The entire network marketing industry is just about to hit critical mass, which means not only a period of tremendous growth but also tremendous profits! Position yourself in this industry today because *less than three percent* of the market has been touched. Forecasters predict that percentage will jump to over 10 percent in the next few years. This means that the vast majority of money to be made in this rapidly growing industry will likely be made in the next few years. In addition, the Internet will have a powerful influence on networking in the next decade. You'll learn more about this in Chapter 3. For now, realize that times are rapidly changing and women who have the vision will position themselves today for the explosion that is coming! So get in, get set, and buckle up!

Consider the Options

Like Danielle, I began to study—really study—the pros and cons of starting my own network marketing business and the advantages were staggering! The start-up cost was minimal. (I had invested a quarter of a million dollars cash in my last business deal, not to mention the bank loans.) Very little, if any, inventory was required. (Inventory at my dealership hit 5 million dollars.) I had no license to apply for, no sales tax reports to file, no employees or payroll to deal with. (I had over forty full-time employees and a staff of five just to run the office.) I did not have to have an office, special equipment, or work from a certain city. (My overhead was $100,000 a month and I had hundreds of thousands of dollars invested in tools and equipment. And I was locked into housing that was close to work.) I could set my own hours, arrange my own schedule. (We were open at the dealership seven days a week!) I did not have to personally guarantee any products—the company had a 100 percent money-back guarantee. (The headaches with warranty issues are too numerous to mention.) With network marketing I didn't have to worry about the rising cost of gas, interest rates, or inflation. My product line wasn't seasonal, trendy, or a luxury item affordable to only a few. I could build a global business, travel, make loyal friendships, and handpick the people I wanted to be in business with.

I didn't have to hire security guards or worry about someone stealing my inventory or manipulating the books. No more worries about sick leave and workman's compensation plans. I could take a vacation whenever and wherever I wanted—and enjoy it! I had the best business and financial advisor that money could buy—and I didn't have to pay for it! It was my upline, already

FOUR MORE REASONS TO SAY YES!

1. In network marketing you can be your own boss, run your own show, call your own shots. You determine the level of success you achieve. You are not held back by anyone or anything.
2. Be in charge of your own life by having choices, real ones, and making decisions that are best for you—for your family and their future.
3. No financial risk! No huge investment of inventory is required in most network companies. There is no risk of losing your hard-earned money.
4. An opportunity to share your dreams and your time with the people who matter most—your family and friends.

a millionaire herself because of network marketing. And best of all, I had nothing to risk!

Sound pretty good? You better believe it! If that isn't enough, I could build a business that would pay me as much money as I wanted to make…forever! Yes, that's right! In network marketing you can develop a business income that is residual and inheritable. I could create a business today that would pay me not only for the rest of my life, but my kids could inherit it. That was more than I could ever hope for in my traditional business. Oh, and did I forget to mention that it was fun too!

The Future Is Bright!

In the next few years, women just like you—perhaps even someone you know from the office, gym, committee, or church—will create tremendous lifestyles in network marketing. Never before in history have so many people been in position to take advantage of such an explosive marketing trend. More and more women will grab their share of the pie. How about you? Will you take a chance and claim your fair share? You have everything to gain and nothing to lose. Dare to dream big, because any woman can find success in network marketing today.

Your future is waiting!

CHAPTER TWO

WHY NETWORK MARKETING IS RIGHT FOR WOMEN

What Makes It Great for Women?

Unlike traditional business, network marketing offers unlimited opportunity for women in today's workplace. A recent article in the *Wall Street Journal* featured an article, "Even Top Women Earn Less, New Study Finds." This article revealed that top executive women with "line" roles collect median cash pay of less than 50 percent received by comparable men.

In traditional business today, women are still somewhat stereotyped by their male counterparts. But in network marketing, women find a freedom

> The *Wall Street Journal* says "Even Top Women Earn Less, New Study Finds." This article revealed that top executive women with "line" roles collect median cash pay of less than 50 percent received by comparable men.

of opportunity unlike anything they might be offered from their typical workplace. Here, women are controlled only by themselves, their own goals, and by the amount of time and energy they are willing to devote to their success.

The Female Edge

You'll be glad to know that psychologists who have studied networking tell us women are naturally better at it! "This type of business draws on our natural ability to network," says Lorene Cron. "We always tell our friends about 'good deal's, great restaurants, schools, teachers, and so on. Women are relationship builders. And that's what network marketing is—building relationships."

Women have been taught to share and express feelings and interests with others. Since much of network marketing is about building relationships, this

THREE REASONS IT'S GREAT FOR WOMEN

1. Women are relationship builders, and that's what network marketing is—building relationships.
2. Women are comfortable in engaging in a multitude of tasks simultaneously.
3. Women have incredible strength and endurance. They can juggle many balls and keep their eye on them all.

research would stand to justify itself. Because of their gender, women have an edge on success in network marketing. Women have more opportunity for success in network marketing because they are female—because they are comfortable in engaging in a multitude of tasks simultaneously, playing many varying roles concurrently, and having the strength, stamina, and ability to keep an eye on it all. These skills, shared by women and superheroes, can launch you on a superstar career in network marketing.

In network marketing, women are driving this fast-moving industry. Not only are there more women monopolizing the numbers (accounting for more than 75 percent), they are also monopolizing the top positions of most MLM companies. Although women are becoming top leaders in all areas of business, they are achieving this at breakneck speed in network marketing. Let's just name a few.

Lorene Cron, started her business just a few short years ago while working as a receptionist in a doctor's office and raising five children on her own. Lorene has made over a million dollars in just three short years. M.J. Michael didn't even know the difference between wholesale and retail—she called them *hotel* and *resell*—has not only developed an international, multi-million dollar Internet business, but has spanned the globe in her efforts to impact the lives of other women. Karen Yamada Furuchi, one of the first women to reach success in network marketing, now shares hope with women around the world.

Women like these leave me with no doubt that network marketing was made especially for women, even more so than any other business venture or income opportunity. Here are some of the reasons why.

SUPERHEROES

Superman, Spiderman, Batman, and Robin all have one thing in common: panty hose. It seems that all superheroes wear panty hose. It's no surprise then that many women of today are called "Superwomen" and it's not just because of the panty hose connection. The Superwoman designation came about because of our ability to do it all.

The other day I took a chance and dropped in on a friend of mine unannounced. She is a top female network marketer who is responsible for leading business groups of hundreds of thousands around the world. Within two minutes of my unplanned visit, Ruth escorted me into her office, offered me a seat, handed me a glass of water, and with a warm smile on her face told me how happy she was to see me. The phone rang. Before even having a chance to say more than a quick hello to this caller, her second line rang and she smoothly transitioned, putting caller number one on hold. She apologized to me and picked up line number two, which evidently was an international call. She juggled these two calls, smoothly and professionally, making decisions and offering support while continuing to smile and make eye contact with me.

Talk about using time productively, distributing energies easily, engaging in many tasks effortlessly, and keeping a pulse on it all. One may surmise that these abilities evolved in women out of necessity, considering the variety of tasks involved in keeping the home fires burning. There may indeed be some truth to that. But these abilities became even more fine-tuned as more and more of us entered into the work arena. Let's face it, many women who work outside the home face a full evening of work once they get home. We'll be discussing more of this in Chapter 12, The Balancing Act, but for now let's talk more about why women are right for this industry and find out how other women, women just like you, have made it big in network marketing.

GETTING IT DONE

"I thought that having my own business would give me the edge, would provide the opportunity for financial success," says Karen Yamada Furuchi. If you think that having your own business would solve the earnings gap, think again. According to a recent Small Business Administration study, women business owners are earning 49 percent less than their male counterparts. In network marketing women are on an equal playing field with men; rewards are commensurate with results.

Karen was the third generation American Japanese in her family. She said that she faced many obstacles because of her race and her gender. "My parents were proud. They taught me to be honorable, to have respect for my culture, for America, and for my family. At an early age I learned by my parents' example to work hard, to strive for excellence in all I did, to be a model citizen, a model American. I lived my life by my parents' example. My father would often tell us, 'Never paint my face red.' Meaning, 'don't embarrass our family or me.' I had such a tremendous respect for my father, for our family and culture, I have dedicated the rest of my life to honor him, our family, and the commitment we share to strive for excellence in everything we do."

"Perhaps this is where I developed a driving desire to win," Karen continued. "After college I married. As the wife of a dentist, I had a certain prestige among my peers. But soon I realized that image did not exemplify respect. And as my father had said so many times in my youth, 'Honor is earned. Commitment is honored.' I spent many years trying to prove myself honorable, respectful, and capable. I started and stopped many business ventures, from a tailor shop to real estate to an auto mechanic shop. I was always looking for the right deal, the right vehicle to move me in the direction of my dreams. I finally found that vehicle with network marketing."

IN THE BEGINNING

"I was one of the first single women building the network marketing business alone," says Karen. "In those days, mostly men ran big organizations and held large conventions. Not having the option of building a business with a male partner, I had to decide if I was willing to do the work and make it happen on my own. When I understood the potential benefits and evaluated my other options, I decided to do whatever it took to get to the top. I knew I might not be as smart as the businessmen I knew, but no one could outwork me!"

TOO GOOD TO BE TRUE

"I had invested over a quarter of a million dollars in cash in my newest business venture," said Cathy Berry, "My husband and I had given every penny, every asset we had to ensure the proper capital of investment to our newest dream, one of the state's largest luxury car dealerships."

Cathy thought that hard work and expertise would ensure their success in this new business venture. "My husband had started his business in Southern California many years before. By the time I met him, he had already achieved a measure of success. With our combined efforts we would have twice the go-power and were sure to succeed. I knew that in time we would have not only developed a comfortable lifestyle, but in addition, a prosperous future."

"When we were first approached about network marketing, my first thought was, No way! It sounds too good to be true. Besides that, I would never want to sell door-to-door. I suppose I had more than a little status in those days. Little did I know how quickly that would all change—status didn't pay the bills," adds Cathy.

Dream On

Someone once told me, "If your income is dependent on your ability to perform, it is temporary." Ok, listen again. If *your* income is dependent on *your* ability to perform, *it is temporary.*

> ### TEMPORARY INCOME
>
> Any income source that is dependent on your ability to perform is **temporary!** Anything can happen.

"It is so interesting to me that often I shared the same message with my friends…that of developing financial security. I talked to people about their children, the costs involved in raising them and the rising costs of a college education," says Cathy. "I encouraged my girlfriends to make investments, plan for their future. I never imagined that I would be the one suffering from a tremendous financial hit in the months to come. I thought that because I had a successful business, a great husband, and a pretty fabulous financial portfolio, I had it made. Was I ever dreaming!"

Security, Where Did It Go?

Security is what most people want in their lives. Research shows that security continues to top the list of what most people desire in their careers for their families and for their futures, too. Sadly, the truth is that today security is slipping away or gone for most of us. And it's going at an alarming rate.

So what about the American Dream? Where has it gone? To network marketing, that's where. Consider for a moment the reality of doing traditional business in today's market. With real estate at an all-time high, just finding a location to open up shop can take most small business owners over the edge. Combine these costs with investment capital, inventory, insurance, employee expenses, taxes, liability insurance—the list goes on and on. Just to open the doors in traditional business today can be more than overwhelming for most small business owners. Then consider that over 90 percent of businesses that open today will be gone in the next five years, and of those 10 percent who do make it less than 2 percent will be around a decade from now. Those are slim odds, and yet people open new business ventures everyday across America. Why? Because they have dreams, hopes, and desires for a better tomorrow, for freedom and security for their families and children. Yet most of those dreams will be nothing more than a nightmare in a year or so.

GET MORE BASKETS!

"When the gas prices started to rise I didn't pay much attention. I had already survived the gas crunch and I thought I had seen it all. Boy, was I ever in for a surprise," said Cathy. Little did she know that not only were gas prices going to continue to rise at a steady pace, but in addition, interest rates would also begin to follow suit. "When money gets tight, so do the purse strings. One of the first things to go is luxury items, such as fancy cars. I noticed the traffic on our dealership floor began to get sparse and fewer deals were being brought into my office," Cathy continued. "I learned valuable lessons amidst the tremendous losses we suffered." Sadly, Cathy's story is much like the story I hear day after day of women living in an illusion that their job or career will be able to provide them with financial security. More often than not it won't. I now understand the meaning of a statement my grandmother told me over and over again when I was a young girl. I first heard her say it one winter morning…

"'Don't put all those eggs in one basket,' grandmother said. As a young girl my family lived on a farm. I never seemed suited for farm living and I especially disliked gathering eggs in the cold winter mornings before school. I always tried to hurry and get the job finished. Often in my haste I would either drop or kick over the egg basket as I attempted to snatch the eggs from beneath the hens. My grandmother would watch me from the kitchen window. I could see her shaking her head as I stepped up on the porch. She would remind me once again that if I continued to try to jam all of the eggs in one basket, I would make more work for myself. Eventually I understood that if you have your eggs in one basket and that basket tips over, you chance losing them all. Life later taught me that if I had all of my income coming from one source and that source ended, I would be in financial trouble. Sadly, most women have their eggs in one basket and often aren't prepared if that basket tips over."

THREE REASONS TO CHOOSE NETWORK MARKETING OVER TRADITIONAL BUSINESS:

1. Over 90 percent of businesses that open today will be gone in the next five years
2. Those 10 percent who do make it less than 2 percent will be around a decade from now.
3. Because you have dreams, hopes, and desires for a better tomorrow, and for freedom and security for your families and children.

In her best-selling book, *The Millionairess Across the Street,* co-author Jennifer Basye Sander talks about the importance of creating multiple streams of income. She practices what she preaches: "As an author, editor, public speaker, and investor I understood the value of creating multiple income streams. I also knew the Internet was a wide-open opportunity. When I heard about the network marketing business launching on the Web, I jumped in running," said Jennifer. We'll learn more about income and investments in Chapter 9, but for now, let's take a hard look at reality.

Today it takes at least two incomes to achieve the same standard of living we were accustomed to while growing up, the standard of living our parents achieved with just one paycheck. There is even talk today of the emergence of the *three-income* family! History has already taught us what to expect in the future. Thirty percent of all Americans lost their job at least once during the last two decades of the twentieth century—30 percent—and those in the know predict that this unsettling trend will continue well into the twenty-first century.

Sadly, most women today are so busy, often overwhelmed, just trying to make ends meet and to juggle their already difficult responsibilities that they don't see the writing on the wall. I know I sure didn't. But I have since learned that the rules that people grew up with about lifetime security and employment just don't apply in today's society.

So women, let's face it, there is no security anymore. We can't turn back the clock to the days when our parents told us to get a good education, get a job with a big company, and work hard for forty years and you will then be taken care of for the rest of your lives. That ship just doesn't float anymore. So let's face reality and get on with it!

To stay competitive in today's market, companies must increase production and reduce costs. That means more machines and fewer jobs. It just doesn't make sense to pay five people $40,000 a year if they can be replaced by a machine that costs $100,000—a machine that never gets sick, never takes a vacation, doesn't go on strike, and doesn't require a benefits package. And you can be assured this machine will never file a sexual harassment suit. Ouch! That one hurts you say? Painful, but true. Today, companies must weigh all the costs while trying to stay competitive in the market.

Against the Wind

A popular song in the '80s was titled "Against the Wind." A local graduating class selected this song for the closing ceremony of graduation that year. Perhaps this class felt that they had "gone against the wind" in many ways that year. Sometimes, when in pursuit of a goal, we often feel pressure, feel as if we are pushing against the wind or swimming upstream. "Swim upstream," the late Sam Walton once said. "If everyone else is doing it," he said, "there's a good chance you can find your niche by going in exactly the opposite direction."

So why not try something new? You have got nothing to lose—and you might win big!

A Day Late and a Dollar Short

Just think for a moment. By the time most of us get into the stock market, or by the time real estate hits an all-time high, the big money has already been made. For the majority of us, all that is left is the crumbs. Sadly, many women feel like they are always a day late and a dollar short.

Here is your chance to be one day early and to make that extra dollar—and much more! Network marketing gives women the definite edge over any other industry in our country today. With network marketing women call their own shots, determine their own future, run their own race. And that is good news! It is clearly time for a change for women—a change for the better—a dramatic change that will turn the tide on what the future holds for the way America does business in the new millennium and a change for the better for you!

FOUR REASONS IT'S RIGHT FOR WOMEN

1. Call your own shots!
2. Determine your own future.
3. Run your own race.
4. Create a dramatic change for your future!

CHAPTER THREE

WHAT THE FUTURE HOLDS

Click On and Cash In

Safe in the comfort of your own home, you decide, at your convenience, to do your shopping. You grab a cup of coffee, snuggle up in your comfy chair, click on, and embark on your shopping experience. You don't have to get dressed, fix your hair, put on lipstick, or even leave home. Sounds great doesn't it? Shopping online makes it all possible.

> **CLICK ON AND CASH IN!**
>
> With the click of your mouse you can have everything from cars to caviar, perfume to peanut butter, delivered right to your door. Women find that shopping online is safe, convenient, time saving, and fun.

With the click of your mouse you can have everything from cars to caviar, perfume to peanut butter, delivered right to your door. Women find that shopping online is safe, convenient, timesaving, and fun. Online shopping is here, and it is here to stay!

The Future of Network Marketing

The Web is everywhere. You've probably heard about it so often that your brain's hype filter automatically begins to screen out any phrase containing "cyber," "network," or "virtual." Big mistake. Network marketers are more high-tech than the average businessman. They have to be. The apparatus of the Web—database software, e-mail, Webzines—could have been invented with this industry in mind. What better way is there to keep in touch with a far-flung organization, take orders from millions of consumers (while computing who should get the commissions), and train new people from a distance? It makes me wonder how our industry worked before all these newfangled tools came into existence.

The Web is also a great place to market the products, services, and opportunities that network marketing companies offer. A survey conducted by Baruch College found that about 30 percent of the U.S. population is now online—comprising 58 million people. That's almost sixteen times the number of Web surfers back in 1995 and a much more representative slice of the population.

Women accounted for approximately 60 percent of the new home online subscribers during the past year. Good news for those selling household consumables and cosmetics. People are getting used to buying online. A recent Roper Starch study revealed that 45 percent of Americans online today have made a purchase over the Net. Of those who haven't, a full 31 percent still go online to research the products they're buying elsewhere.

Forecasters predict that by the year 2003 consumers will spend in excess of *three trillion dollars* on the Web. The world is undergoing a massive transformation. Deregulation in many industries is opening markets to new players, creating a global opportunity for people who are ready to take action and help lead others into the twenty-first century.

As electronic commerce continues to evolve, new networkers will quickly learn how to utilize the combination of e-commerce and network marketing to start developing a business of their own. For the network marketing veteran, the Internet will introduce you to the greatest opportunity of your lifetime. You can now tap into (or click on) to a limitless business opportunity so explosive that you will ride the wave all the way to the bank.

E-commerce brings the world to your fingertips. It is the superhighway to success in the new millennium.

In this chapter we will build a bridge between the benefits of high technology and the demands of the mass consumer marketplace. By combining the power of one-on-one relationships with the emerging global Internet opportunity, the possibilities are unlimited. As we progress through the dawn of a new age of computers and communications into the global promise of a new millennium, this timely book will introduce the next revolution in network marketing—and it's here! Women can take full advantage now of the phenomenal growth and profits available through network marketing on the Internet.

The New Wave

We stand on the edge of a new age, where people of vision are beginning to bring technology, communications, and commerce together in a way that has never before been possible. Women can learn how to profit from this revolution with network marketing, where now, more than ever before in history, technical knowledge, business experience, and endless potential join to bring the world to their fingertips.

> ### THREE REASONS WHY E-COMMERCE PLUS THE INTERNET = SUCCESS!
> 1. E-commerce brings the world to your fingertips.
> 2. It is the superhighway to success in the new millennium.
> 3. The possibilities are unlimited.

In his best-selling book, Wave 4, author Richard Poe says that the merger of network marketing and the Internet will be the biggest wave of growth in the MLM industry than ever before in history. Women are searching for a way to jump on this new wave of business on the Web. Those who capitalize on the amazing boom known as e-commerce will be on the superhighway to success. Women who grasp the understanding of this new market, how to transition from their current business to networking on the Web and explain it to prospective distributors, will develop businesses beyond their wildest dreams and ride the wave all the way to the bank.

THE FUTURE IS NOW

The Internet changes what is possible, and for women this is especially true. Virtually everyone—whether computer savvy or novice—understands that a networked economy changes the way we do business. The Internet will do for knowledge what the steam engine did for manpower: leverage it, move it, and use it more efficiently. Information and communication will become by far the most important component of the economy. The arrival of the networked economy, the gurus say, will be as dramatic as the transition from an agrarian economy to an industrial one. The networked economy will happen ten times faster than the industrial revolution. Multilevel marketers need to be poised to benefit from this once-in-a-lifetime opportunity and cash in on this new market.

People are flocking to the Web. It has about 100 million users worldwide now; it should have 320 million by 2002, according to the International Data Group. As more people get on the Web and as the Web gets better and more useful, it becomes an increasingly integral part of living. And as people use the Web to shop for clothes or groceries, find repair services, and get information about vacations, schools, or piano lessons, they plug into and enhance the networked economy.

Add up the business and consumer activity and the effect is enormous. By 2002 the amount of commerce on the Internet will exceed $400 billion, a compounded annual growth rate between now and then of an astonishing 103 percent, IDG says.

The realization is sinking in that the networked economy is not just about Silicon Valley, computers, and Web surfing. "This is about our entire economy," says Kevin Kelly, executive editor of *Wired* and author of *New Rules for the New Economy*. The geography of wealth is being reshaped. Those who play by the new rules will prosper, while those who ignore them will not.

Although this new economy may seem unfamiliar or even uncomfortable to some that may feel frustrated and forced to change in the face of a new paradigm shift, they need only to understand the phenomenal opportunities that await them. The Internet is responsible for radical changes in information delivery and product purchasing. IDG predicts that by the year 2015, retail businesses as we know them today will

FOUR HOT FACTS FOR THE FUTURE OF BUSINESS

1. Currently the Web hosts over 100 million users worldwide. It is predicted to swell to over 320 million by 2002, according to the International Data Group (IDG).
2. People use the Web to shop for clothes and groceries, find repair services, and get information about vacations, schools, or piano lessons. From cars to caviar, the Internet is becoming the place to find goods and services.
3. By 2002 the amount of commerce on the Internet will exceed $400 billion, a compounded annual growth rate of 103 percent, IDG says.
4. IDG predicts that by the year 2015 retail businesses as we know them today will be nonexistent.

be nonexistent. Emerging trends in the development of technology and the marketplace are creating business opportunities for those who understand how to take full advantage of this vast and growing market.

Leaders with vision will expand their thinking to embrace a new business opportunity and understand that they too can create wealth on the Web. Imagine a business in which you prosper and that your children can inherit and have the opportunity to create even more income for themselves and their families. With network marketing the American Dream is alive and well and it will endure, not only for another generation, but with e-commerce, generational income is available to all.

Dreambiz.com

Many people are wondering how the Internet will change their businesses. How big will electronic commerce be? When will it take off? What will happen to our current business? Can I make a business on the Internet work for me? "It's as if we're sitting on a beach wondering what the weather will be like today," says Don Tapscott in his book, *Blueprint to the Digital Economy.* "But we haven't noticed that just beyond the horizon is a 100-foot-high tsunami, which will not only affect the weather today, but will sweep us all away if we don't get ready."

There is a tsunami approaching that few have noticed. This tidal wave results from the intersection of the technology revolution and a demographic revolution, which Tapscott refers to as the Net Generation or N-Gen (children aged 2-22 in 1999). "This baby boom 'echo' is the largest generation we've seen, and because they are the first to come of age in the digital era, they have a different culture, psychology, and approach to learning, consuming, working, and playing than their baby-boomer parents. As these kids enter the workforce, they will blow all our estimates for electronic commerce right out of the water." The N-Gen is potentially the largest group of prospective network marketers in the history of multilevel marketing.

"When I began to understand the power of the Internet, combined with network marketing, a thrill of excitement hit and I don't think I've been able to sleep since," said MJ Michaels. "The Internet changes everything. It provides a vehicle where any dream is possible. The power of merchandising and networking over the Web is mind-boggling. Suddenly the gold ring is within every woman's grasp."

MJ started her network marketing business as a college student in her early twenties. "I think I was the most unlikely person to succeed in any business. I had never taken a business course, I didn't know how to use a computer or keep records. I didn't even know how to balance my own checkbook. I remember trying to do a business meeting and explain the opportunity to a group of my friends. I got a little confused at the new terminology, and called wholesale and retail, *hotel* and *resell*," laughs MJ.

Like many women, MJ thought that because she lacked business expertise success was just beyond her reach. She found out, like other women, that network marketing was a "learn-as-you-go" business and if she was willing to study, council with her upline, and work hard, she could make it big. And make it big she did!

"It took several years for my husband, Scott, and I to reach a level of success. There were many times we felt disappointed, our goals unmet. We reset many of the same goals, over and over again. We were just determined to make it. We didn't believe we had any other options. Somehow, someway we were going to make it work. Quitting was never an option for me," adds MJ. "Then came the opportunity to begin the development of an Internet business. A new opportunity, an entirely new business model designed specifically for the Internet. When we opened for business on September 1, 1999, cyberspace rocked. Over 20 million hits in the first 10 hours! We created history that day."

Today MJ Michaels's business spans the globe. She has not only developed a tremendous organization, but has helped many others to do the same as well. MJ has indeed become a professional businesswoman and is well respected in the industry. Recently elected as President to the Women's Auxiliary Council, MJ says that the Internet makes network marketing the perfect business model. And today, more than ever before in history, women have the opportunity to make it big in network marketing.

Why Online and Not in Lines?

"After working all day, skipping lunch, and fighting the commute, the last place on earth I wanted to go was the supermarket," says Marie. "Joining the throngs of exhausted people, all frantically pushing their shopping carts through overcrowded isles, attempting in vain to remember what they had written on their shopping lists that were forgotten on their desks back at the office. And the crying children, that almost sent me over the edge— "Mommy, Mommy, Mommy..." Kids, all tired and hungry after hours at the day care, wanting nothing more than some food in their tummies and their mother's attention, often put on quite a show for the audience at the supermarket," adds Marie.

You know. You've been there too. Rush to the store after work just to pick up a few things for dinner. "Oh look," you say. "Tommy's favorite cereal is on sale today—only $2.99 a box. Better get two, no three, or maybe four. And doesn't that salmon look fresh today? I wonder if it will keep until tomorrow night. I guess I'll get some now because I don't want to do this again tomorrow. Oh, no! Tomorrow night I have that dinner party. I forgot! I better grab some salad and pate too. What else have I forgotten?"

Sound familiar? There is a faster, easier, and smarter way to shop today thanks to technology and the Internet. The Internet is responsible for radical changes in information delivery and product purchasing. Emerging trends in the development of technology and the marketplace are creating business opportunities for those who understand technology and know how to use it. As worldwide markets continue to deregulate, this

FOUR GREAT REASONS TO SHOP ONLINE

1. Choices, ah choices. The Internet offers more choices than any of our local markets or shopping malls. Everything from music to macaroni, cars to caviar, or platinum rings to peanut butter can be found via the Internet.
2. Convenience. Shop anytime of the day, any day of the week, in the comfort, safety, and convenience of your own home or office.
3. Save time and energy. With the click of your mouse you can have goods delivered to your door and buy back all those hours of shopping, standing in lines, fighting crowds, and making returns.
4. The Internet, combined with network marketing, offers the best way to make money. Cash in on the explosion of e-commerce by starting your own network marketing company online today!

phenomenon will expand to encompass even greater opportunities. For women, this means not only simpler, more convenient shopping but big savings of both time and money.

"I was kind of timid about shopping online in the beginning. I had many concerns at first. Would the quality be the same as I was used to? What if I wanted to return something? When I factored in the shipping costs, was I really saving money?" wondered Marie. "After placing a few small orders, I was completely relieved of my previous concerns. The products were great, the delivery was prompt, and the convenience was unbelievable. I soon realized that even if I had to pay more for the convenience, it would have been worth it. But after I factored in all of the time and energy I spent running from store to store, I realized that shopping from home not only saved me time, but money too!"

We are often taken in by the mass of advertising of major companies that try to get us to buy more stuff. Many women have even convinced themselves that they *like* shopping. I once heard a woman say that grocery shopping is her *time to get out!* Ok, you are thinking, "I like shopping too." So do I, but not for toilet paper and aluminum foil! That is not my idea of a fun night out. Have we convinced ourselves that we are not worth it, not worthy of some personal time for simple pleasure or relaxation? Do we really believe that pushing a cart up and down aisles in harshly lit warehouses, lifting heavy cartons in and out of cumbersome shopping carts, standing in long dreary lines only to buy more stuff than we really need because it looked like such a good deal is fun? Then it's pulling stuff out of our carts and onto the checkout belts, pushing those massive carts to our cars that are parked in the distant and poorly lit parking lots only to drag our products once again out of the cart and into the car. Finally we make the trip home, haul those same products out of our cars and into our houses, then once again unpack them and rearrange them in our cupboards only to realize that we forgot to buy bread. Whew! I'm worn out just thinking about it! And we say that this is fun! Come on girls—think again.

Camp Clueless

Ok, so you don't know how to turn on your computer, much less surf the Net. How can you do business online you ask? Simple. Find the best networking companies online, the ones that are well funded, have a diversified product line, a good compensation plan, and a strong training system. Develop a close relationship with your successful upline. In Section 2 you will learn some tips from top networkers to get your business off to a fast start. After you have picked your winner, your next step is to duplicate the pattern for success taught through your own marketing system and offered by your own upline. Then magic happens! The success of network marketing combined with the power of the Internet and you've got a winner. Anything is possible!

> **FIVE FABULOUS REASONS TO START NOW!**
> 1. Low start-up costs and overhead.
> 2. No inventory.
> 3. Low risk.
> 4. Set your own schedule.
> 5. Unlimited income potential.

So How About You?

As you evaluate your own options, what do you see in your future? Network marketing, combined with the power and opportunity of the Internet, is reaching people who might never before have been interested in developing this type of business. Successful, goal-oriented young women like Rachel Stewart are jumping onboard everyday, making career changes and choices to build the future of their dreams. "I wasn't interested in getting involved in network marketing. I had recently graduated from the University of California at Berkeley and was off to build my career," Rachel said. "I knew a little bit about network marketing because my parents had been involved many years before. They had certainly made some money at it, but they never really made it big. Perhaps this is one reason that I didn't see it as a valid business opportunity or career choice. But that all changed for me last year," she adds.

Rachel, like many college graduates, was hot and heavy on the fast track to success—or so she thought. "I was so excited to get my degree from Berkeley. Being a student athlete, I understood the value of commitment and persistence. It took me five years to finish school, and when I finally hit the workplace, I was ready to run," Rachel says. "I had a job offer before I even graduated. At the time it looked like a great opportunity—a new company— opportunity for advancement. I could see myself in a couple of years driving a new car and buying my first home. Things didn't quite work out that way," she adds.

"I was driving in gridlock traffic for 2-3 hours everyday just to get to and from work, then coming home at night to the same cramped apartment I could barely tolerate living in when I was a student. Sure, I had more spending money than when I was a starving college student, but I never seemed to have enough to make a difference, enough to invest for my future. I kept thinking, 'Is this all there is?' Dreams of that new car and home were slipping further and further away. Then something happened," Rachel said.

About the time Rachel had begun to accumulate a little nest egg and started looking for a new car her boss called her into his office. "Rachel, if things don't turn around for us in the next couple of months, I am going to have to throw in the towel," he said. Like many companies, his was under capitalized. And when sales had not hit the level that he had projected, he was in big trouble. "The dream job that was going to give me the moon and the stars—hit the dirt. It was only three months later that we closed the doors," Rachel said. The day the doors shut on her job, Rachel said it felt like the doors to her dreams had closed as well. "I stuck it out with him until the end, hoping they could turn it around—but they couldn't. I was forced to apply for jobs that didn't meet any of my dreams for the future. What other options did I have? I still had bills to pay!"

Women have so much responsibility today that often they feel trapped, even suffocated. They are working at jobs they don't enjoy, for money that isn't enough, with people they don't want to be with, yet it is that sense of responsibility that keeps them on the commute and in the rat race—because they don't know that there is a way out.

E-commerce and network marketing provide a bridge between earning money and having a life. With network marketing women can build a business at their own pace and around their own busy schedules. They don't have to quit their jobs or give up their paychecks to get going with network marketing. Little by little, day by day, consistent effort can give women the perfect opportunity to build up a little nest egg, replace their income from jobs or careers, or create tremendous wealth.

THERE IS A BETTER WAY!

Women have so much responsibility today that often they feel trapped, even suffocated. They are working at jobs they don't enjoy, for money that isn't enough, with people they don't want to be with, yet it is that sense of responsibility that keeps them on the commute and in the rat race—because they don't know that there is a way out.

"Because of this disappointment, I was much more open-minded the day my mother called," Rachel said. "She was so excited about a new company that was starting on the Internet. The possibilities were staggering and I decided that if it was even half as good as it sounded, it was better than anything else out there. I jumped in and ran hard. Sure, it took work, but soon I was able to quit my full-time job, stop the commute, and even move out of that crummy apartment and into a comfortable home. I still doubt if I would have seriously looked at network marketing if it hadn't been this new business model on the Internet. Thank goodness I did!"

What about your future? What does it hold? What is important to you? In the next chapter we will unfold a secret to success: defining your dreams. With the advantages of network marketing, combined with the power of the Internet, *any* dream is possible!

SECTION TWO

How It Works:
Seven Steps
to Success

CHAPTER FOUR

DEFINE YOUR DREAMS

Why Your Dreams

Most of us have heard the story of *Alice in Wonderland,* written by Lewis Carroll. At one point in the story Alice, reaching a fork in the road, was feeling somewhat perplexed about which path to take. "Shall I take the road to the left or perhaps the right?" she wondered. In the center of the road stood a large tree. Glancing up, Alice saw a cat grinning down at her from his perch on a branch of the tree.

Alice asked, "Would you tell me please, which way I ought to walk from here?"

"That depends a good deal on where you want to get to," said the Cat.

"I don't care much where—," said Alice.

"Then it doesn't matter which way you walk," said the Cat.

"—So long as I get somewhere," Alice added.

"Oh, you're sure to do that," said the Cat, "if you only walk long enough."

This fairytale holds an important truth for us all. If we do not know where we are going (or what we want out of life) then any path we are on will get us there. But in the end, will that be the place where we really wanted to go?

In the absence of clearly defined goals we push forward in life, sometimes aimless and misdirected, often working hard only to discover at the end of the day or year that we are both unsatisfied and unfulfilled. Where did the time

DEFINE GOALS

In the absence of clearly defined goals we push forward in life, sometimes aimless and misdirected, often working hard only to discover at the end of the day or year that we are both unsatisfied and unfulfilled. Where did the time go? Where did we go wrong? Often one rudimentary missing element in our lives—taking the time to define our dreams or goals—creates this feeling of demise.

go? Where did we go wrong? Often one rudimentary missing element in our lives—taking the time to define our dreams or goals—creates this feeling of demise.

What's Your Destination?

If you were planning a trip across the country by car, what would you do? Where would you start? First you would decide what your ultimate destination would be. You would get out a map to decide which route is best. How long would it take to get there and how much time would you be able to devote to such a journey? You might consider what stops along the way would be important to you. Where would you spend the night or stop to eat? You would get your automobile in tip-top shape, perhaps even investing money in a tune-up or new tires. What about expenses? How much would this trip cost? You would take steps to prepare for unexpected emergencies that might befall you.

The weather could be a consideration. Will you have a backup plan for bad weather days? You would need to arrange your schedule with your job, family, or other commitments. Packing for this cross-country trip would take some planning and preparation. In your absence you might arrange to have your mail retained at the post office, your paper cancelled, your pet fed, or your residence looked after. There would be many considerations to make such a journey. It would take thought, time, money, and careful planning to make a trip like this a successful experience.

What a lot of planning! Most of us have planned for a trip, perhaps not a cross-country car trip, but an extended trip or vacation. We invest so much precious time in the planning and preparation and we think nothing of it. And yet most people have never taken the time to sit down, pen in hand, and contemplate their future, making a thoughtful, detailed list of their goals and dreams. Most people spend more time planning a vacation than planning their lives.

Put First Things First

It's a quiet Sunday evening. The crisp chill of winter is just outside your window, but inside by the fire it is warm and toasty. You are relaxing at home, curled up on the couch, enjoying your one and only day of solitude. Feet propped up on cushions and comforter draped across your lap; you reach for your cup of tea. The phone rings. "Mary," the frantic voice on the end of the line exclaims, "Did you hear? You won the lottery! Twenty million dollars, Mary, twenty million dollars."

Many of us have jokingly made remarks about what we would do with the money if we hit the big one or received that unexpected inheritance. It is so easy to ramble off a long wish list, isn't it? So how about it—what if you did strike it rich, hit the lotto, or even just doubled your present income? What would you do?

Cathy found out that making the right choices led her to success in music as well as in network marketing. You'll find out more about her success and what she did to hit the big time in another chapter, but for now, understand that your life, your future is in your control. The choices you made yesterday brought you to the life you live today. If you want to change some things in your life—you will have to change some things in your life. Start today to make smart choices—the ones that will lead you in the direction of your dreams.

> ### THREE GREAT WAYS TO START DREAMING
>
> 1. Set aside some private personal time to reflect upon your life, your future. Start writing a list, and write down everything!
> 2. Organize and prioritize your list. Get pictures, preferably of yourself enjoying each item on your list, and look at these pictures 3-4 times everyday. Visualize how it will feel when you reach this dream.
> 3. Start checking them off your list! As you accomplish a goal, check it off. Update your list frequently and keep adding new dreams.

Would you pay off your debts, buy a new car, get a dog, donate to your favorite charity, learn to fish, get a new wardrobe and maybe a new house to go with it? Or would you take flying lessons, get a massage, finish school, quit your job, start a new business, help a friend, open a scholarship fund, adopt a child, or write a novel? What would *you* do? What is important to *you*?

Think about it for a moment. How would your life be different? How would you feel if you were able to live your dreams? The first thing you need to do is decide what is important to you.

Write It Down

Imagine it is New Year's Eve. The party is great! Throughout the day you have evaluated your past year and tonight, as you raise your glass to toast the New Year, you make a decision, a commitment that this coming year will be different, exceptional! You will do all of the things left undone in the previous year, finish all of the projects, fix all of the relationships and, of course, lose all of the weight from the past year. Yes, this year will be different. Oh, really?

There is a famous tale often told among motivational speakers about an Ivy League college and a research project conducted several years ago. A group of research experts selected a particular graduating class and after an exhausting study compiled the personal information of each student, such as age, demographic, nationality, income level, degree received, etc., into their file and then they waited. They waited for five years, and at the conclusion of that time the researchers located each of the graduating class members from five years prior and entered their current data into the system. They tracked the success of this graduating class and the result of that research was remarkable. Of that particular graduating class only 3 percent had achieved a level of success in their chosen careers—only 3 percent! Astounding! After a careful, calculated evaluation, this research team discovered only one thing that differed from the successful 3 percent and the others: the successful 3 percent had written down clearly defined goals, the others had not!

So you say that this year your life will be different? Your life can be different and you have the power to create any kind of life you choose, in fact, you already have. Ouch! I remember the first time I heard a statement like that. I agreed to attend a seminar for work—a "positive thinking" seminar of sorts. I certainly could have used a positive attitude on that day. Sales were down at the dealership, gas prices were up at the stations, and customers seemed to delight in a sadistic ritual of visiting our dealership just to kick the tires and make comments like, "You think you are going to sell any of these gas hogs? With the gas prices sky high? Ha!" The nightly news preached doom and gloom and the daily paper was filled with headlines of gas short-ages, lines at the stations, and the rise of interest rates. Day in and day out we faced this kind of negative attitude. I decided to go to the seminar to learn something that I could take back and moti-vate the sales crew. I believed I was in attendance only for the benefit of my sales department. I never dreamed the seminar message given that day would impact my life personally.

> ## FIVE IMPORTANT STEPS
> 1. Take out a clean sheet of paper.
> 2. Throw out of your mind any past fail-ures and fears.
> 3. Think of what is really most important to you.
> 4. Write it all down.
> 5. Set no limits!

I remember sitting on a cold metal chair that afternoon, in the third row, next to a rather large man who had the sniffles so loud I could barely hear the speaker. Tired, uncomfortable, and definitely out of my comfort zone, the speaker made a comment that caught my attention, in fact, it changed my life. He said, "You are in life exactly where you want to be."

"Excuse me!" I thought. I am not at all where I want to be. I do not want to be sitting on this cold chair, next to a sick man, worried about possible sales opportunities I was missing at work, not to mention listening to you tell me that I am exactly in life where I want to be. I almost left. Thank goodness I didn't.

That afternoon I grasped an awareness that I had not previously consid-ered. *I* was responsible for my position in life. All of the past decisions and choices I made brought me to this exact place. *I had chosen it all.* I did not particularly like my life at the time, but accepting responsibility for my situa-tion gave me the understanding that if I could create this mess, I had the power and ability to change it. And I did.

That night I took the speaker's advice and stole a quiet moment alone. Taking out a clean sheet of paper, I began to make a list of all the things I wanted to be different in my life. Everything! There was no turning back. The gas prices were still high and interest rates were up, yet something was dif-ferent. Somehow writing this list down made my goals real, and in the days, weeks, and months to follow I expanded this list, implemented the speaker's tips, and began to enjoy the new life I was creating.

You can do this, too! Take out a clean sheet of paper. Throw out of your mind any past failures and fears. What do you want to do? Where do you want to go? What kind of person do you want to become? What kind of relationships do you want to enjoy? If you had the life of your dreams, how would it feel? Write it all down and remember—set no limits!

The Power of Goal Setting

One night, while reviewing the family budget, Amy Sandler found she was $200 short every month from making their balanced budget goal. Even as a successful executive, Amy faced the reality that they were unable to meet their family expenses. Working sixty-plus hours a week while her husband, Bill, completed his master's degree, Amy knew her options were limited.

One afternoon her long-time school friend called. "Amy, I am coming to visit you next week. I have found a way that we can retire early!" she exclaimed. Ready and willing to escape the doom of her finances, Amy eagerly agreed to meet with her friend the following week. Many sleepless nights followed as she contemplated the promise of freedom her friend so eagerly offered. What could this be? Could this business really work for me? Is this the answer I have so desperately been searching for?

Days turned into that long awaited week and finally her long-time friend appeared, bearing good news. "Amy, we can do this. We can be free in five years!" exclaimed her friend.

After listening to her friend's presentation about a network marketing business, Amy did indeed get excited about the possibilities. She had a goal: to earn an extra $200 and balance the family budget. Enthusiastically, she began her own business, part-time in the evenings, and within a short six months Amy matched her income as an executive. After another seven months of working this new business, she matched both her income and her husband's income, and within five years they were millionaires! How, you may ask yourself? This sounds too good to be true.

From the first day, Amy became a student of the business, devouring training manuals, books, training cassettes, and constantly making calls to her sponsor for more information. The first step, she was told, is to write down your goals. Amy thought, "But I know what my goals are—to make an extra $200 a month, and my next goal is to make enough money to retire. Why do I need to write this down?" However, Amy was committed and so she followed the counsel of her sponsor and made that list of her goals and dreams. At the top of her list was the $200 a month, followed by a new car for Bill, clothes for herself and the kids, and the list went on and on. Amy tells me that every single goal she had written on her list she had accomplished within the first year of her business. What do you think she did then? She wrote down another list of goals!

> ### FIVE GREAT WAYS TO SET GOALS FOR A BALANCED LIFE
>
> 1. Goals for financial independence.
> 2. Goals for physical and mental health.
> 3. Goals for family and personal relationships.
> 4. Goals for your spiritual being.
> 5. Goals for education and career advancement.

Of course, we all know that it takes more to succeed than simply writing a goal on a sheet of paper. But history has taught us that successful people know what they want, know where they are going, and have a clearly defined dream. In Chapter 5 we will discuss the next step Amy took on her path to financial independence, but for now, let's concentrate on step one.

Get Real

You know that there is more to life than paying bills, making the commute, watching TV, and just plain old getting by. You don't have to settle. Now that you have made your list, let's start to prioritize it. Have you written goals in all areas of your life? Is your list complete with goals that involve not just monetary pleasures but goals involving your family or relationships with others, physical or health goals, your career, the continuing education of life, or your spiritual side? A balanced life is one that has a sense of fulfillment in many areas. Why not write your lists of goals to encompass every part of your life, your being?

And what about setting short-term goals in addition to those long-term ones? Often I meet with people who want to review their lists with me. Many times they will have written only goals that are so lofty, distant, and far-reaching that they cannot create a feeling of accomplishment for months or even years. If your only goals are those that are so huge that to accomplish them will require a tremendous effort and amount of time, often success will seem so far from your grasp that you may become discouraged. If your only goals are so far from reach you may decide that it really won't matter if you start today or next week, or not at all.

Be honest with yourself. Don't put something on your list because you think you *should* want to have that thing, or look that way, or be that kind of person. Make an honest evaluation of your life. What is truly important to *you*? What stirs your soul and motivates *you*? It is futile to write a list for yourself of things that are not meaningful to you personally. Have you ever gone shopping, knowing exactly what you were looking for, only to have someone suggest that you would look smashing in that orange pantsuit with the brassy metallic belt? "It will be perfect for you. Trust me!" the salesperson says. You come out of the dressing room feeling like a clown and someone says, "It's you! You look fabulous. I can see that orange is really your color." But you don't feel fabulous, you still feel like a clown. Listen to your feelings. Be honest with yourself.

Marilyn, a single mom with two young boys to raise, started her network marketing business under challenging circumstances. "I was living alone for the first time in many years, trying to juggle my new job, the challenge of living on a limited income, and the needs of my two sons. When I first started my business and wrote my first list of goals, I wrote down everything I thought I was suppose to want—a new car, new house, clothes, and travel. When I hit my first bump in the road to success, that old car of mine started looking pretty good."

Marilyn readily admits that although she would enjoy a new car and clothes, those were not the things that were most important to her and definitely did not motivate her to move forward in her business. "When I honestly evaluated the things in life that were most important to me, I realized that what I truly wanted was more time with my boys. I wanted to be the one to take them to their baseball games and cheer for them as they got that first home run. I didn't want to always have to tell them no when they asked if I could take them to field trips at school or come to a class party. I wanted to be at home when they burst through the door in the afternoon, bubbling over with enthusiastic descriptions of their day. Most of all, I wanted to be the one who at night, when tucking them into bed, was not too tired to listen to the soft, sweet words they so longed to share with me," Marilyn says.

What are your priorities? Evaluate your list and consider what things are the most important. What is first, second, third? Remember when setting goals for your business to begin with the end in mind, asking yourself with each step, "Will this short-term goal help me along the path to my ultimate goal?" For example, as Marilyn began to outline her priorities and set her goals, she defined her ultimate goal as time with her children. In order to achieve this lofty goal, many smaller goals were set along the way. Some of your goals might be to decide how many people you will talk to about your business in a day or how many presentations you will give in a week. Remember to set goals in all areas of your life, not just your business. As women we understand that each part of our lives overlaps another part; a business goal and the results from the achievement of it will overlap into our personal or family life. We will discuss creating balance in Chapter 12, but for now remember, as Marilyn found out, making the commitment to a goal will only work if the goal is worthwhile.

THREE GREAT IDEAS TO CREATE SPECIFIC GOALS

1. Determine what is really most important in your life. Then decide what is second and third. Take time to reflect.

2. Do your homework. How do you know if you want to move to Vermont if you haven't spent time there in the winter, or if you want to drive a Ferrari if you haven't driven one? Research and find out if they are everything you hoped they would be.

3. Visit your dreams often. If you decide Vermont is the place for you but you live in Nebraska, get videos of Vermont, pictures, travel guides, etc. and look at them everyday, imagining how your life would be if you were actually there. Do the same with cars or travel. Feel the wind in your hair as you drive through the windy streets of Monaco or the sun on your face as you lay on the sandy beaches of Bermuda.

Be Specific

When Marilyn finally determined that quality of life with her family was the most important thing to her, she needed to evaluate what it would take to achieve that goal. Simply writing, "I want time with my boys," was not enough. What would getting that time entail? Marilyn had to determine how much money would be required to replace her present job. At first she set a short-term goal of making a specific amount of money that would enable her to work part-time, being home in the afternoons for her children. Then Marilyn set other goals that would give her the freedom to work her own networking business from her home, completely eliminating her outside job. She was honest and specific about her goals and what it would take to make them a reality.

So what is in it for you? If a new car is on your list, what model, make, or color is it? Would you have leather seats, a sunroof, security system, and top of the line sound? Have you seen this car of your dreams? Have you sat in it? Driven it? How do you know if that model is the car you want unless you spend some time investigating, evaluating, and testing it out? What if your goals include travel? Where would you like to go? Shouldn't you go to a travel agency or library to get information about possible trips? Would you ski down the Swiss Alps or bury your toes in the warm sand of the Caribbean? What would be your means of transportation? Would you fly to Europe on the Concorde or take a round-the-world cruise? Perhaps you would get a motor home and drive across the United States, sail the Atlantic, or speed down the Autobahn in a sporty European car.

"When I would come home after a grueling day at the office, fight the commute, and drag myself into my apartment only to find my kids eating ice cream in front of the TV, homework abandoned at the front door, and mounds of dirty laundry on the bathroom floor, I wanted to quit! It was during those discouraging times when I had to make a conscious effort to focus, not on the disarray before my eyes, but on the mental image of my dreams and goals. After turning off the TV, helping the boys start their homework, and putting in a load of clothes, I would take a moment in my room and visualize what I wanted my life to be like—visualize my dream. More often than not, that was enough to give me a boost of energy to shake the discouragement and get moving!" says Marilyn.

Can you feel the wind on your face as you race down those Swiss slopes? Does the warmth of the sun and the sound of the ocean lull you to a restful nap as you gently swing from a hammock on the beach? This same principle holds true for all of your dreams and goals. Can you see yourself doing, having, enjoying, and loving the life you are creating with this list? You might want to try them on and see if they fit the image you have in your mind and then you must get really specific, detailing as much as possible, to help you reach that goal or destination.

> ### FIVE GREAT SHORT-RANGE GOALS
>
> 1. Set up separate checking account.
> 2. Study training material everyday.
> 3. Attend every seminar possible.
> 4. Outline a list of perspective business partners
> 5. Schedule regular time with sponsor.

Go for the Gold!

Olympic athletes have shared their secrets of success with the world. Each of them had determined their goal, outlined specific short-term goals to track their progress, formulated a plan of action, made a commitment, and then worked for the gold. Every successful person, whether in athletic competition or in life, has set big goals. People often say, "Shoot for the stars." Sometimes we are afraid to aim high, fearing failure or embarrassment. If you shoot for the stars and miss, you might hit the treetops, but if you only shoot for the treetops you may hit dirt. When setting goals, set no limits on yourself. Anything is possible.

As I mentioned earlier, when setting goals it is important to not only get real and be specific, but also to set a variety of goals in all areas of your life. First let's talk about short-range goals. These goals might be steppingstones to larger goals. For example, if I wanted to lose weight and my ultimate goal was to lose twenty pounds, I might set a short-range goal of losing five pounds at a time. With each five-pound loss I would have achieved success. This would give me a sense of accomplishment and motivate me to go for the next five pounds. In contrast, if my only goal was twenty pounds and after two months of diet and exercise I had only lost eight pounds, I may feel like a failure and grab that gallon of ice cream.

In your business you should first set short-range goals. "At first," Marilyn explains, "my goals were simple and attainable. I needed a feeling of success and control in my life where previously there had been none. My first goal was to complete my goal list! I did it. My sponsor told me to pat myself on the back even for the accomplishment of little things and as I did that, I began to feel better about myself and more committed to my next set of goals."

Your first short-range goals might be to set up a separate checking account for your new business. You might want to set a goal to study your suggested training material everyday for a specific amount of time, attend meetings and conferences suggested by your organizational leaders, outline a list of prospective business partners, or develop a professional approach.

Put a Date on It

A goal without a date on it is merely a wish. By setting a date for the accomplishment of each goal we have not only created another goal of sorts, but more importantly we have put an urgency to it. By setting a date we can then develop a plan for the achievement of that goal. If you were planning a trip from California to New York by car, wouldn't it be important to know how much time you had to give to this trip? By determining the amount of time required to get from California to New York, you would then be able to chart your course step by step, breaking down your final goal into smaller goals such as how many miles you will drive the first day or where you will stop for the night. Wouldn't the time you had allowed for this trip be the single most determining factor for what you would do first, second, and third?

By putting a date on each of our own personal or business goals, we then can break each one down into smaller ones. Marilyn's ultimate goal was to be at home to raise her two sons. She set a date for retirement from her job. "When I finally realized that the most important thing in my life was quality *and* quantity of time with my children, I had to first determine how much money I needed to match my present income from my job," says Marilyn.

"After determining the total income I needed to develop in my network marketing business that would allow me to be home full time, my sponsor suggested I consider a shorter goal, one that would be attainable sooner. She helped me to break my long-term goal down into smaller goals, such as working only four days a week. Then I set a goal to work only part time, until I was able to finally realize my dream of quitting my job completely and creating more options, more choices in my life. By putting a time frame or a date on each of my goals, they became real to me and I could then develop a step-by-step plan to achieve them. I could see that they were realistic and attainable where in the beginning the goal of totally retiring from my job seemed so far away I did not really believe I could do it."

> ### FIVE POINTS TO PROPEL YOUR SUCCESS
>
> 1. Set a date for accomplishing your goal.
> 2. Review your list of goals daily.
> 3. Evaluate your progress each day.
> 4. Set daily goals.
> 5. Consult with upline regularly.

Review and Report

"Every night before my head hits the pillow I review my written list of goals from the previous day, evaluate my progress, and make a new list of goals that I want to accomplish on the following day. The next morning when my feet hit the floor I am off and running, not having to stop and wonder what I am going to do first," says Amy. "Then I set aside one hour every Sunday night to evaluate the past week. Did I accomplish my goals? Where could I improve? I would then call my sponsor and discuss the events of my past week. My sponsor would offer suggestions and ideas for my consideration that would help me to attain my goals. After consulting upline, I would determine my goals for the next week, breaking them down into a daily list, which I would modify each night before going to sleep. Knowing I would be talking to my sponsor every Sunday night really kept me on track. My success rate increased tremendously and I found I was able to accomplish more things in less time as I reviewed my goals and reported my achievements and even my shortcomings."

Breaking into a new future doesn't mean working enormously harder. It means knowing perhaps for the first time what you are working *for*. It means choosing what you will do based on your deepest passions rather than trying to motivate yourself to work harder at something that you are only partially committed to. By reviewing your goals each night and reporting your successes and even lack thereof to someone who has a sincere interest in you and in your success, you begin to realize a feeling of accomplishment. In following the path you have chosen to walk—even if you have never really succeeded before—you'll know that you never again will have to do it alone. You are learning not to work harder but to work smarter.

Thoughts Are Things

Author Earl Nightingale once wrote, "We are what we think about." Thoughts are things. Every word we have spoken, every step we have taken, every action we have made first began with a thought, whether conscious or not.

As a young girl the hot days of summer often found my family at the lake. Boating was my all-time favorite summer activity. The sound of the motor combined with the wind in my face seemed to offer great relief from the scorching heat of the Texas sun. We would jump into the boat, waves slapping against the sides, until we found the perfect spot for swimming. My father, not at all interested in swimming, would be looking for the perfect fishing spot. Determining that he had found just the right place to catch the big one, he would lull the motor to a crawl and set the automatic pilot to maintain a very slow course.

Before he could even get in his first cast, my brothers and I would splash into the icy cold water of that deep lake and promise to swim away from his perfect fishing place. I was a strong swimmer and would swim quite a distance from the boat. After getting sufficiently far enough distance between myself and my two younger brothers, I would float on my back, sun baking my face, looking up at the blue sky and puffy white clouds while my younger brothers would take turns dunking each other with squeals of delight. Soon my father would whistle and we would each return to the boat while he looked once more for the perfect spot to catch the big one. Determining once again to have found it, he would again lull the motor and make us promise to swim quietly away from his fishing place.

On one occasion he forgot to reset the automatic pilot in the boat and I wasn't watching close enough. When I finally looked up he seemed to have drifted quite away from us. Both of my brothers and I began to call out, "Hey, Daddy, over here." When he turned the front of the boat and crept carefully towards us we asked him where he was going. He explained the automatic pilot, how it worked, and what had happened when he forgot to reset it. It had taken him unknowingly back on the previous course he had programmed in, which was not the course he had wanted.

Later in life I realized that each of us has an automatic pilot of sorts—a program in our minds. Teachers, parents, siblings, family, and peers have

> "Whether you think you can or you think you can't, you are right."
>
> —HENRY FORD

helped us set some of these programs. Other thoughts we have created, and whether they are true, we operate our own course in life based upon the settings. In order to change the course of our lives, we need to reprogram our thinking about ourselves and what we think we are capable of or think we deserve. If it is true that we get what we think, would you agree that it is important to be aware of the things we think?

"Whether you think you can or you think you can't," said Henry Ford, "you are right." Our thoughts and attitudes are among the few possessions that are totally ours and cannot be taken from us. We are totally in control. It is only when we continually exercise control over our own thoughts that we can manage external circumstances. Real change comes from the inside first and our behavior naturally follows.

Reward Thyself

Women, caregivers of the world, are often so busy giving to others that we forget about ourselves. As important as setting goals, rewarding yourself for the accomplishment of goals that you have set will play an important role in your success. Amy says, "In the beginning money was so scarce that I did not have anything to reward myself with, nor my family, so I set little rewards. For example, if I accomplished each of the items on my weekly goal list I might treat myself to something as small as a new nail polish. As I progressed in the business my rewards would progress too. Soon I was able to afford to reward myself with a manicure and later a full day at a luxurious spa. When I would set goals with my children, I would also set a reward for them as they accomplished their goals. In the beginning it might have only been an ice-cream cone. Later came the new cars and trips to Hawaii. I have learned that by giving myself little rewards along the way, I felt positive and that motivated me to do more—to go the extra mile."

Amy put into practice the principles taught in this chapter, and in only six months she matched her income as a professional and within five years was a millionaire in her business. As you set your goals and put a date on the achievement of them, add a list of the rewards you will give to yourself and others as you attain these levels of success. And most of all—enjoy it!

Give Yourself Permission to Succeed

Allow yourself the privilege of success. Often people justify their lack of success saying to themselves, "I am doing Ok," or "I have attained more in life than my parents." We have often been told that in order to be happy we have to be humble, and sometimes we associate humility with a lack of monetary success, often believing that it is somehow wrong to be successful.

You deserve to succeed. You deserve a good, joyous, productive, happy life. It is yours for the taking. Give yourself permission to have it all!

Enjoy the Journey

Have fun along the way to success. If you can only feel great once you have reached your ultimate goal and dream, you will miss the sweetest experiences of success along the way. Success is not a destination; it's a journey. You can gain satisfaction, joy, and happiness as you move forward toward your dreams.

"I learned to enjoy the feeling of satisfaction as I accomplished the little things I learned as I pursued my goals and plodded forward along the path to success. I made many mistakes and I learned to laugh at myself instead of being so self-critical. I learned from the mistakes I made and I was grateful for the experiences that have led me to these important lessons in life," said Amy. "If I had waited to achieve my ultimate goal before finding joy and happiness in my business, I would have cheated myself and my family out of richly rewarding experiences along the way."

Have fun. Smile at yourself. As you hit roadblocks or obstacles along the path to success, look for the positive things in every aspect of your life and business. Above all, remember you are moving in the right direction!

> **THE JOURNEY**
>
> Success is not a destination; its a journey.
>
> 1. Have fun.
> 2. Smile at yourself.
> 3. Look for the positive things and focus on them.
> 4. Remember, you are moving in the right direction.

Dream Stealers

Something was terribly wrong!

Immediately upon stepping on my front porch I knew that something terrible had happened. The door was ajar and through its opening I could see past the hallway and into my ransacked living room. Gone from its shelf was my favorite sculpture. Ripped from the wall above the mantel, my grandfather's sword. Upon further inspection I noticed that not only was my TV and sound system missing, but also my daughter's collection of antique porcelain dolls. My stomach in knots, I felt suddenly weak. Oh no, I thought, what else did they steal?

Someone had broken into my house, rifled through my personal belongings, and ripped me off. If this has ever happened to you, you probably remember the feeling. It was awful. I felt cheated, violated! But no matter how terrible I felt or how angry I got, I was absolutely powerless to do anything about it.

Six Steps to Your Success

1. Write down your dreams and goals.
2. Be specific. If you want a yellow car, —what make and model and with what options, and specify the color of yellow or you might end up with a lemon!
3. Put a date on it! When do you plan to accomplish these dreams or hit the goals? Dating each one puts a time limit on it and moves you forward in a specific motion.
4. Review and report. Look at your list daily. Check off and date each item as you reach it. Constantly upgrade your list. Progress is improved by review and reporting your progress to a particular person on a regular schedule.
5. Reward yourself. Remember to let yourself feel satisfaction and joy as you reach each goal, no matter how small.
6. Enjoy the journey. Have fun along the way. True success is measured by the joy you have as you move along the path to success. It is enjoying the journey, not only hitting the destination.

That is how we feel when someone steals something from us. Yet most of us think nothing of it when others come into our lives and steal something so priceless and precious as our dreams.

As you begin to hit some of the milestones along the road to your success, you will notice other benefits not previously considered. When you are in the pursuit of a worthwhile goal or dream, you will find you have added energy and enthusiasm for life. Others might notice that you have a spring in your step, a twinkle in your eyes, or a smile on your face. People may comment that you look younger, more relaxed, and happier. They may compliment you on your enthusiastic attitude.

There may be others, however, who appear less than excited about the improvement they see in you. They may feel uncomfortable or even intimidated by the "new" you. Sadly, it is often those closest to us—friends, family, or coworkers—who may be the most powerful dream stealers of all. Dishing out sarcasm, stirring up guilt, feeding you a line of garbage, they may attempt to stop your progress and keep you in your "proper place"—the one *they* feel comfortable in. Some may scoff at you, even implying that something is somewhat strange about you as if it were inappropriate to feel so happy, look so good, be so successful. Don't you dare fall for it! Don't you dare let anyone steal your dreams.

Define and Accomplish

Determining your dreams, defining your goals, and visualizing your success could be the single most important step in achievement of your success in network marketing and in your life.

"While attending a conference in my network marketing business, I learned the importance of setting specific goals and defining them with as much detail as possible," says Marilyn. "One of our speakers that evening was discussing the subject of defining goals and dreams and suggested that once we have defined our dreams that we need to get a picture of them and place those pictures in places around our homes or office where we will see them often, thereby focusing our attention upon our goal. The speaker told a story of his path to success and how he had written a detailed list of goals, placed pictures of them around his office, and daily visualized his life as it would have been had he been in possession of his particular goals and dreams.

"One of his dreams was to own a red Ferrari. As he began to investigate and search for information and details of this car, he followed the advice of his sponsor and found a picture of the car of his dreams. It was on the cover of *Road & Track* magazine. It was a feature article of that particular issue and he removed the picture and placed it on his refrigerator door where he would be sure to see it several times a day. Every morning when leaving for work he would look at that picture and say, 'Someday that car will be mine.' He would repeat the same each night upon returning home from work.

"As he continued to develop a bigger and more profitable networking business the day finally came that he was able to order his car and he did. He ordered a red Ferrari, just like the one on the cover of the magazine he had looked at for so long. Finally his car had arrived and he met the sales representative on the dock to await the delivery of his dream. However, when the car was delivered to the dock, instead of being the beautiful red Ferrari he had ordered, it was an orange-red one. He was terribly disappointed! The sales representative was embarrassed and quickly tried to save the sale by telling him that only a limited amount of cars were delivered to the United States in a year and that rather than wait again for many months, perhaps he could be satisfied with the orange-red Ferrari.

"'No thank you,' he replied. 'I have waited this long for my dream and although I am extremely disappointed, I will not settle for anything less than the car I have worked for, dreamed of, and paid for. I will wait.'

"The sales representative, feeling as though he had exhausted all possibilities of keeping this customer, happily took one more chance. 'Well, I do know where I could get my hands on a red Ferrari, just like the one you ordered, but it is a little bit used. You see, it was the demo car for *Road & Track* magazine.' He then took our speaker to see the exact car that was hanging on the fellow's refrigerator at home, the exact car! The power of a dream was proven."

Define your dreams. Write them down and be specific. Visualize your life as if you were already in possession of the dreams you desire. The next step in your journey to success is making a commitment. We will talk about commitment in the next chapter and how commitment affects the outcome of your level of success in business and in life. So come on—enjoy the journey. Beware of dream stealers. Most importantly, give yourself permission to succeed and, above all, *dream big!*

CHAPTER FIVE

MAKING A COMMITMENT

What Does Commitment Have to Do with Success?

A conclusive, clear-cut, definitive decision is often the singular element that separates the winners from the losers. Nothing worthwhile in life is obtained without commitments. Commitments can be scary for two reasons: We are afraid that they won't be able to fulfill us, or we're scared that we won't be able to fulfill them. Often women shy away from commitments because they already know how awful it feels to be committed to projects they don't believe in, job titles they don't enjoy, or relationships they've outgrown. Plans change; commitments don't.

This chapter will help readers learn the difference between commitment and completion, offering clear-cut steps that outline the path from commitment to achievement of your goals.

Launch Your Dreams

A burning desire to be and to do is the launching pad from which anyone who wants to succeed must take off. Dreams and success are not born from laziness, indifference, or lack of ambition and drive. Consider that everyone who succeeds in life has gotten off to a bad start at least once and has encountered heartbreaking struggles before they hit it big. Often they will tell you that their turning point came during the most challenging crisis where they were often introduced to their true selves.

Let's hear what Elaine has to say about turning tragedy into triumphs. "My husband's shining career of 20 years went out like a match after corporate merging. Bob was at the top of the pay scale when it happened. I had not worked since putting him through college. We had a nice lifestyle, but even with our savings and investments, we weren't prepared financially for unemployment. I was devastated," says Elaine.

When Elaine's sister heard the news, she immediately called Elaine and told her about a new business opportunity and suggested she and Bob go to a meeting the following week. She encouraged Elaine to check it out. Feeling like her options were limited, Elaine went to the meeting. "At first Bob was totally turned off by the idea of network marketing, but when I came home from that first meeting, he saw my excitement and enthusiasm. I think it gave him hope," says Elaine. "In the beginning I was only hoping for a little extra money to help tide us over until Bob could find another job. I never dreamed that we'd match Bob's income after only 12 months!"

Elaine's story typifies that of many others who have turned tragedy into triumph. Sometimes it is the very challenge life slaps in our face that forces us on a new path and drives us to find our dreams.

In Chapter 11, Overcoming Obstacles, we will discuss in detail how other successful women, women like Terri Gulick who built her business through terrible personal challenges, have emerged through insurmountable odds to become the biggest and the best in network marketing. For now, let's get off the launching pad and turn the lemons in your life into lemonade.

The Game Plan

Armies never go into battle without a plan. Coaches don't send players into a game without clearly outlined plays. Chefs don't begin preparations for a great meal without checking ingredients and recipes. Contractors don't begin construction of their buildings without blueprints. And you can't start down the road to success without a plan, either.

You are what you are and where you are because of countless choices that you've made during your lifetime. Each choice has an influence, however slight, upon your path in life. You can choose to be cheerful, or you can choose to be sad. You can choose to be rude, or you can choose to be courteous. You can choose to love your neighbor, or you can choose to hate your neighbor. You can choose to be prosperous, or you can choose to be broke. When you understand that every choice has an end result, you place yourself in a position to become successful in every area of your life.

Every choice that you make takes you either toward what you want in life or away from your heart's desire. In Chapter 4 we discussed defining your goals and dreams—determining what your personal driving force will be. In this chapter we will define what your plan or strategy will be to attain those goals and dreams. In this chapter you will get focused on the course that will get you heading down the right path if you aren't there already.

Smart Choices

To make your dreams a reality and achieve the balance and lifestyle you seek, you must first make good decisions. Wise decisions are vital to the fulfillment of your dreams. For example, if you desire to be a professional football player, you should turn down the offer of a cigarette. If you want to be a CIA agent, don't involve yourself in any illegal activities. If you want to be accepted at a particular college, find out what its requirements are and decide to exceed them.

> ### FOUR GREAT TIPS TO WIN BIG!
>
> 1. Develop a game plan. Decide what you want and how you plan to get it. Know what your first, second, and third move will be and how it will relate to your ultimate success.
> 2. Make smart choices. With each decision you face ask yourself, "How will this affect my business? Will it be better or not?"
> 3. Develop a burning desire. Desire is critical to your success. It is something you cannot buy or borrow. Determine what yours is and you will find out that nothing can stop you from attaining it.
> 4. Stick with it! Never, ever, ever give up on your goals and your game plan. You cannot fail unless you quit trying.

"I remember as a young girl, watching my grandfather as he listened to his favorite music album. He would close his eyes and lean his head back a bit. Engrossed in the sounds and sensations the music created within him, he would smile, eyes closed, and tears would slowly creep down his face. I knew then that someday I wanted to be a singer. I wanted to make music like the music that moved my grandfather to tears," says Cathy Combden. "Every choice and decision I made from that day until now was affected by my drive to sing. Even deciding to pursue a network marketing business was connected to my ultimate goal of being a famous recording artist. I knew if I hit it big in Quixtar, I would have the money to produce my own music," she adds. And she has. Cathy has recorded many albums and has had several top hits. Cathy made smart choices, each one building upon the last. By knowing what she wanted and making the commitments necessary to fulfill her dreams she did experience the day she dreamed about as a young girl.

"I was performing in Canada and my grandfather was in the audience. I could see him from the stage and I hoped beyond all hopes that he would be pleased with my performance. As I began my first song, I tried not to look at him, still concerned about pleasing him. Soon the music consumed me and I no longer thought about pleasing my grandfather—I almost forgot he was there. Then as I wrapped up the last chorus, something caught my eye and I turned my attention towards my grandfather, sitting second row from the stage. In his old burgundy button down sweater, beret tilted slightly on top of his balding head, he sat, head back, and eyes closed. I saw the smile on his face and the tears as they gently ran down his weathered cheeks and I knew that dreams really do come true!"

Cathy found out that making right choices led her to success in music as well as in network marketing. You'll find out more about her success and what she did to hit the big time in another chapter, but for now, understand that your life, your future, is in your control. The choices you made yesterday brought you to the life you live today. If you want to change some things in your life, you will have to change some things in your life. Start today to make smart choices—the ones that will lead you in the direction of your dreams.

Masters of Fate

When Henley wrote, "I am the master of my fate, I am the captain of my soul," he should have informed us that we are the master of our fate, the captains of our souls, because we have the power to control our thoughts.

He should have told us that our brains become magnetized with the dominating thoughts that we hold in our minds, and, by means with which no person is familiar, these "magnets" attract to us the forces, the people, the circumstances of life that harmonize with the nature of our dominating thoughts. He should have told us that before we can accumulate riches in great abundance, we must magnetize our minds with intense desire for success.

Helen Keller became deaf and blind shortly after her birth, yet despite her greatest misfortune she has written her name in the pages of history of the great. Her entire life is an example of the power of intense desire. Beethoven was deaf in his later years, Milton was blind, and van Gogh was mentally unstable, but their names will last as long as time endures.

The Power of Desire

Long ago a great warrior faced a situation that made it necessary for him to make a decision that ensured his success on the battlefield. He was about to send his warriors against a powerful army whose men outnumbered his own. He loaded his soldiers into boats, sailed to the enemy's country, unloaded his soldiers and equipment, then gave his men the order to burn their own ships. Standing bravely before his men just before the first battle, he said, "You see the boats are burning, going up in smoke. That means that we cannot leave these shores alive unless we win! We now have no choice—*we win*—or *we perish*!" They won.

> ### THE DESIRE
>
> When our *why* is big enough, we are able to do the impossible.
>
> When the *dream* (desire) is big enough, *the facts don't count!*

When our *why* is big enough, we are able to do the impossible. When we burn our own ships, we are able to do the unimaginable. Time and time again we hear stories of a frail woman who lifts a heavy car from her grandson's leg, or a little child who courageously pulls his buddy from the icy water of a frozen pond, or a father who breaks open locked doors to rescue his children from fire. How do they do it? Desire! When the *dream* (desire) is big enough, *the facts don't count!*

THE COMMITMENT

Trying is just a noisy way of not doing something. There is a vast difference in being involved and being committed. When you are "interested" in something you do it when it is convenient, but when you are "committed" you follow through no matter what—no excuses!

Making a Commitment

Trying is just a noisy way of not doing something. There is a vast difference in being involved and being committed. When you are "interested" in something you do it when it is convenient, but when you are "committed" you follow through no matter what—no excuses!

Many people are involved rather than committed. They talk about *trying* to do something, rather than actually *doing* it. They make lots of noise but fail to follow up. An *interested* exerciser wakes up in the morning to rain and says I think I'll exercise tomorrow. A *committed* exerciser wakes up to rain and says I better exercise inside.

When a person is committed to doing something he or she will find ways to suppress rationalization even when it is inconvenient. Such a person will keep his or her commitment. Persistence in life is characterized by this mental and behavioral toughness.

Which Came First?

Lorene Cron says that commitment is the single most important ingredient in success. "I worked all day in a doctor's office and often got home at night to pull another eight hours with my family," says Lorene. "Raising children is a full-time job and I certainly put in many hours of overtime with mine. When I decided to take on the challenge of my own business, I wondered if I would be able to make the time to do it all. I later understood that there isn't a person out there who works, has family or other responsibilities outside their jobs, and is developing a business on the side that can do it all. The secret is to define your priorities, make a commitment, and never renegotiate your decision to succeed."

Many have heard the story of the chicken and the pig when discussing issues of commitment. It goes something like this: Over breakfast one day a mother was trying to teach her son about commitment. She looked at the breakfast before them, eggs and bacon. After a moment she said to her son, "You see these eggs and bacon? The chicken was involved, but the pig was totally committed."

So how about you? Are you just involved or are you totally committed to your dreams and goals? The difference in mediocrity and monumental success is often hinged on commitment.

Walking the Walk

Commitment is about sticking to your guns. Someone once said that true commitment could be described as a person who stays committed to a goal long after the excitement of the moment has past. Look around. Who is the loyal leader in your organization? More often than not it is the person who is the most successful—and often the busiest. That person has learned to look upline to her leader and has duplicated her pattern for success. She has walked the walk, not just talked the talk.

"When I make a decision and then a commitment to that decision, it is a done deal," adds Lorene. "Oh sure, things come up, roadblocks are always along the highway to success, but a committed person finds a way to get through the obstacles."

Perhaps you have heard the saying "A dog on the hunt doesn't know he has fleas." Or "A happy shopper doesn't know that she has blisters." If we are truly committed and continue to focus on our dreams and not our obstacles, they seem to get smaller and smaller until we often don't notice them at all.

To Thyself Be True

Being honest with yourself is one of the most important parts of your progressive development and success in life. Dr. Norman Vincent Peale kept a poem in his wallet and referred to it frequently. It was written by Dale Wimbrow.

You may fool the whole world down the pathway of life
    And get pats on your back as you pass,

But your final regard will be heartaches and tears

    If you've cheated the man in the glass.

While the message is loud and clear, you might ask, "But don't some people do the wrong thing and then rationalize what they've done?" Yes, people do that, but if they take a good hard look at themselves, down deep they know they have done wrong.

You can't go against your image of yourself and what you think is right without feeling bad. It's counter to your purpose—the picture you have of yourself as an ethical person. A clear purpose is the foundation upon which sound, ethical behavior is built. When we make commitments—to ourselves and to others—we feel good when we have fulfilled them, just as we feel bad when we don't. If we make a commitment to do something, we must do that thing which we said we would do. This promotes good self-esteem. So a large part of our success depends on our honesty—both with others and especially with ourselves.

Paralyzed by Procrastination

After analyzing several hundred millionaires, analysts disclosed this fact: Every one of them had the habit of reaching decisions promptly and following through on those decisions completely. "Procrastination is a certain failure in any business, but especially in network marketing where we deal with people everyday," said Kathy. "When I make a decision to do something, whether it is convenient or not, I do it. I wasn't always this way. In the beginning I let many things come up to take my focus off my business plan for the day. It might have been something as important as a child who needed some extra help with homework, or something as little as a phone call that could throw me off schedule. Often I would then try to rationalize why I should wait until later to finish a business project or appointment. My business was paralyzed by procrastination. It was always a mistake to wait, to put off doing what needed to be done," says Kathy.

Lack of persistence is one of the major causes of failure. Moreover, history has proven that lack of persistence is a weakness common to most people. It is a weakness that can be overcome by effort. Where there is a will, there is a way! The more intense your desire to succeed, the easier to conquer this weakness. If you find yourself lacking in persistence, perhaps your desire isn't what it should be. Get a bigger dream!

> **FIVE TOP COMMITMENTS FOR SUCCESS**
>
> 1. Commit to your dreams and goals.
> 2. Commit to your personal game plan for success.
> 3. Commit to read books and review tapes and training material daily.
> 4. Commit to 100 percent product loyalty.
> 5. Commit to start today!

"While at a training meeting I learned about a big promotion for top achievers—a trip to Hawaii! Oh, how I had dreamed of going to Hawaii, basking in the sun and sticking my toes deep in the warm sandy beaches. I had talked about going for years. I knew that with consistent effort I could finally take that dream vacation," adds Kathy. "I set my goals, evaluated my plan of action, and made some clearly defined commitments. As I followed through each day I began to see such amazing growth in my business. I realized just how much I had been 'putting off' and just what it had cost me. When the day finally came and I was splashing in the warm waters of the Pacific Ocean, I understood very clearly that procrastination is pitiful but *persistency pays big*!"

Commitment Is Critical to Your Success

Now that you understand how critical commitment is to your success, have you evaluated your own commitments? Start with your *why*—your reason—or your dreams, then evaluate your commitment to your particular business plan, which should include not only your own product line, training system, and support material but your upline leaders as well as your own downline partners. In Chapter 13 we will discover some key ingredients to success through development of loyalty and leadership, but for now, decide today that you will be in the 100 percent club—that you will be *100* percent *committed* to your own business, products, and, most importantly, to you!

"Sometimes people get involved in network marketing and just seem to 'play' at it. They say they want to make big money, yet they treat their business as if it is just a little hobby, something that they can do in their spare time. I wonder if their dreams and goals are just not very important to them—mine were. I spent 40+ hours a week at my job. Why would I imagine that I could make serious money in a business of my own if I gave it less effort?" said Lorene. "I knew that some things in my life were nonnegotiable—my kids, my job, etc. I also knew that some of the other things I gave my time to each day were not really important. I found that doing a few simple things differently every day gave me many more hours of discretionary time every week. I used this time to make a life for my family and myself. I worked my business for a few hours after work and almost every weekend. In just a few months I had exceeded my income from my day job, and within that first year I was free from that job altogether. Today I enjoy life, my family, and friends—money is definitely not a problem. I believe that because I stayed consistently committed to my goal that I am able to enjoy such a great lifestyle today."

On Your Mark

Now you are ready to get in the race for success—the race to financial freedom. You know that network marketing is big and it's getting bigger. You have only seen the tip of the iceberg. The future of business is network marketing and the Internet will be a big player in your future. Now that you know this is the best business opportunity for making money, you have a list of clearly defined objectives and goals, made some commitments, and now you are ready to get started! What's next, you ask? Well, it's time to get started on another list—of prospective business associates. In Chapter 6 we'll talk about who, why, and how, then offer step-by-step guides to help you off the mark and into the winner's circle.

On your mark, get set, go!

CHAPTER SIX

SHARING THE IDEA

So you've decided to take the challenge. You have set your goals, made the commitment to move forward, and started to think of all the people you know on a first name basis. You lock yourself into the quiet solitude of your office and reach for the phone, and you stop—dead in your tracks. "I don't know what to say," you gasp in horror. "What will I do if they say no? I need to know how to handle their objections, answer their questions. I need a plan, a script to follow." So you stop, wipe off your sweaty palms, and do the smart thing. You call your sponsor.

Every network marketing company has its own unique prospecting system.

> ### THREE GREAT WAYS TO SPOT YOUR LEADER
>
> 1. Your Upline has developed a successful business.
> 2. Your upline follows closely the pattern of success taught by their leaders.
> 3. Your upline is "walking the walk," not just "talking the talk."

You should always follow the system your upline uses. After all, they are the experts. No matter what minor differences in style or approach your upline may practice, the fundamental principles of prospecting will always be the same. But remember, follow the leader.

Who Is My Leader?

Who is your leader? Your leader is the person in your upline who has developed a successful business and is teaching the pattern or system of success that is being taught by his or her upline leaders. In other words, they are duplicating a proven outline for success. Unfortunately, this person may not be your sponsor. Be careful whom you take your lead from. Ask yourself, is this person following my organization's pattern or system? Does this person teach by example? Following a successful leader can be an important first step for women who are beginning their business. We will discuss more about the development of a pattern for success in Chapter 9, but for now let's find out what Amy did to jump-start her business.

First Things First

"My sponsor lived over 3,000 miles away," says Amy Grant. As a top executive with a leading department store, Amy understood the power of duplication and of a proven training system. "I knew if I was going to make this business work I would have to get my hands on every piece of training information available, so I called my sponsor and asked for help. She sent me a box of training material that I quickly digested, and when I called her, hungry for more information, she knew just what to do. My sponsor was new in this business too, but she was smart enough to get me in touch with someone in our upline who had already reached the level of success I was searching for." Amy learned from her upline how to jump-start her business, and that is just what she did.

Who Do You Know?

Recognizing Amy's potential as a leader, her upline immediately went to work to help her learn the basics of success in her new business. This included developing a list of potential business partners, or those who might be interested in making money in a business of their own. "My upline told me that only second after defining my goals and dreams was writing a complete names list. At first I didn't think I knew very many people. I was quickly surprised at all of the people I did know and could include on my list," Amy said. "If this was step one, I wanted to do it right. My upline told me that I should include every person I knew, even if we weren't close personal friends or associates." Amy says this was a beginning to her success.

Fundamental to the establishment of a network marketing business is the creation of a list of potential distributors. Some people refer to this as a "warm list." A warm list is a group of individuals from your past or present whom you know well enough that were you to pick up the telephone and call them, they would recognize you after they heard your name. Developing a large warm list can be your first, most powerful resource in your race towards success.

Get a Big List

"I was told that to develop a big business I needed to develop a big list, and I did!" says Amy. "My sponsor told me to write down at least 200 names, so I went for more. First I wrote down the obvious—family, friends, and coworkers. Then I reached a little further and wrote a list of past friends, those who had moved away or changed jobs and I hadn't seen for awhile. I looked at my Christmas card list, my wedding reception journal, and even my college and high-school yearbooks."

Making cold calls is one of the quickest ways to burn yourself out. Why? It's so stressful. In a cold call, you constantly face the anticipation (and the reality) of rejection and abuse. I don't know about you, but to me, making cold calls every day would be like being on a starvation diet for the rest of my life. Miserable! Torture! The good news is that there are much better ways to find your ideal distributors and customers that don't make you nearly as uncomfortable. To attract qualified leads, consider developing a large warm list.

The larger your warm list, the easier it will be to develop a solid business. By age thirty, social psychologists have noted, the average person literally knows 2,000 people on a first name basis. One of the first steps for new networkers is to begin making a 2,000-person list of people they know personally. Did I hear a faint sigh, or was it a gasp? Ok, I know that may seem like a lot of people. I

THREE GREAT WAYS TO BUILD A HUGE LIST

1. Utilize your resources. Refer to your address book, Christmas list, wedding list, high-school or college yearbooks, civic or church directory, etc.
2. Don't try to prejudge who will or who won't. A common mistake made by new networkers is to look at their list and try to pick who will and who won't do the network business. This is a fatal mistake. You can't pick them— they will choose themselves.
3. Constantly add to your list. You meet new people everyday. Get their name, business card, or phone number.

can imagine you may be thinking that you know only 100 or 200 people, tops! But, if I told you to make a list of 200 names, you might only come up with 150 names. If I suggest a 1,000-names list, the odds are that you will manage to get a substantially larger list written. Maybe you won't reach your target of 2,000, but if you shoot for the stars, you may reach the moon.

Blast from the Past

As a teenager living in Texas, summers for me often consisted of lazy days, floating on the lake, or going to the drive-in with a car full of girlfriends, top down and music blasting the night away. Only last week I was driving down the interstate, the wind blowing in my hair and music playing on the car radio, when an old familiar song began to play on the car stereo and suddenly I was taken back to the days of my youth. The memories that flooded my mind were so thick I could almost brush them away with my hand. I could even recapture the emotions of those days gone past as I listened to the old familiar tune. The smiling faces of friends long gone spring to my mind as this song brought me a blast from my past.

Just as a song can conjure up memories of days long gone, so can other memory joggers bring forward names of people you had almost forgotten. Amy said that her upline suggested she find some memory joggers—something that would help her remember all of those people that she seldom sees or thinks about. You know, people like the insurance guy, a local firefighter, mail carrier, or city official. "As I began to consider all of the people in my surrounding neighborhood and community, my list got longer and longer," says Amy. "It is amazing the number of people we each come in contact with in our day-to-day lives. When I stopped thinking, 'I don't know anyone,' and started looking, really looking at my life, I found that I knew a lot more people than I had ever imagined."

What about you? Who do you know? Probably, like Amy, at first you thought you didn't know enough people to make a 100-name list, much less a 2,000-name one! The following is a memory jogger, a triggering device that will help you recall people from your past and present.

Remember, think BIG!

Who do you know that...

You admire or respect;

is active in their church;

always seems to have a smile on their face, or a kind word for others;

is a professional;

is a teacher;

is the president of a club or organization;

does professional counseling (such as doctors, church leaders, school therapists);

deals with the public (such as police officers or highway patrol, firefighters,

city officials, mail carriers, tellers at the bank, flight attendants);

is assertive or ambitious;

is a leader;

has children; wants to have children;

is a grandparent or big sister or brother;

has children with special needs;

has children in an athletic program;

owns a business;

wants to have freedom;

wishes they didn't have to leave their kids with a childcare person everyday;

holds a responsible position;

is under stress at work;

wants to own their own business;

has recently been laid off or changed jobs;

is unable to advance in their current career;

has talents and strengths that are being overlooked at work;

is held back because of lack of education, gender, or age;

in sales or marketing (such as insurance, real estate, health products, stocks

or money market accounts, cars, boats, planes, pharmaceuticals, elec-

tronics, etc.);

is headed for college or just graduating from college;

> ### WHO DO YOU KNOW?
>
> 1. People you admire.
> 2. Relatives.
> 3. Professionals.
> 4. Business associates and co-workers.

was recently married;

knows everyone in town;

has a network of friends;

goes to the gym;

plays tennis;

plays golf;

lives across the street;

used to live in your neighborhood;

sold your home to you;

bought your last home from you;

painted your house;

does landscaping, pool care, or design;

takes care of your car;

you take your cleaning to;

does your taxes;

styles your hair;

gives great massages;

runs the spa;

is on a diet;

wants more time with family;

wants to relocate;

is concerned about their health.

Relatives...

Who are our parents, grandparents, stepparents, sisters, brothers, uncles, aunts, cousins, children, and stepchildren?

Professionals...

Who is our dentist, physician, minister, lawyer, accountant, religious leader, veterinarian, optometrist, chiropractor, congressional representative, pharmacist, professor, dean of our university, teachers, surgeon, podiatrist, dental hygienist, physical therapist, interior decorator, florist, artist, author, publicist, nurse, hairstylist, insurance agent?

Who sold us our...

House, car, boat, motor home, business wardrobe, wedding rings, jewelry, shoes, bicycle, furniture, appliances, business supplies, office equipment, computer, cell phone, stereo or entertainment system, spa or bath products, health products, car insurance, health or life insurance?

Who do you know that...

Teaches your children in school;

teaches music, art, or dance lessons;

was at your wedding or in your wedding party;

is a photographer;

was in your sorority or your friend's fraternity;

goes camping, hunting, or fishing;

drives a limousine;

owns a taxi service;

rents you cars;

makes your travel arrangements;

is in a car pool;

works on computers;

owns real estate;

is in an investment club;

does day trading;

sews or does alterations;

sells gasoline or car washes;

owns a nursery;

designed your house;

high-school principal or teacher;

athletic instructor or coach;

does CPR;

drives a truck;

delivers parcels;

repairs furniture;

makes cabinets;

works at the coffee shop;

delivers your food?

Who is a professional...

Model;
office manager;
baseball, basketball, golf, tennis,
    or football player;
fire chief;
highway patrol;
detective;
security guard;
welder;
musician;
forester;
carpenter;
pilot;
banker;
tailor;
editor;
lifeguard;
race car driver;
librarian;
mortician;
bus driver;
ticket agent;
grocery store owner;
trucking company owner;
insurance adjuster;
cement finisher;
furniture dealer;
motel owner;
judge;
paralegal;
typesetter;

news person;
restaurateur;
paper delivery;
dietitian;
mortician;
oncologist;
swimming teacher;
soccer coach;
tool-and-die maker;
sawmill operator;
industrial engineer;
waiter or waitress;
notary public;
statistician;
horse trader;
shoe repair;
fisherman;
telephone line person;
exterminator;
research technician;
professor;
missionary;
choir director;
actress or actor;
opera performer;
brick mason;
contractor;
television anchor or producer;
farmer;
antique dealer.

The List Goes On

Now that you have opened your mind to some new ideas, has your list gotten bigger? "It took me several days to complete my list. After I had exhausted my resources and had written down everyone I ever had known, I still would find myself remembering new people. I might be driving down the street, or waiting in line at the ticket counter and suddenly a light would come on and I would remember another name! I immediately would write it down," Amy said. "I am still constantly adding to my list."

How about you?

Keep Reaching

"There is not a day that I go out of my house that I do not meet new people. Standing in line at the store or bank, dropping off packages to be mailed, picking up kids from school, or picking up clothes at the cleaner. It is just so natural to have a conversation with those around us. We do it everyday and think nothing of it," says Amy. "My list is ever growing with each new day and each new person I meet."

What about you? Are you the kind of person who speaks to those around you, or are you the quiet type? Perhaps if you find yourself to be somewhat quiet or reserved you might consider trying this effective technique that makes talking with strangers really easy. Amy learned it from her upline.

> **THREE EASY WAYS TO REACH NEW PEOPLE**
>
> 1. Smile! People are drawn to happy, positive people.
> 2. Show genuine concern for others.
> 3. Reach out a helping hand to those in need.

"As a professional, I had to talk to my employees daily, but I didn't find it comfortable to strike up a conversation with total strangers. With children at home and a house full of responsibilities waiting for me, I never took the time after work to socialize, certainly not with people I didn't know well. I began to use a formula my upline taught me. She called it F.O.R.M., which stands for family, occupation, recreation, and money," said Amy. "It not only worked, but it was easy."

THREE GREAT WAYS TO BUILD RELATIONSHIPS

1. Ask questions, then listen—really listen. People are tired of being brushed off and put aside. Showing sincere interest in people will draw them to you. And if you are listening to them, you will hear what they are missing in their lives.
2. Speak kind words. Sadly, many people are hungry for a kind word or gesture from their fellow humans. By being the kind of person who offers a kind word or a helping hand, you set yourself apart.
3. Genuinely care about others. When you really care about another person, truly care about their interests and well being, they know it by the things you do as well as the things you say.

Here is how it works. You are standing in line and the person next to you looks your way. "Hi," you say. She turns towards you and replies, "How are you?"

"Just fine," you reply. "How was your day today?"

More often than not, these total strangers, hungry for a smile or a genuine kind word, will tell you about their day. You might ask, "What is your occupation?"

She replies. You begin to inquire about her job. "Have your worked there long? How do you like working for…?" Typically people will tell you their concerns about their jobs, the layoffs, cutbacks, or concerns about their employer. Often they express negative feelings, either lack of time with their family, a cut in pay, or an unsettling feeling about job security.

"Do you have children at home?" you ask. Most people are happy to talk about their kids, usually sharing with you the various activities little Johnny is participating in at school. This is a great opportunity for you to talk with them about their family, the time they do or don't have with them, their personal goals, or recreational activities.

Often you will hear comments such as, "I missed Rebecca's dance recital last week. I had a pressing deadline at work. I seem to miss a lot of my kids' activities lately. I wish I had more time with them." And the ball is now in your court. This is your opportunity to talk with them about your business. "Perhaps I know a way you could spend more time with your kids and never miss another one of Rebecca's dance recitals again," you reply.

Relation-shipping

The bottom line in your business is not profit. The real bottom line—the one that shows whether your network marketing business will work or not—is relationships. That's what the biggest and most successful networkers have told me. "I want to make absolutely certain," my upline said, "that if you only take one thing away from our meeting today, it's this: *network marketing is the relationships business.*"

After two hours of training at my upline's leadership conference, I began to look back over my most recent approaches and contacts with the people on my list. How did I measure up to the council I had received today? As I looked back over each conversation, I realized that more often than not I had been thinking more about myself, what *I* would gain by sponsoring that person or *what's in it for me,* than I had been about what advantages she/he would gain as a result of working this business.

"You'll notice," she reminded us, "I didn't prattle on about products, convey my company, even *discuss* my deal. Why? Because I don't have to. The next time I am with so-and-so, or the time after that, *she will ask me!*"

"How do I know this? We live in a relative world. Human beings are connected, related. They are always, in some way, in a relationship," she told us. "And relationships are reciprocal. Give and take. You scratch my back and I'll scratch yours. It's so simple. I've shown an interest in this person, and you can bet she's going to show interest in me and mine. Next time—or the next—I'm going to ask her what she does for a living. And when she's finished telling me all about that—because I *really, really listen,* and because I ask all kinds of genuinely curious questions, and because I'm interested in who she is and how she is—she's going to ask me what I do.

"I promise you that she will," said my upline. "She will not be able to help herself. How do I know she will do this? We like people who like us. We're interested in people who are interested in us. We care about those who care about us. We love people who love us! It's just the way we are put together. The most important thing we can do today is develop relationships, true ones. Make new ones. Keep old ones. Manage crazy ones. Warm up cold ones. Fix broken ones. Engage in them. Explore them. Enjoy them. Enrich them. Empower them."

"Every day you choose to go to work, you should have your attention focused on building relationships," she continued. "That's what we do in the business of network marketing. It is fundamentally the singular most important aspect of everything we do. We speak and listen to create relationships that we grow into friendships, which evolve into partnerships. We develop and duplicate them into a powerful sales and marketing organization through leadership," she said.

"Network marketing is *relationshipping, friendshipping, partnershipping*—and also *leadershipping*. We really are in the distribution business. Shipping and receiving—that's what we do."

"Relation-*shipping*, friend-*shipping*, partner-*shipping*, leader-*shipping*. And then we *receive* money in the mail. Shipping and receiving," she laughed. "What an incredible business."

True prospecting involves people, their hopes, their needs, and their dreams. Ask other people about their lives. When they answer, *really listen to them*. Think about what they are truly saying, what might be between the lines. Be patient with them. Genuinely care about the part of them they are sharing with you. Inevitably, they will ask what you do. Then, tell them.

The Chicken List

So you have compiled your list of hundreds of people, constantly meeting new ones at every turn, and now you are poised and ready to make the approach.

"I was told to evaluate my list, consider the top 25 people that I would like to work with, people I respected and thought were dynamic go-getters," Amy says. "I retreated to my office, closed the door, and immediately began to re-evaluate my list. I started thinking that maybe so-and-so wouldn't be interested because he was a successful doctor. Then I went on to eliminate my friends who were really busy, thinking they certainly wouldn't have the time to devote to this new business venture. After a few minutes, I had scaled down my original top 25 down to about 5 people. Then I remembered what my upline told me."

What Amy remembered was that one of the first, and most tragic, mistakes made by many new people in the business is to prejudge people—failing to contact people whom they consider to be too busy or too successful to want a business such as ours. In reality, nothing could be further from the truth. Take my word on this: If you want something important done quickly, find a busy person to do it.

Statistics state that 20 percent of the people do 80 percent of the work. Just look around your office, children's school, or community activity group. More than likely you will notice that the same people who are heading up these organizations or who are responsible for the most leadership are also the people who seem to get the most accomplished.

"Everywhere I went, I saw Sandy. Whether it was at the PTA (which I seldom had time to attend), or church activities, or at a local community group program, Sandy was always there—usually leading the group. I began to wonder if she had a life. I mean, did she have a family, a job? How could she possibly find the time to organize and run these huge projects? I felt I was a go-getter, but she was even making me look bad!" said Amy.

What Amy found out was that Sandy did indeed have a family, and many other commitments. Sandy was an achiever. She got things done. And although she seemed over-involved and much too busy, it turns out that she was the perfect candidate for a business of her own. She was looking for a way to excel and Amy's business opportunity gave her the perfect vehicle.

> ### THREE TYPES OF PEOPLE TO LOOK FOR
>
> 1. People who are busy. They get more accomplished.
> 2. Ambitious people who strive for excellence.
> 3. People who help others—those who are willing to give.

As you look at your list, look for people who are hungry for success. They can be really well-to-do or lacking in the financial department, but they are still looking for more meaning in their lives or more financial security for their families. Try to think of people who want to help others and, again, don't prejudge. Many distributors have done just that only to see a friend or associate who later achieved a tremendous level of success in someone else's business group! Don't let that happen to you!

Tap into the System

Every good network marketing business has training material to help you. Smart networkers will quickly tap into their upline's training system and learn from the success and mistakes of others. Great leaders are first good students. How teachable are you? When I first started my networking business, I owned and operated several very successful RV dealerships. I had made a lot of money, and lost a lot of money. A college student who was working on his Ph.D. introduced me to my particular network business. I could have taken the attitude that as a successful business owner I could not learn anything from this young man, but instead I recognized that no matter how much success I had previous to this business, I did not understand the workings of this networking business. I eagerly became a good student and I believe that has made all of the difference.

How teachable are you? Are you willing to invest in the learning materials your upline offers? Do you attend every training meeting sponsored by your organization's leaders? Are you promoting the system your upline teaches? If not, perhaps you should reconsider. Remember, listen to the experts.

Are You Ready?

Remember your first love? Every waking hour was spent thinking about, talking to, or spending time with this person. It was your first waking thought in the morning, and that person consumed the majority of your day. At night, your last thought before drifting into a blissful sleep was of your love. And often even your dreams were filled with him or her. Network marketing is the process of sharing your belief in a marketing concept that is so unique and about which you are so enthusiastic that you can hardly go to sleep at night. In fact, you lose sleep. You can hardly wait to tell people of your discovery. When this level of conviction is lacking, people tend to hold back. It is a catch-22. If you wait for your belief level to reach this peak, you run the risk of missing the opportunity. If you try to move forward without it, your friends can hear the reservations and uncertainty in your voice. So first, do your best to work out whatever reservations are holding you back.

Contacting and Inviting

So you have a huge names list and a big dream. Now comes the true test. Will you have the courage to make the first call? And the second? Successful networkers tell me that the success of any MLM business is all in the numbers. If that is true, what are yours? Are you prepared to make 30-60 calls a day? What if that is what it takes for your success?

Someone once told me, "If you had one hundred rocks in your backyard, and under at least six of them was $100,000, how quickly would you get those rocks turned over?" Pretty darn fast I imagine! Your business works much the same way. You will never be able to discern who will make it in your business. Sometimes the people who are most likely to succeed will be the first to quit. Then there will be those that you would never imagine could make anything out of this business who manage to make it to the top. So if it truly is about numbers, how fast do you want to get through yours? If you understand that your success is directly related to the speed in which you share this opportunity with others, would you run faster?

As far as the particulars on inviting, your upline can guide you as to what to say and what works and doesn't work. The most important information that I can give you is that if you want to build a big business, have financial security, and enjoy a comfortable lifestyle, you will have to talk to a number of people. So let's get going! What are your other options?

FOUR TIPS TO SUCCESS

1. Just do it! Don't procrastinate or put off this important step toward your financial success. Just make the effort and overcome whatever challenges may face you.
2. Create momentum. It is much easier to build your business fast than slow. Talk to one hundred people as quickly as possible and watch what happens in your business.
3. Focus on your dreams. Keep your eye on the goal, not the obstacle.
4. Care about others. People don't care about how much you know until they know how much you care. When your main objective is to help others succeed, you can't help but win.

SIX STEPS TO RETIRE IN 2-5 YEARS

1. Talk to 100 people a month.
2. Give 20 presentations a month.
3. Sponsor 10 new people.
4. Focus on the top 3 who are ready now!
5. Teach those 3 and help them duplicate the first four steps above.
6. Repeat often.

Set Your Pace

Action is essential in building momentum for your downline. Procrastination is a killer. If you jump in the race and set a pace for yourself, you will surely succeed. "As an executive, wife, and mother, I wore many hats," says Jody. "I had to develop my own pace, working with the variety of other obligations that I had in my life. I knew that adding one more thing to my long list was going to be a difficult commitment, but I constantly focused on the prize, not the price."

Jody learned early on that to make it to the level she desired in her business, she would have to dedicate herself and her time to consistent effort. "I was told by my upline that if I shared the business opportunity at least 20 times per month on a consistent basis, I could retire in 2-5 years. That was more than I could ever hope for in my present career," Jody continues. "In order to secure 20 meetings a month, I found I had to talk to at least 100 people a month. I found out early on that most people are not willing to make the necessary changes in their lives in order to gain financial success. I found out that by talking to 100 people, I could usually confirm at least 20 meetings. From those meetings, I could usually sponsor at least 10 new distributors, and my averages were about 3 of those that joined ended up being leaders and duplicating the pattern for success taught by our upline leadership."

Jody was able to do in only a few months what few had ever done. She was able to replace her income. Shortly afterwards she replaced the income of her husband, a teacher and counselor with a master's degree. In five short years Jody was a millionaire. She has since spread this great opportunity around the world and has had the opportunity to see firsthand the great benefits network marketing can offer other people.

Believe and You Can Achieve

Sincere enthusiasm can go far, but in order to really capture an audience you have to be sold before you can sell. If you are passionate about your product or compensation plan, prospecting has a strange way of taking care of itself. But if you are not, all the technique and marketing savvy in the world won't win you a single new business partner. You have got to believe to achieve.

All Jody wanted to do was to retire. Her primary focus was to be able to spend time with her three boys, whom she had left with a sitter almost everyday of their lives. "My mother always scolded me, telling me over and over again that no success outside of my home would ever compensate for failure within it," says Jody. "Everyday when I would drop my little boys off at the sitter and head out to another day of work, I would cry. I was torn. I knew we needed my income to manage our finances, but I felt guilty spending so much time away from my children."

Many mothers feel much the same way, especially single moms like Karen Yamada Furuchi. "Every time I missed one of my kid's school activities, I felt like a failure. Whenever my in-laws made comments about my absence in our home, or my travel agenda, I felt guilty. The worst times were when my children themselves would cry and plead with me not to leave them. Those were the times when I would really start to do a number on myself. I would go into a kind of frantic self-abuse cycle. Eventually if my kids even got a temperature, or had a difficult day at school, I felt responsible, felt guilty. Somehow I imagined that if only I were home more with my kids that life would be perfect."

Of course, life isn't perfect, and children will have trials, as each of us will, no matter what our availability in the home might be. Karen learned that in order to get out of the rut she was in she was going to have to dedicate even more time and energy away from her family. Even though she knew it would only be for a few short years, there were times when she didn't think she would make it. "Sometimes, after working all day and doing meetings for my downline at night, I would get home, just in time to put a load of clothes in the washer and get the dishes cleaned up. Even then I would fret over not having been home to get dinner for the kids. I would wait until the clothes were finished with the wash cycle, while going through the mail or my children's school papers, and eventually get the clothes in the dryer and myself into the bed. Though I was often exhausted, I sometimes couldn't get to sleep, thinking about my kids, what I might have missed that day, or would certainly miss the following. I often thought I might just lose it altogether. Then I would somehow get a grip on myself—remind myself just why I was going at this neck-breaking pace. It was for my children. I wanted more for them and I knew as a single parent that it was all up to me," she said.

In Chapter 11 we will discuss in detail the special obstacles women face while developing a business of network marketing. We will hit head-on the issues that can become stumbling blocks, if not barriers, to women today. But for now, let's continue learning tips and techniques to develop a huge and profitable business of your own.

What Is Your Market?

If the 80/20 rule is correct, then we already know that 80 percent of your business will be done by 20 percent of your organization. Wouldn't it make sense that you might increase your odds a bit by finding motivated and successful people to work with, people who have already paid a price for success? People who understand delayed gratification? People who have a proven track record for success? Some of the greatest networkers say that it is easier to find a leader than to develop one. If that is the case, where are all of the leaders?

I believe that luck does have a small part in your success. If you are really out there, truly out in the market making yourself known and available, working your list and talking to new people, you are much more likely to run across an individual who is looking and ready to take the challenge of your particular business idea. However, I must admit, the harder I work the luckier I become!

"I learned that it was really a matter of going through the numbers. In the beginning I believed everything anyone told me," said Deborah. "If I talked to a prospect and they told me they really wanted their own business, that they were really committed to making it happen, I totally believed them. I soon learned that my business, like anything else in life, required focused energy and commitment, something most people chose not to give."

"My sponsor told me to watch who I was dancing with. She meant that I needed to make sure I wasn't dancing with too few who really never wanted to dance in the first place," said Deborah.

Often networkers will sponsor a few people and then sit on them and try to get them to perform. These networkers think that they have found their leaders but eventually drive them out of the business for two reasons: first, because they have not set the proper example of continuing to sponsor, and second, because they have so few people sponsored they feel they must get those people to perform or reach a certain amount of volume. Networkers drive prospects out of the business because they won't allow them the room to grow and develop at their own pace. They pressure them too much.

LOOK FOR THE ACES

There are fifty-two cards in a deck. Out of those fifty-two cards you will find only four top cards, or four aces. If you know that your odds of finding an ace (or a leader) are four in fifty-two, why do you constantly try to make someone be an ace who is a jack or a ten? Just keep turning over the cards and you will find your aces, your leaders.

"I was told that there were three kinds of people: quitters, carriers, and builders. Since I knew most people have quit everything they ever started, from a diet to a class at college to even a relationship, I didn't expect most people to stick. I did understand, however, that people that got in my business, whether they ever developed into leaders or not, could certainly lead me, or carry me and this business plan to someone who would be a builder. So I allowed people to go at their own pace. Giving them enough room to grow, to develop. I encouraged them, but didn't push them so hard that I pushed them out," says Deborah. "If nothing else, I wanted them to lead me to someone who was ready, who had that window of expectancy and desire open. I knew I had the perfect vehicle to fill it."

One of the primary complaints I have faced in prospecting new people is the sour relationship of a past acquaintance. More often than not, I have been told lengthy and detailed descriptions of an acquaintance or individual that has pressured their friends to the point of alienation. That is not only terribly unprofessional, it is most unnecessary. A common mistake made by many new distributors is to pressure a few of their closest friends or relatives into getting in their business (and they do just to get them off their back!); the new distributor then spends the next few months or years trying to drag them across the finish line. For many well-meaning distributors, they feel it is their duty, if not obligation, to make their downline successful. Unfortunately, that is exactly the opposite of what our business is all about. Our job is not to do it all for them but to teach them how to do it for themselves.

Many have heard the common saying, "Give a man a fish and feed him for a day. Teach a man to fish and feed him for a lifetime." We are educators. We teach people a new way to buy and sell products and service and a new way to make a living and build a financial future. The more people we educate, the more money we all earn. Ask for referrals with every contact you make. And the more people we approach with extreme enthusiasm about our business, the more big money and free time we will generate.

FOUR WAYS TO SUCCESSFULLY SHARE YOUR PLAN

1. Reach out to everyone. Don't pre-judge people.
2. Ask for referrals from everyone you meet.
3. Be enthusiastic not over bearing.
4. Build solid relationships.

Reach out to everyone on your list. Leave no one out. Can you imagine the following scenario? "Because I knew this business was not for everyone, there were just some people that I did not approach about it. I tried not to pre-qualify people, but sometimes I was just so busy with those I did have in my business, I overlooked people who really might have either been great at it, or really could have benefited from it. One such case was my own secretary. I was so thrilled to have finally found that special "office angel," at least that is what I called her, that I wasn't about to risk it by telling her about the business or encouraging her to join. I had already lost several office managers in just the same way and I really needed help!" Katie said.

"So when Vicki came into my life, I wasn't about to let her go. Little did I know of what was to come. It was only one short year after she joined our staff that she and her husband took that long awaited vacation. They loved the mountains, often taking their children on day hikes at local state parks. This particular trip they had planned was high up in the mountains of Wyoming. Little did they know that trip would prove to be a life changing vacation, for while hiking high up in those beautiful mountains, Vicki's husband suffered a sudden stroke. Unable to get him down to medical help, he died," Katie sadly adds. "It would have been tragic to lose your husband, but somehow with seven children to raise, it seemed even more devastating to me as I contemplated Vicki's limited options. I decided right then that there would never be another person who crossed my path that I would not share this great business with. I didn't ever want to feel such a burden of responsibility again."

So reach out and touch someone. You may never know the impact your initial approach may have in the lives of another person. Reach out to everyone. Don't prejudge. After counseling with your upline, researching all of your training material, and making a huge names list, start talking. Contact your top twenty-five people first and remember to utilize your greatest asset—your upline. If possible, your sponsor or upline should be there with you for your first two or three meetings. It's best to present the opportunity to small groups of four to ten people at a time. Remember the rule of thumb: always invite twice as many guests as you want to attend. You must always allow for the no-shows, which are an inevitable part of this business. Focus your first ninety days to *relationshipping,* reaching out to those closest to you and extending the invitation to create a business partnership intended to enhance the quality of their lives.

You will constantly get better at contacting and inviting as you continue to move ahead in your business. Become a great student. Follow closely and duplicate the pattern for success taught by your upline.

Points to Ponder

Remember, the work of your business is in the presentation of your particular marketing plan. Thinking about it will never count for anything. It is only in the *doing* that the results will come.

Keep your eyes focused on your dream, your *why*. Remember Chapter 4, Define Your Dreams? Always keep in the front of your mind your reason for doing this business, for doing what you need to do.

The individual who continues to do what she planned, long after the emotion of the moment has passed, measures true character. Stick to your goals. Focus on your dream.

This is a numbers game and to play big you have to talk to lots of people. Believe in everyone and wait for no one. Keep going forward and carve out a path for others to follow. Create a vacuum. You will draw people in.

Everyone wants to get on a fast moving train. If you are the leader, create the momentum and never, never, never give up! If you stick with it you cannot help but find those who are looking, those who will do this business and do it big, no matter what you do.

Remember that people don't care how much you know unless they know how much you care. Relationshipping is more important than products or personal income. First come people, then product and profit. Keep your perspective and priorities straight. The money will naturally follow.

CHAPTER SEVEN

AVOIDING PITFALLS

I'm Doing Ok

"Many new prospects don't have the experience to know how truly great the opportunity really is," said Jamie Carlin. "They look around their office or neighborhood and say to themselves, 'I am doing pretty good, compared to my colleagues at the office.' I say, pretty good compared to what?"

Whatever you do, don't make the mistake of falling into a state of mediocrity. In the beginning you thought this network marketing business was really great. You saw it as a vehicle to get you from your present situation into a different one. Don't fall into the trap of succumbing to your fears by using the excuse that you are really doing Ok. Look around. Look at the person who has been at your job, doing what you do for five years longer than you have. Ask yourself, "Does this person really have what I want in life?" Then look at the person who has been in your chosen career for ten years longer than you have. Again, ask yourself, "Does this person truly have what I want?" If the answer is no, why even consider doing what you do for five or ten years longer just to get what you don't want?

> **ASK THESE FOUR QUESTIONS:**
>
> 1. Do they have the lifestyle you dream about?
> 2. Do they have the income you want?
> 3. Do they have the kind of relationships you desire?
> 4. Do they have peace and happiness in their lives?

"As an attorney at a leading law firm, I held a pretty prestigious position," says Jamie. "People in my circle of influence thought I had it made. I had a new custom home, a successful career, and a happy family. What they didn't know

How to Qualify People:

"I've recently heard about a new business that has me so intrigued I just had to tell you. There are people making more money in one month than I make in a year, but that is not what really got my attention. I really got excited when I saw their lifestyle. They are working from their homes, spending more time with their families, going at their own pace, and creating a permanent, residual income that is staggering to me. I don't know if this will interest you or not, but I couldn't stop thinking about you. Maybe it would be smart for us to get together for a cup of coffee and talk. Would Wednesday or Friday be better for you?"

is that I didn't have any furniture to go in that big luxury home. I got started in my networking business to get some new furniture. My next goal was to make up the difference in my budget and to set up a retirement fund. At the time, I really never imagined I would be making the kind of money I make today."

Until you have the confidence or belief you need, you might try this idea when you approach those on your warm list:

"I've recently heard about a new business that has me so intrigued I just had to tell you. There are people making more money in one month than I make in a year, but that is not what really got my attention. I really got excited when I saw their lifestyle. They are working from their homes, spending more time with their families, going at their own pace, and creating a permanent, residual income that is staggering to me. I don't know if this will interest you or not, but I couldn't stop thinking about you. Maybe it would be smart for us to get together for a cup of coffee and talk. Would Wednesday or Friday be better for you?"

Jamie said that she really got a lot of mileage from qualifying people. She understood that not only her success depended upon having a big names list to start with, but success was also about qualifying her prospects. "I knew that this business would not appeal to everyone. Oh, I believe whole-heartedly that this business would be of benefit to everyone. I just understood that not everyone would see it the same way I did and I allowed them to have their opinion," Jamie said. "In the long run, by telling my prospect that I knew this business was not for everyone, it let them off the hook, or took the pressure off. Some of those same people later came back to me and asked me if they could join my business. They said that they respected me, not only for my belief and commitment to my business, but also because I allowed them to say no without making them feel awkward."

Accept the fact that success in any network marketing business is strictly about numbers—how many are on your list and how many you contact everyday. In addition, understand that it is simply not for everyone. It may be simply the timing in their lives, or something else that you just can not see from one simple meeting with them. Allow people to say no with dignity. If you do, they may come back to you later and be your biggest leaders.

What Will My Friends Think?

What will people think of me? This is a classic scenario with new networkers. They often become so concerned about what their so-called friends or acquaintances will think of them that they let it immobilize their effort and success.

"I was certainly concerned what people would think of me," says Donna Parks. "After all, I held a high ranking position with a respected company. I was obviously concerned about keeping my job, and at first I hesitated sharing this great business idea with friends and colleagues at work."

While you certainly must protect and respect your present employment opportunity, it would not be wise to let it stifle you into inactivity. As more professionals enter the network distribution industry, it is natural that they will want to postpone acknowledging their participation until the time is right. For example, some will pretend that it's their husband's or wife's business. The problem is that if you're a professional and people sense your doubts or uncertainty about the industry, they will also be suspicious. Some will choose not to join while others will join but build through someone else such as their spouse. But the reality is that once someone of stature has joined our industry, the floodgates start opening for everyone. And sometimes it's the ordinary, everyday people who make it to the pinnacle, not the "big hitters" of traditional business, law, or medicine, though they certainly can earn enormous wealth.

I can tell you countless stories of people who have failed at this business because they were afraid to let their peers know how very serious they were about building a networking organization. "I remember one of my first 'learning' experiences," Donna adds. "I had recently registered a doctor and her husband, who owned a successful car dealership. I just knew that they were going to be my next stars! After bringing them to their first seminar, my upline wisely took me aside and said, "Get under them quickly."

"Of course I didn't really understand the powerful message she was sharing with me that night. But I later understood that if you want to hold a person's interest who is wavering in their belief, sponsor a downline for them."

A downline will help keep them in the business because now they have something to lose.

I'll Do It My Way

"I can do it all myself," thought Sally. As a successful executive, she did not understand at first the power of utilizing an upline. "I thought I was pretty smart. After all, I had a college degree and a measure of success in my career. But when I got started in network marketing, I quickly understood that I didn't know it all—couldn't do everything by myself. I soon learned that if I took the limelight off of myself and put it where it belonged, to my successful upline, I was able to free myself up to be not only more helpful to those I was prospecting, but also more relatable."

> **THREE SMART MOVES**
>
> 1. Put your ego aside.
> 2. Be willing to learn. Be teachable.
> 3. Utilize your upline; their success and their knowledge.

"I learned to utilize the credibility and success of my upline to support my business," Sally said. "By taking all of the spotlight off of me, of my past success, I was able to be more relatable to those around me. It was easy for me to say that my upline was great—that they had acquired enormous success." By utilizing one of her assets, her upline's credibility, Sally didn't have to worry about being perfect, about knowing everything. In addition, she didn't have to worry what others thought of her. " I did not have to worry that others would judge the success potential of this business based on what they saw from my present lifestyle," she adds.

Many leaders find that it is often easier to talk about the success of their upline rather than their own. First of all, it makes the person they are talking to feel more at ease. In addition, they are not parading their own success in front of a prospect's face. The opposite is also true. Let's take Gail as an example. "I was barely out of high school when I got married," Gail says. "I went to work right away while George, my husband, finished college. After he graduated, I came home and we started a family. After ten years I thought we would have been further along financially than we were. But with a family and mortgage our funds were limited. When I first saw the network marketing plan, I saw a way to bridge the gap between George's salary and what I wanted for my family."

Like many young married couples, Gail and George were barely making ends meet. Gail was tired of being embarrassed when friends or family would come over. She wanted to do some home improvements—get some new furniture and a fresh coat of paint. "I was thrilled at the idea of finally being able to do some of the things to our home that I had dreamed of. We were still sitting on the $45 couch George bought when he started school. It was used when we got it and that was over 10 years ago."

Although Gail was excited about the possibilities, she soon became intimidated when she realized that she would need to have some meetings in their home to get started. "I was mortified at the thought of standing in my living room, upholstery faded with wear, permanent stains on the carpet, and trying to tell people what a great opportunity I had—a great way to make money," Gail adds. "I knew if people were going to look at my current lifestyle to determine the financial possibilities for themselves in network marketing, I was in big trouble! I didn't want prospective distributors to look at me, at my level of success, or lack of, and think that was all they could expect to have."

By utilizing her upline, their stories of success and lifestyle, Gail could take the pressure off herself. If you feel you might not have the credibility you need to reach a certain group of people, consider utilizing one of your greatest assets—your upline and their success.

Standing Strong

Some professionals hold back in developing a network marketing business because they are concerned about conflict of interest. Brenda Baker was no exception. "I knew that my boss wouldn't like me doing a business outside of my career, but I never dreamed he would take the stand he did," said Brenda.

While she was in a highly respected position in the company, Brenda knew that she should be careful not to step on any toes. For this reason, she was very careful about whom she talked to within her company about her new business venture. "I was so respectful and so cautious about my job that I was literally afraid to talk about my new business at work. In fact, I didn't think anyone knew I was involved with an outside business. I was so careful that I was almost surprised the day the company president called me into his office."

"Mrs. Baker," he said. "We do not allow our top executives to have outside business or income. You need to decide which is more important to you, your little side thing or your promising career. You have 30 minutes to think about it and I will call you to hear your decision. Your job or your little side thing."

"I was overcome with fear," says Brenda. " I left his office that morning to go to my own and decide which would it be: my promising career or the business that could potentially give me the freedom and lifestyle I so desired."

After thirty minutes had come and gone, Brenda had made up her mind—she would tell her boss that she had indeed made a choice. She chose her future potential in her new marketing business over thirty more years with her present company. Surprisingly, her boss never did call her to his office, never did demand an ultimatum.

While most of us will never be faced with that decision, would we have the courage or the commitment to let go of those things in our lives that we know will not give us what we ultimately desire, or would we give in to the pressure of those around us, letting go of our dreams to hold on to the mediocrity of our lives?

Brenda has gone on to develop an international business that spans the globe. Her influence is felt around the world and has been shared from generation to generation. "What if I had given in?" says Brenda. "I have had the opportunity to see families reunited, lives in upheaval healed, finances restored, and dreams revived. Nothing can compare to the feelings I have in my heart for the people I have come to love around the world."

Relationships

Every leading networker has told me that developing strong relationships with people was a key to their success. The business of networking is about relationships. It takes time and effort to develop strong bonds with people. Experts tell me that it can be the one thing that makes the difference between a small business and a huge one.

Last summer my four-year-old daughter, Rebecca, wanted to "grow a garden." I spent hours in the hot sun, clearing weeds from an unused and badly neglected area at the side of our property. After hours of preparing the ground I then went to the nursery and spent a small fortune on topsoil, mulch, fertilizer, plants, and irrigation supplies. Many days later we stepped back and admired our little garden. Rebecca was delighted. I was exhausted!

Everyday for the next two months Rebecca would inspect each plant, determining if any progress had been made. Each morning when she found a new bud emerging from a plant she would ask me if she could pick it. It took several attempts and a lot of patience to help her understand that these tiny plants weren't developed yet. They weren't yet ready for harvest. She had a hard time understanding why it would be towards the end of the summer before she could pick the tomatoes and various other plants.

Rebecca learned that summer how to care for her plants, to water them, and that pulling the weeds was acceptable. We tried everything to keep her little hands busy and off of the budding tomatoes. Some of the plants died. Others didn't produce very much. But some of them thrived. I noticed that

---

FIVE WAYS TO GROW SUCCESSFUL RELATIONSHIPS

1. Prepare the soil. Take time to get to know the person—her interest, dreams, or fears.
2. Plant good seeds. Teach correct principles and live by them yourself.
3. Plant in the best locations. Give thoughtful attention to where you want to "grow" your business.
4. Water and fertilize often. Relationships take time, nurturing.
5. Plan for the harvest. Develop long-term relationships and "reap" the reward for years to come.

the plants toward the front of the garden, the ones that were the most obvious, got the most attention and were the plants that not only survived but also grew the biggest and tallest. The plants in the back, along the fence, didn't fare as well.

At the end of the summer we finished pulling the last of the produce from the vines and took pictures of Rebecca holding a huge basket of plump red tomatoes. When I showed this picture to her older brother he said, "Mom, you could have gone to the store and bought bushels of tomatoes, cheaper than it cost you to grow the ones in your garden."

I told him, "I didn't plant that garden to grow tomatoes son. I planted it to grow a little girl."

Relationships are the same. They must be planted, carefully tended, nourished, and fed. In network marketing the top income producers will tell you that you have to plant a lot of seeds and take good care of them. And if all goes well, a great harvest is sure to come.

FIVE WAYS TO AVOID FAILURE

1. Keep sponsoring new people.
2. Don't try to push people to success.
3. Build width to find leaders.
4. Create depth with those leaders.
5. Don't wait for anyone! LEAD!

I've Got Mine!

A common mistake among networkers is to think they have found their big leaders among the first few distributors they sponsor. "When I first saw the marketing plan I though it would be so easy," says Amanda. "All it would take is to sponsor six people. When I started sponsoring people, I thought I had found my six in the first month." A common pitfall among new distributors is to sponsor a few people and then try to *push* them into productivity. It is like trying to push a rope. It never works.

Amanda learned the hard way that by sponsoring only a few people she stunted not only her own growth but the growth of those first few as well. "Because I only had a handful of people in my group, I needed them to perform. I was always trying to get them to do more. They weren't growing. Everyone was frustrated," she adds.

Her people were only doing what they saw Amanda do—sponsor a couple of people then wait for the money to roll in. When Amanda finally talked with her upline and began to listen to their advice, everything changed. "My sponsor told me I needed to keep sponsoring until I found some people that were ready to run. Instead of trying to get those first few groups to grow, I went out and sponsored ten more people that next week. Out of that second group, I found a couple of people that were open and ready to go for it. I didn't have to do much of anything for those two groups. They just took the ball and ran with it. When I finally understood that I couldn't *make* people ready, but I could *find* some that were, I went out and found more!"

By building width you will find people that want to go fast. Then you'll find it is easy to build depth. There is a balance between width and depth. Each network's compensation plan is different. You will need to research yours and counsel upline for advice on the most effective way to create wealth with your particular plan. However, I have found that in most plans width translates to immediate income or profitability, and depth is equated to long-term financial security. The key is not to wait on the first few people—get wide fast!

Spinning Plates

"I spent most of my time the first few months running around in circles," says Karyn. "I didn't know anything about focused effort or building team leaders. When the phone rang—I ran!" Jumping from group to group without a plan for success not only discourages a new distributor, it exhausts them. As Karyn soon found out, working smart in an organized pattern will not only promote fast growth, it will also develop long-term financial security.

"Then one day my upline, Sue, invited me to bring my family to go with her to the circus. I enjoyed a break from my fast and furious routine, and I wanted to spend time with my kids. The children laughed as they watched acrobats swing from the trapeze high above our heads and clowns in bright costumes, riding funny bikes and doing tricks. Suddenly Sue leaned over and whispered in my ear, "See that man over there?" she pointed. "The one spinning plates. He reminds me of you," she said.

I looked across the tent and saw him, a fellow in a purple costume running back and forth, trying to keep plates spinning. Then I understood what Sue had been trying to tell me for weeks. "Work with groups of three," she said. "And build depth under them. Focus, Karyn, focus."

Sue had been telling Karyn that to be the most effective she needed to pick three or four personal legs and focus her efforts with them until she duplicated herself and created leaders. Karyn had been jumping around twelve or more legs, trying to keep them all spinning. She might have been doing twenty presentations a week, but in twelve or more groups that might have only been one per group. By focusing in groups of three, Karyn was able to get more than six presentations a week in each group. She created more momentum in just a few weeks than she had in many months. Focused effort yields big results.

When You're Down, Go Up!

"The fastest way to destroy your business is to dump negatives to your downline," says Stephanie. "It is like pouring poison on a plant. No matter what you do to try to clean it up, once you have poured it on it's too late. It usually dies." Stephanie knows that negative situations or problems are to be taken upline, not downline. You downline doesn't need to hear your problems or negatives; they already have enough of their own. What they need is support, encouragement, and a strong leader with a positive attitude who is telling them, "You can do it!"

"My sponsor used to come to big group meetings and find something to gripe about. I couldn't believe it. Sometimes what he said was true—the lines were too long, the sound system wasn't working properly, or the brochures were on back order—but who cared? I didn't want him to point out what was wrong—I only wanted to know what was right," Stephanie adds. "He occasionally even made cutting remarks about our upline leaders. I knew right then that I could never have him working in my downline. He would kill them." Stephanie got smart and went upline for help. She found a great leader that was positive and could help her get her own business off the ground. A great relationship was formed. Her sponsor eventually quit, as did some of the people he had sponsored. Stephanie was glad she hadn't let him drag her down with him. Today she runs a successful and profitable business and teaches her people to throw up, not down!

> ### FIVE FABULOUS WAYS TO BUILD STRONG LEADERS
>
> 1. Stick to the basics! Stay focused.
> 2. Train and teach; show, don't just "tell" people what to do.
> 3. Help your people build confidence in themselves.
> 4. Let people fail and learn from their own mistakes
> 5. Praise people often and offer support.

Trying to Do It All

Network marketing is a people business, and because it is, it's natural for us to have a drive to help other people. It's one of the most wonderful aspects of our business; one of the things that sets us apart from other enterprises and industries. It's also a trap.

Jeanelle was a sales manager with a leading computer company when she first started her business. "I had lots of experience in sales and in giving compelling sales presentations. I wanted to help my downline to get off to a fast start. So I offered to help," Jeanelle said. "At first I helped them make their calls. If they didn't want to do it, I offered to do it for them. When I set up the meetings for them, often they asked me to come along. I ended up giving the presentations. That was okay with me. I wanted to help. But after several months of doing everything for everybody, I knew something had to change."

What Jeanelle explained was that she got caught in a trap—one that she had created. Of course, she wanted to help her people, and she should help them. But by doing it all for them, she wasn't teaching them or preparing them to go out on their own. When she did sponsor a person for her distributor, she started the pattern all over again. Eventually she had a group that couldn't do anything without her, or so they thought.

"I got back to the basics, the fundamentals. I began to train and teach my people—not just what to do—but how to do it," she adds. "Once they stepped out a little on their own they began to get the confidence they needed to take the next step. The people I sponsored in the beginning never did take that first step on their own and eventually quit. But the next group of people, the ones I trained, some of them have gone on to be great leaders in this business."

When we see a new distributor struggling, it's only natural to want to step in and ease his or her way. They're having trouble getting past their fears and doubts, so we say, "Hey, I'll call them for you. No problem, I'll do the interview. You just sit there and watch. Don't worry, I'll present the compensation plan for you."

WRONG! Let me tell you a story—about a tiny moth.

One day a man found the cocoon of an Emperor moth and excitedly took it home to watch the creature emerge. Soon a small opening appeared, and for several hours after the moth struggled but could not seem to fit its body past a certain point.

Deciding that something must be wrong, the man took a pair of scissors and snipped away the hindering part of the cocoon. The moth then came out easily, but its body was large and swollen, with small and shriveled wings.

The man expected that in just a few short hours the moth's wings would unfold in all their majestic, natural beauty—but they did not. Instead of developing into a magnificent creature, free to fly, the moth spent its existence dragging around a bloated, misshapen body with small, shriveled, and completely useless wings. It soon died, and the man mourned its fate.

What he did not realize was that he was the cause of the moth's deformity and untimely death. For the constricting cocoon and the struggle to pass through the tiny opening are nature's way of forcing vital fluids from the moth's body into its newly developing wings. The creature's struggles were required for its survival and fulfillment. The "merciful" snip of the scissors was, in reality, the cruelest cut of all.

Often in our desire to help our people we take away from them the opportunity for growth they need to become successful. Helping others does not mean doing it all for them. Like the moth, people need to stretch and sometimes struggle to develop into leaders.

Points to Ponder

Stay out of the I'm Okay club. Don't compare yourself to your neighbors, coworkers, family, or friends. Decide what is important to you—what you want out of life—and find someone in your upline that has already attained it. Learn all you can from that person and you'll soon in the I'm Doing GREAT club.

Worrying about what others think won't pay your bills, won't help you feel safe at night, and won't get you the dreams you hope for. Stick close to your upline and be the kind of person that you think they would be proud of knowing.

> ### EIGHT GREAT TIPS
>
> 1. Don't compare yourself to others.
> 2. Stop worrying about what people think.
> 3. Be a great student.
> 4. Stick with your commitments.
> 5. Remember the golden rule.
> 6. Keep sponsoring new people.
> 7. Go upline with challenges.
> 8. Encourage your people to grow.

Great teachers were first great students. Being the best student of your business training system is what will take you to the top. Be humble and teachable. Then you will be rich!

Plans change—commitments don't. By setting goals and making plans and commitments you can get from where you are right now to exactly where you want to be in the future. Stay focused on your dreams and stick to your guns!

Remember the golden rule. Treat other people the way you would like to be treated. Treat your upline the way you wish your downline would treat you. Treat your downline the way you would like your upline to treat you. You will have the best of both if you do unto others as you would have them do to you.

By sponsoring a few new personals every month, you will always have fresh excitement in your group. You will always have someone to work with. Stay wide. Set the pace.

Keep problems out of your downline. Take challenges upline, to someone who can actually do something to help you. Stay positive. Be the motivation and inspiration for your downline. People want encouragement—you can make a difference in their lives.

Like the beautiful butterfly has to struggle to get strong, people need to stretch in order to develop. Help your people, but don't stifle their growth by trying to do it all for them.

CHAPTER EIGHT

HAVE A SUCCESSFUL MEETING

Ok, so you love your new business. You've been around the network marketing business for a while, and—quite honestly—you've never had your first meeting. What do you do? Get with your sponsor and get going!

Have a Successful Meeting

The first get-together is extremely important for you and your business. It is crucial to remember why the people you invite would consider giving up an evening of relaxation at home to drive over and listen to your business plan.

Why would they come? You will find some people who are simply not interested in making more money. However, most people feel that they are underpaid, overtaxed, and overrun by inflation and the insecurity of their financial future. Keep in mind what that new prospect might be looking for in a business and you will have a leading edge on a successful meeting.

FIRST MEETING

Often a new distributor's first meeting can make or break her. Prior planning and preparation will help create a successful meeting for that new person and give her the confidence and enthusiasm to move forward to the next meeting.

Often a new distributor's first meeting can make or break her. Prior planning and preparation will help create a successful meeting for that new person and give her the confidence and enthusiasm to move forward to the next meeting. Kathy and Nadia, both top networkers, said this was especially true for them. "In the beginning my sponsor helped me to make a list of prospective partners and even helped me make those first few appointments," Kathy says. "I think if I had been left alone to make those calls, I would have put it off. But because I did not want to look silly in front of my sponsor, I had the extra courage to pick up that phone."

New people often tell me that their sponsor motivated their initial success. Helping that new person make calls, and stepping in for a conference call, will give her the confidence and assurance to take another step. "I thought I had to know everything, be prepared to answer every objection or question, before I could get started," says Nadia. "If my sponsor had let me wait until I was sure I could handle everything on my own, I would still be waiting."

Successful networkers help their newest people make calls and set appointments, answer questions, and offer encouragement. "My sponsor just kept smiling at me and saying, you can do it! For some reason, I believed her." Kathy said her sponsor helped her set up the first four or five presentations and helped her prepare in advance to maximize her success. "She told me that first impressions are often the most important ones. I learned some important tips to make that first great impression and it gave me the confidence I needed," she adds.

Qualify and Confirm

"An important part of having a successful meeting," says Lana, "is knowing you are going to have one!" Often new networkers, in their haste and excitement, neglect to qualify and confirm their appointments. "In the beginning I was so nervous, so excited, that I sometimes forgot to pin down my prospect and confirm our appointment. There were a few times that I showed up and the

FOUR GREAT WAYS TO OVERCOME YOUR FEAR OF COLD CALLING

1. Start with a huge list—your possibilities are as long as your list of names. Increase your percentage for success by getting a big list.
2. Stop thinking about yourself, your fears or challenges, and focus on what this opportunity can do for your prospect.
3. Ask your upline for support. Conference calls or three-way conversations can take the feeling of pressure off of you. By using the help of your upline, they can be the experts.
4. Make more calls! The faster you face your fears and make those calls, the faster your fear will subside. Soon your confidence will skyrocket!

prospect wasn't home! I had piqued their interest, but forgotten to get a commitment," she said.

In Chapter 6, Sharing the Idea, we covered tips and techniques for inviting. So we know that qualifying and confirming is critical to having a successful meeting. Qualifying your prospect means to determine his or her level of interest. Are they really looking, truly interested in hearing more about your business plan or are they simply courteous? Asking qualifying questions in the beginning will save you time and headaches.

"I quickly learned to ask qualifying questions such as 'If I could show you a way that you could increase your income without jeopardizing your current job, would you be interested in getting together to discuss the details?' Or, 'Jan, you told me last week that you really wanted to stop commuting and wished you could work from your home. Did you really mean it? Yes, well then I think it would be smart for us to get together. I have some great ideas for a home-based business that I think you'll be excited about,'" Lana adds.

By asking qualifying questions, Lana could determine the prospect's level of interest. Then

> ### THREE GREAT WAYS TO QUALIFY AND CONFIRM APPOINTMENTS
>
> 1. Ask questions. By asking leading questions you can quickly determine the level of interest a person has in your business opportunity.
> 2. Offer a choice of appointments. Ask your prospect if Tuesday or Friday would be better for them. Let them feel like they have a choice and are making the decision to meet you.
> 3. Confirm your appointment. Let your prospect know that you are great at keeping appointments and you expect them to be as well.

she could go to step two, confirming the appointment. "When my prospect expressed a desire to meet, I immediately pulled out my calendar and asked that they do the same. 'Jan, I have my calendar in front of me, do you? I have Tuesday or Saturday open. Which is better for you? Would you prefer 6 P.M. or 8 P.M.?'" By offering her prospect a choice of two dates, Jan could have better control over her calendar as well as get a specific day pinned down. "Ok, I'll be at your house on Tuesday at 8 P.M. And I want you to know, Jan, I am very good at keeping my appointments. Are you?" she asks. Lana is confirming the appointment and taking it one step further. "I want my prospects to know that they can count on me, that I keep my word. And I want them to know that I expect them to keep their appointment. By taking just a moment to ask a couple of questions, I have been able to keep my calendar full. And I seldom knock on a door and find nobody home!" she laughs.

The Purpose of a Meeting—the Next Meeting

Every appointment I make is with the intention of securing the next one. If I am going to share the marketing plan with a new couple, my goal is to get to that next meeting with them whether it's to sign them up, get them started, or to simply follow up and answer their questions. I never leave a meeting without securing an appointment for the next one. This way my calendar is always full and my time is used more effectively.

Put Your Best Foot Forward

In his latest book, *New Women's Dress for Success*, John Molloy discusses a proper, professional business look for women. He says, "Today the debate is not over whether a women *should* dress for success, but *how* they should go about doing it." Molloy tells us that 80 percent of the time it's better to choose a traditional cut, color, and design of clothing when doing business. "A woman who starts to dress for success immediately has a measurable statistical advantage over her competitors," he adds.

We have only sixty seconds to make a good impression. Within that amount of time people have sized you up and decided whether they want to get to know you better—whether they want to hear about your business idea. "I wanted to stack the odds in my favor," says Coleen. "We are in a highly competitive industry. There are many good network marketing companies with many good product lines. I knew network marketing was a great business opportunity. I wanted other people to feel the same way. By dressing for success I had the edge or advantage over other women—women who did not take their business seriously—who didn't take the time or energy to look professional," she adds.

Coleen knew that by dressing professionally she attracted a larger market. This gave her more of an advantage. "If I dressed in my blue jeans," she says. "Then the only people that would relate with me would be those dressed in jeans. If I dressed in khakis, then I increased my odds. Both those in jeans and those in khakis would relate with me. But if I dressed in a conservative, professional attire, I had everyone!"

What most leading networkers told me is:

- Wear color combinations that work well together, for example, a blue blouse with a beige skirt or a dark suit with a white shirt.
- Avoid the newest weird fashion—even if it is the latest rage.
- No cleavage and definitely no mini-skirts.
- Avoid tight fitting clothes.

Now you are dressed for success and you have made that great impression as you enter the room. What's next you ask? Eye contact! Looking people straight in the eye is one way you build confidence in your prospective distributor.

"Rachel sponsored me the first time I met her," said Deborah. "She looked me straight in the eyes and I knew she meant business. I also felt I could trust her." Eye contact is critical in communication and in building trust between you and potential distributors. "If a person can't look me in the eyes, I find it hard to believe anything they say," she explains. "I always wonder what it is they are hiding—what they aren't telling me."

By looking at people directly in their eyes, you let them know that you are honest, trustworthy, and confident. Another important technique in creating a good step towards a successful meeting is to show genuine interest in the other person. Marlene says that the people she meets love to talk to her because she shows a sincere

> **FOUR WAYS TO PUT YOUR BEST FOOT FORWARD**
>
> 1. Dress for success by wearing conservative, professional clothing.
> 2. Look people directly in the eye.
> 3. Offer a firm hand shake and remember to smile!
> 4. Speak in a professional manner and choose your words carefully.

interest in them. "When I meet a stranger in the store, I don't immediately try to recruit them," says Marlene. "I ask them questions. Then I listen intently to their answers. People get tired of being ignored or brushed off. They want to be appreciated, cared about."

Often people will get in business with you because you showed a genuine interest in them. After all, who couldn't use another friend?

Perhaps you have heard the phrase words are weapons? I am sure this is intended to make the point that we can use words to injure others. However, words can also be used to build up, to create, to inspire. What you say and how you say it can have a great influence on others and definitely can affect the success of a presentation or meeting. Proper, professional verbiage will set you apart from the crowd and let others know that you are educated, informed, and successful.

Rene Watkins says that appropriate language is important in developing a big business. "In school, I was always known as the class clown. I got a lot of attention being funny," Rene said. "I had a portfolio of jokes an inch thick and I could toss one out without even thinking about it. I found out one night that business meetings might not be the best time to crack a joke."

Luckily, it was not Rene who was clowning around at the meeting, but she learned from another's unfortunate mistake. "Our upline had flown in from California to do a presentation for us. The room was packed and the crowd was excited. When our upline finished his presentation, he invited the group to ask questions. In his excitement, a fellow in the back raised his hand and cracked a joke. The joke was funny, and at another time or place I might have been the one laughing the loudest. But that night you could have heard a pin drop. His comment was not appropriate and I was so thankful that I didn't have to learn this lesson the hard way," Rene said.

Although humor is important, jokes, no matter how funny, usually don't belong at a business presentation. Neither does questionable language or insinuating remarks. If you aren't sure what is acceptable, ask your upline leaders. They will be sure to fill you in.

Get Informed

Have you ever heard of the five P's? Prior Planning Prevents Poor Performance. Being informed helps promote successful meetings. You might agree that having a clear sense of the product line and an understanding of the compensation plan would be essential to a successful presentation. Most new distributors will thoroughly study their training material before doing a meeting on their own. Do you think it might be equally important to study your prospect? What do you know about her/him? Knowing as much about your potential prospect can help you maximize your time by prequalifying potential clients and eliminating those who don't have a dream or motivation to make changes in their lives.

"My sponsor taught me how to ask qualifying questions," said Darlene. "When I started building my downline, I wanted to find out who was really interested and who was not. I worked full time in a bank and my hours were restrictive. I needed to maximize my time and eliminate early people who really weren't looking."

Ask questions. If your prospect isn't open to making money or having their own business, why waste your time or theirs? There are plenty of people who are ready, willing, and able—people who are out there looking for you! Go find them.

> **FOUR GREAT TIPS TO EXCEL**
>
> 1. Understand and know your product line.
> 2. Present a professional presentation.
> 3. Don't be afraid to use notes.
> 4. Relax.

Rehearse

The most successful networkers tell me that they were not salespeople, nor were they public speakers when they started out in business. Often they are terrified of speaking in front of a group. Some of them even told me they didn't believe in the beginning that they would be able to build a successful business because every time they even thought about giving a presentation they got sweaty palms and weak in the knees.

Two Great Ways to Prepare a Great Presentation

1. Study, study, study. Attend as many presentations as possible with your sponsor or upline. Glean the tips from the superstars.
2. Rehearse, rehearse, rehearse. Practice your presentation in front of a mirror, the neighbor, or even your dog. Practice makes perfect!

But they all say that you can learn to be good at making presentations, and many said it is a part of the business that they enjoy the most. What is the secret to the big change in their attitudes? Practice, practice, practice!

When I decided to give my first presentation, I prepared well. I wrote down every word I intended to say and read those pages over and over. Then I took those pages and scaled them down into an outline format and placed them on 3 x 5 cards. I again rehearsed my presentation out loud, often in front of my huge mirror in the bedroom. Finally I gathered my family together and positioned them on the couch. Standing before them I gave my first "official" presentation, using my note cards of course! Even though it was only my family, I still was nervous. I knew that there was only one way to get really good at giving a compelling presentation—just get out there and do it! So I did. I found out that it was not only easy, it was fun! I continued to get better and better with each presentation. This, of course, motivated me to want to do even more.

And a really interesting thing happened. One night, after my second presentation, a prospect approached me and asked if he could get started that very night. As we signed him up and discussed the steps to start building his business, he told me that when he saw me using note cards, he realized that he could do this business after all! "At first I thought I wouldn't be able to make a go of this business," he said. "I am not a salesman and I have never been good at speaking in public. But when I saw you used note cards to give your presentation, I realized that I could do it too! If I could use note cards, I didn't have to give a perfect presentation or memorize each fact. It gave me the confidence to say yes to my dreams."

I decided to continue to use those cards long after I had memorized each word. If by using these cards I could encourage new people to get going right away, it was well worth it. Many people told me that when they saw me using cards they thought, "If she can do it, I can do it, too!"

So rehearse, rehearse, rehearse—in the mirror, to your dog, your neighbor, or an artificial plant. It can be helpful to tape-record yourself and critique your own presentation. Work with someone in your upline to smooth out the flow of information and make yourself as confident as possible. Most importantly, start giving presentations!

Most of us have been in presentations when the speaker was out of touch with his or her audience, rambling on long after any audience interest had left the room in despair. Think in bulleted points and headlines. You want people to come out of your presentation with just a handful of learned benefit points.

If you use equipment to make your presentation (flip charts, computer printouts, PowerPoint on a laptop, interactive CD-ROM, interactive holograms, laser light shows), bulletproof your equipment and carry spares of essential parts like disks, bulbs, and power cord. People tend to understand when you have a little technical trouble, but they do expect you to fix it.

Share the Benefits

In the Hall of Marketing Fame, the distinction between features and benefits sits on a raised marble pedestal in the center room under a ring of spotlights. This distinction separates marketers and everyone else in the business world just as sharply as the Berlin Wall divided Berlin. Many entrepreneurs talk about their products or business plan in terms of its features: capacity, strength, durability, or other technical capabilities. Marketers (that's you) are different. They speak of the product or the bonus plan, often as dramatically as possible, in terms of how it will benefit the prospective distributor. In other words, they sell the "what's in it for me" plan, the benefits. People are usually most interested in themselves—their needs, their plans, their dreams. Successful networkers learn to listen, really listen, to their people, defining what the other person's wants are then sharing the benefits of their particular business plan with them, wrapped around their wants. Successful networkers make a living by wish fulfillment.

Benefits are the satisfaction of a need or desire. Let's take the following example of a coffee maker.

FEATURE	BENEFIT
10 cup or 42-oz capacity	Make a full pot and have fresh coffee for hours
Special filter switch allows pot to be removed while filling	Grab a quick cup without spilling a drop
Digital timer is programmable	Wake up to freshly brewed coffee on a 24-hr basis
High-impact polypropylene	If it breaks in 3 years, we'll replace it free
Used paper filter #4	Standard filter available everywhere
High rated filter eliminates solids to 8 microns	Clean, smooth, great tasting coffee

What sells you—the features or the benefits? Most people would agree that beyond wanting value for our money, when it comes to coffee makers, or anything else, we want to know what the benefits are for us. The same is true in network marketing. Tell people what benefits are offered in your own business. Is it the *quality* of the products or the *concentration of value*? Will your compensation plan meet the expectations and goals of your new prospect? At what stage of development could your prospect attain one of the goals she/he shared with you? Could one of the benefits be to have the flexibility to arrange her own schedule or set her own hours? What could this kind of control over her time mean to her? Remember to listen to your prospects. Find a need and fill it by sharing the *benefits* of your business plan.

Invite a Dialogue

Most people can't stand to be preached to or lectured. They usually, however, like to be in a conversation with people. Ask questions and encourage your guests to ask questions as well. By inviting and encouraging their participation, you enlist their help in figuring out all the ways your product or service or compensation plan can benefit them.

Listen, really listen, when they share their questions and concerns. Often people will not tell you their real concerns at first. If you listen and don't interrupt, they will begin to feel at ease with you and more often than not will eventually tell you what they are honestly concerned about.

"I was pretty nervous about speaking in front of people," says Sally. "When I held my meetings I always got my prospects involved in conversation with me. I would ask them leading questions like, 'What is your occupation? Do you enjoy your job? If you could change one thing about it, what would that be? Have you lived here long? How do you like this area? Do you have children? 'By asking questions I got people involved with me and they opened up. It made it so much easier to then share the information with them."

> **SAMPLE DIALOGUE**
>
> "When we spoke last week, Doug, you mentioned your company had been experiencing major cutbacks. I know this is a widespread issue and a tremendous concern for most of us. As you look at your financial future, what is most important to you, Doug? Would it be helpful to you to develop a substantial income on the side that is permanent and inheritable to your family?"

Don't Panic

People who give objections are at least taking you seriously, so don't panic! "I learned how to handle objections early in my networking career," says Eileen Sargent. "Business on the Internet was exciting to most people, but because we were a relatively new business model, people had lots of questions. I was always happy to get the questions. I knew that meant they were interested and wanted to know more."

When you get in a presentation where everyone is smiling at everything you are saying you might be in trouble. This could be a polite way of cutting you off or getting through the presentation quickly. However, I find that when people object, they're looking for more information, or they want you to clarify their perception of your business plan. Questions indicate that they are at least interested enough to get more facts. I encourage questions. I want to address their concerns up front and head on. Encouraging questions lets the prospect feel comfortable and safe which allows them to open up and really talk with you. You should be prepared for objections and whatever you do, don't panic. Objections mean, "tell me more."

Asking for the Sign Up

I have seen so many people give great presentations, get people at their peak interest, and drop the ball on the follow-up. "My background was in education and I was great at giving a professional presentation," Eileen adds. "However, none of my education and training had prepared me for selling and I didn't want to hear the 'no.' I was so afraid of getting rejected that even after giving a top rate presentation, I would often not even ask them to get in business with me. In the beginning, I sometimes wouldn't even follow up after that first meeting, again fearing a no."

If you want to have people join you in business, there is one simple way—ask them!

Eileen learned the hard way that giving a great presentation wasn't always enough. After doing a couple of great meetings and getting no sign-ups, Eileen called her sponsor for help. "Cindy knew exactly what I was feeling. She was so great—she never made me feel foolish. She told me that there were times she had felt the same way—that she too had often feared rejection. What she found out was that by *not* asking the prospect to join, she got an automatic *no*! I changed my approach that very night. I started asking people at the first meeting if they were interested in getting started right away," she adds. "I was so surprised the first few times when they wanted to get started that very night! Now asking for the sign-up is automatic. Not everyone joins that night, but many do, and by asking I eliminate a lot of work for myself—and for them."

If you want to have people join you in business, there is one simple way—
ask them!

Combine Steps

Although I never recommend trying to skip a step in your pattern of success,
I often find that *combining* steps can speed your business along and will often
eliminate the hassle of going over the main points again in your second
meeting. "I found out fast that I could give my presentation, answer questions, and get them signed up in the first night,"
says Karen. "By getting on the other side of these
first steps, I could get a fast start, not only for
myself, but for the new distributor as well."

Some people hate to talk about money or
signing up on the first night. I don't think that's
effective. People want to know the price of getting
started, regardless of how little importance you try
to attach to it. Don't apologize for your price,
either high or low. Most people don't expect to get
something for nothing.

"I always assumed the best in people. Every
time I gave a presentation, I talked to the people
as if they were already in. I treated them with
proper respect, never pushing, but treating them like my newest partners.
People that were interested anyway often followed my lead," she adds. "I
gave them an easy way to say yes without putting them on the spot."

> ### FIVE STEPS TO A
> ### SUCCESSFUL MEETING
>
> 1. Identify your prospect's needs, con-
>   cerns, or their "why."
> 2. Offer information to eliminate their
>   objections.
> 3. Leave follow-up material; tapes or
>   books that support your business.
> 4. Schedule a time to meet again—
>   within 24 to 48 hours.
> 5. Ask them for referrals.

Yes, No, or Maybe

When I had a motor home dealership, I taught my salespeople that a *maybe*
was a polite way of saying *no*. In networking I find that, more often than not,
the same is true. If someone gives me a maybe, I try to identify what his or
her concerns are, and without "selling" this person, I try to help him or her
overcome those objections if I can. Unless they tell me no, I schedule a

follow-up meeting with them, giving them a tape or other material to review. This gives me a reason to get back with them without seeming as if I am going to cram it down their throats. Some people just need some time to think it over, to talk among themselves, and often they will overcome their own objections if I allow them that time.

If a prospect does say no, I always ask for a referral. I might say something like, "Well, Joe, I know that this business is not for everyone. I certainly respect your decision and I always want to leave the door open for you if you change your mind. But in the meantime, who do you know, if anyone, that might be interested in an opportunity like this?" Sometimes they actually give me a list of names, and, more often than not, I am able to get another meeting. Sometimes I have even been able to get Joe's referral signed up and have given Joe a call back. "Joe, I know you said you were not interested at the time we met, but your friend Bill just got in and I wanted to give you another opportunity. Bill is really sharp and very excited. Do you want to sponsor him or should I?"

Turbocharge

The most successful networkers will tell you that to get a big business going fast requires effort, but it's easier than many people think. Doing just a little bit more pays big dividends. Take Lorene Cron, for example. "I loved the network marketing business, I loved the products, I loved the people, and I loved the compensation plan. So I went to work. I made a commitment to talk to 30 people every day, either by phone, fax, or mail. I figured that the faster I got the word out, the faster my business would grow," she said. "That first month I made over $1,000. That motivated me to talk to more people than ever before. I turbocharged my business. I talked to more people, made more contacts, did more meetings and presentations. The money just kept rolling in. In the next three years I made over one million dollars! Doing more paid off!"

Stay Strong Through Training

Do you know what the greatest asset you have in network marketing is? It's *you*! Keep razor sharp and stay on the leading edge by utilizing your company training system. Check with your upline for recommendations. Some companies offer a standing order tape of the week that provides information and motivation. Does your business group offer monthly meetings, seminars, or training videos? Some of the bigger networking companies have satellite broadcast and online Web event support. Almost every organization offers a wide variety of recommended reading materials. Whatever your organization offers, use it! The key is to invest in yourself—your personal growth. Information combined with motivation and confidence is unstoppable.

Mark Victor Hansen, mega best-selling author of the *Chicken Soup for the Soul* series, says the back seat of his BMW is filled with self-help and motivational audiotapes. As a top paid motivational speaker and network marketer himself, Mark says, "Being active in a network marketing business helps you sculpt yourself. It is literally the fastest self-growth and personal development plan on the planet. You can actually see your level of self-growth expand. Just watch your bankbook!"

> ### YOUR GREATEST ASSET
>
> Keep razor sharp and stay on the leading edge by utilizing your company training system. Check with your upline for recommendations. Some companies offer a standing order tape of the week that provides information and motivation.

"I wanted to get my hands on any and all of the information my upline had available. I just couldn't get enough," says Suzanne. "I wanted to get profitable fast and I knew I had a lot to learn. I poured myself into training system. Weekly training just wasn't enough for me. I wanted it all!"

Every successful leader knows that it is her responsibility to be on top of the latest information and get it to your downline fast! "Our industry is growing by leaps and bounds. Just to keep up with the increased product lines takes effort," Suzanne adds. "I have always been grateful for an organization that is strong in product awareness and training. I recommend to every new distributor that joins my business to get into the training system that we offer.

I feel it was a major key in my own success. It sure has worked for me! I want it to work as well for my newest person."

Secure your success by investing in your business—in *you*!

Customize Your Presentation

"Every night when I went out to share this great business opportunity I knew it was 'opening night' for that new person," says Amy Grant. "And what I said that night could have an impact on their future. So it was important to me to give them the best presentation possible—the best information to help them make an informed decision. I tried to learn something about my prospect, such as their education, occupation, hobbies, etc. By knowing something about them, I could customize my presentation around them."

What Amy did was speak to their needs, their desires. If she was giving a presentation to a doctor, she might talk about the changes in health care, HMOs, or developing residual income. If she was doing a meeting for a salesman who traveled extensively, she might talk about territory cuts, commission structures, demands and sacrifices on the family, or time freedom. The issues that were most important to the salesman would not be of any interest to the doctor and vice versa. By developing a presentation that fit the concerns or needs of the individual, she was able to increase her sponsoring rate and build a huge business.

Types of Meetings

You have prepared, rehearsed, qualified, and confirmed your prospect and the meeting. So where is the best venue to sponsor, you ask? Although there is a mixed opinion among networkers, most top moneymakers tell me their highest sponsoring came from small group meetings or one-on-ones.

"If success in networking was a numbers game, then I figured the one with the highest numbers wins!" said Annette. "I had grandiose ideas of holding huge hotel meetings and bringing people in by the hundreds. I quickly learned after spending over $100 to book a meeting room and having a turnout of under 20 people that perhaps there was a better way."

What Annette found out is that in the beginning it is often more effective to give presentations to small groups of four or five, sometimes called house meetings, rather than to spend the money for meeting rooms. "My sponsor told me to begin by scheduling small house meetings and then sponsor a few people. So I did. It wasn't long before we outgrew the living rooms and had to move to a larger place. Then it was the right time to go to the expense of renting a larger room," she adds.

Larger venues, such as a business center in a hotel or an auditorium in a college, can be costly. While these are great places to hold meetings when you have the numbers to support it, they are not always the best place to bring first-time lookers. "Large hotel meetings can be intimidating for the new person," says Annette. "I found that sharing the business plan at house meetings and sponsoring a few folks was easier than getting them to come out to a hotel or meeting room. My best results were to sponsor a few people first, or at least give a presentation, and then pull them all together for a second look at a large group meeting. In addition to being more effective and less intimidating, this type of business building can be easily duplicated," she adds.

While some people may have the finances to support renting a large meeting room, most don't. Remember that people do what they see. If a new distributor's only experience in building the business is to go to large meetings, she may think that she can only have a meeting at a hotel. This will stop most distributors from growing. They need to understand that the name of the game is sharing the idea with as many people as you can, as quickly as possible. By waiting until someone in your upline is holding a large group meeting, you will postpone your own growth as well as the potential new distributors.' Holding house meetings and small one-on-ones is affordable to everyone and is also easily duplicated by even the newest person.

SEVEN KEYS TO A SUCCESSFUL MEETING

1. Know why you are building a business and focus on your dream.
2. Qualify your appointments.
3. Confirm you appointments.
4. Schedule a meeting from a meeting.
5. Dress for success.
6. Ask for the sign up.
7. Remember: the one who shows the most marketing plans, wins!

So there you have it! Having a successful meeting begins with knowing why you are building a business and knowing what you want to achieve. After defining your why, just follow a few simple steps such as qualifying your prospect and confirming your appointments. Always scheduling a meeting at the meeting will make your time effective and speed up your steps to success. Put your best foot forward by dressing for success and rehearsing your presentation. Then you will present a professional and compelling marketing plan and ask for the sign-up. This will move you even further ahead. By inviting your prospects to participate in the presentation and encouraging their remarks, you can easily sell the benefits of your own particular marketing and compensation plan. And most importantly, it doesn't matter much *where* you hold your meetings; what ultimately counts is *how many* people you talk to about your own business plan. The one who shares the most plans wins!

In Chapter 9 we will discuss ways to be an effective teacher. Leading network experts share some of their own inside secrets to help you reach success. As you learn to hold successful meetings and teach your own system of success, you will be teaching teachers to teach, thereby creating huge numbers and tremendous volume in your business. By utilizing the counsel of your upline and learning the power of duplication, you can plug in and power up!

CHAPTER NINE

TEACH THE SYSTEM FOR SUCCESS

Every network marketing company has its own training system—its own system of success. While this chapter is about how to teach your downline to be successful, it will not promote a particular teaching plan. This chapter will help you learn a critical lesson: how to teach success principles to your downline. As you learn how to become an effective teacher, you will be developing your own huge business organization.

Without the Why Nothing Happens

Last year a good friend of mine began a building project in San Francisco. It was a huge project, a fifteen-story office complex. Every couple of months I made it a point to drive past the building site. Each time I drove away disappointed. To me it seemed nothing was happening; no progress was being made. I asked my husband, who is also a contractor, why the building seemed at a standstill. He said, "Cynthia, the project is moving along just fine. It takes months for the engineering department to complete their job, the architects to finish the design, and the city to issue all of the required permits. Once that is complete, the land must be cleared and prepared. The foundation must be dug and supports poured. Then comes the sub-floor, and afterwards the steel work begins. Throughout the entire project there are building inspections and changes that must be made. Sometimes it takes years before you ever seen the building completed."

Every time I saw my friend, he was always excited. He saw something I didn't—the finished product. He clearly knew why he was working on this particular project. When I drove out to the site, I saw mounds of dirt, equipment, and workers. When he went there, he saw the finished product. He saw the building reaching up to the sky, the parking garage, and the money rolling in. In his mind he saw it all—years before it actually was completed.

Why would we expect to build a huge business with any less planning, any less effort? Dreams such as this skyscraper take planning and effort. Without it nothing gets accomplished. Dreams and goals are the *why*, the reason behind the action. A clearly defined goal is a major first step in success. Helping your people understand this fundamental first step can make a huge difference in the size of your business. "I was a facts and figures kind of girl," says Marjory. "When I went to my first meeting all I could think of was, 'Will this guy just get on with it? Get to the point.' I couldn't stand the dream session, the part of the marketing plan where we talked about our reason, our why. I just wanted to get past that and find out what to do next."

Marjory learned that the dream *is* the next step and without it nothing happens.

The Power of Duplication

As J. Paul Getty once said, "There are only two ways to be rich—leverage money or leverage time. Most of us don't have enough money to leverage to make us really rich, but we all have the same amount of hours in a day. What we do with those hours is what separates the winners from the losers. By utilizing the power of duplication in your business and teaching your downline to do the same, you will create more time and energy and have more productivity invested in your business.

Richard Poe, in his book *Wave 4*, talks about the power of duplication. He says that duplication is how successful networkers build big businesses. Have you ever heard of the doubling concept? The word "duplicate" originally meant *to double*, and this concept of doubling is one of the most powerful forces at work for you in your network marketing business. Here's how it works:

Suppose I offered you a million dollars cash, this very minute, or offered to give you a penny, doubled every day for a month. Which would you choose? If you are like most people, you'd probably choose the million dollars. But take my advice, don't do it! Take the penny doubled. Why, you ask? Just check this out.

A penny doubled every day for a month doesn't sound like much, and it doesn't look like much in the beginning either. I mean just look at what you would have after five days—sixteen cents! After fifteen days, you'd have a whopping $163.84. Are you beginning to think my advice was all wrong? Hold on, there's more.

On day nineteen, you'd have $2,621. Six days later, day twenty-five, only five days before the end of the month, you'd have just over $167,000. Still not impressed? The next day you'd be up to $335,000. The day after that you'd hit around $671,000. On the next day, the twenty-eighth, you'd have over $1,340,000. And two days later, on the thirtieth—the last day of the month— you'd have a grand total of $5,368,709.12! That's over 5 million dollars! All from one penny, which simply doubled every day.

> ### DREAMS, GOALS
>
> The first step in the system for success is the dream. Dreams and goals are the why, the reason behind the action. A clearly defined goal is a major first step in success. Helping your people understand this fundamental first step can make a huge difference in the size of your business.

This doubling principle is the way a business grows in network marketing, and it's made network marketing the fastest method of expansion in the history of free enterprise. You know, McDonald's didn't start off with 10,000 restaurants all over the world. They started out with just one. That's just how you can start building a huge network marketing business—you and another person. By teaching this success pattern, the pattern of doubling or duplication, you will create a huge organization.

People Do What They See

Keep in mind, however, that if you want people to duplicate success principles, you have to be the example for them to follow. Have you ever heard the statement, "Your actions are speaking so loud I can't hear what you are saying?" People tend to duplicate what they see, not what they hear. Think about the little boy who tries to walk just like daddy. Your business partners will follow your lead, duplicating what they see you do, even if they don't understand why. This is illustrated in a story I once heard about a pot roast. A young married couple was preparing their first meal together. The new groom asks his sweet bride, " Honey, why do you cut the pot roast in half

THREE TIPS TO
ACHIEVE SUCCESS

1. Strive for excellence in everything you do. Give everything you do everything you've got and you are certain to succeed.
2. Detest thinking average. Think big and big things will happen.
3. Look forward to competing with the best. Work and reach to achieve a higher level of success by running with the upline leaders in your own organization.

before you cook it?" Her reply, "Because that is the way my mother did it."

Shortly afterwards, at a family dinner the young groom asked his mother-in-law, "Why do you cut the pot roast in two parts before you cook it?" Her reply, "Because that is the way my mother did it."

The new groom quickly ran to find the grandmother. He leaned towards her and gently asked, "Please, I beg you, tell me why you cut the pot roast in half before you cook it?"

The grandmother leaned towards the young groom and whispered in his ear, "Because the roast was always too big for my little cooking pot!"

For years, even generations, women had been duplicating what they had seen as little girls standing around the kitchen stove. They continued to cut the roast in half and yet they did not know why they were doing it, other than it was the way they had been taught—the way they had seen their own mothers do it. Make sure you are on the right track and are duplicating your upline leaders' proven and successful pattern for success. Then and only then will you be an effective teacher.

Strive for Excellence

It is much easier to teach people who are eager to learn. Bet on people who strive for excellence, not on those who are second-rate performers. Remember, average is the best of the worst and the worst of the best. As you fashion a stronger, more successful business, keep three points in mind.

First, *strive for excellence in everything you do.* See the wisdom in the old saying, "If something is worth doing it's worth doing well." All work is important and should be performed in the best manner possible. Remember that you'll make more money when you are an excellent performer. And you'll enjoy more satisfaction, which is the source of the real wealth you seek.

Second, *detest thinking average*. Thinking average will never help you realize your dreams. No kid likes to say, " My dad is an average dad." No boss wants to tell his superior, "Jack is only an average salesman," and no one will ever brag about you if you look, think, talk, and act as an average person does.

Third, *look forward to competing with the best*. You'll never know how good you are until you match yourself against a big challenge. Mediocre people want company. They delight in seeing others sink to their level. Deny them their devilish delight. Don't let average associates pull you down to their performance level. Get your advice from winners. Model your behavior after the best. Keep moving toward excellence and enjoy the rewards.

Network Marketing Is a People Business

Last fall I attended a convention in Phoenix for the kickoff of a new network marketing business. The America West Arena was filled to capacity. The top networkers in the country were in attendance, celebrating the opening of a new network business on the Internet. Across the country in St. Louis, another convention was being held. Satellites were sending broadcasts back and forth between the two conventions. I saw one of the most famous, highest paid networkers in all of network marketing, Birdie Yager, as she presented a compelling speech. In it she said, "Focus on the people, not the products. This is a people business, not a product business. The Internet in all its glory doesn't do anything—the people do. If someone doesn't turn on the computer, nothing happens."

> ## NETWORK MARKETING IS A PEOPLE BUSINESS.
>
> "Focus on the people—not the products. This is a people business not a product business. The Internet in all its glory doesn't do anything—the people do. If someone doesn't turn on the computer, nothing happens."
>
> —BIRDIE YAGER

Birdie Yager is right! It is people who make things happen. People move the products, not the other way around. And people lead people. The people who learn to lead others and effectively teach a success pattern make everything work. Network marketing is truly a people business.

Importance of Attitude

Our attitude may not be the only asset that makes us great leaders, but without a good one we will never reach our full potential. Our attitudes are the "and then some" that allows us the little extra edge over those whose thinking is wrong. Walt Emerson said, "What lies behind us and what lies before us are tiny matters compared to what lies within us." Researchers at the Carnegie Institute teach us that 15 percent of success is due to technical training. The other 85 percent is due to personality, and the primary personality trait identified by the research is *attitude*. Success is determined more by *how* we think, rather than by *what* we know.

> Success is determined more by our attitude than our level of skill. Success is 15 percent training and 85 percent attitude!

Rachel Stewart is convinced that attitude is everything. "My Dad always told me, 'Success in life is 10 percent what happens to you and 90 percent how you handle it.' I heard that statement over and over again in my youth. Dad never made excuses himself, and he never let us make them either. He once gave me a plaque that he was especially fond of. He had it in his office for years and I have it in my own today. It reads:

> If you think you are beaten, you are.
> If you think you dare not, you don't.
> If you'd like to win but think you can't,
> It's almost certain you won't.
> Life's battles don't always go
> To the stronger or faster man,
> But sooner or later, the one who wins
> Is the one who *thinks* he can.

"So in high school, when my basketball coaches told me that I was too short to play college ball, I didn't accept it. I knew that if I kept my attitude up and focused on what I wanted, not what they told me I could have, that I would win." And she did.

Rachel went on to play college basketball for an NCAA Division I team. She attended the University of California at Berkeley on a full-ride scholarship. As a 5'5" basketball player, Rachel knows that her success was 90 percent attitude. "When I started my own networking business, I applied the same lessons that helped me win on the court, namely building on a strong, positive attitude," she adds. "I teach my group that same winning principal. Over and over again I watch my downline reach levels of success that in the beginning they thought were impossible. When your attitude is right, everything is possible."

Teach by Example

People catch our attitudes just like they catch our colds—by getting close to us. There is a law in physics that states for every action there is an equal and opposite reaction. If I bounce a ball against the wall it will rebound from the wall with precisely the same force with which I threw it. That law is also true in the realm of influence. In fact, its effects multiply with a leader's influence. The action of a leader multiplies in reaction because there are several followers. To a smile given, many smiles return.

Remember the four-minute mile? People had been trying to achieve it for decades but couldn't break the four-minute barrier. "Our bone structure is all wrong," the experts claimed. "Wind resistance is too great. We don't have enough lung power." A million reasons were given. One man proved that they were all wrong! Roger Bannister broke the four-minute mile, and the year after he did the impossible thirty-seven other runners broke the four-minute mile.

What happened? There were no great break-throughs in training. Human bone structure and lung capacity didn't suddenly improve. But human attitudes did. "I wanted to be in the top money-making bracket," says Joyce. "So I saw myself, visualized myself as a leader, a success, long before I had gotten there. I taught my people to do the same thing. In order to make it big, you have to *know* you are going to be there. You have to make success real in your mind before you ever achieve it. When you have that positive attitude, that attitude of expectancy, people will catch it, and when they do, magic happens!"

> "When your attitude is right, everything is possible."
>
> —RACHEL STEWART

A leader's attitude is caught more quickly than his actions. An attitude is reflected by others even when they don't follow the action. "My upline taught me the power of a good attitude," Joyce adds. "I always felt great being around her. She was an up person—high energy—positive. One particularly distressing day I was complaining to her about one of my distributors. This couple just never seemed to do anything right. In fact, I often wondered if they didn't mess up just to bug me! My sponsor told me that sometimes people *act* they way they *think* you *think* they are. In other words, I had a negative attitude about that couple and so when I was with them, negatives were all I could see. They would react to me—to my attitude about them. I expected them to be a problem and I got what I expected," she said. "Boy, did I start changing my attitude fast! I realized that if I wanted to build a large organization, not only did I have to have a good attitude myself, I had to have a good attitude about my people."

An attitude can be expressed without a word being spoken. A leader's attitude is of significant importance when teaching the system of success. Our attitudes determine what we see and how we handle our feelings. These two factors greatly impact our success. Teaching your people how to have a great attitude can be accomplished—if they are willing to change.

Words Make a Difference

As a young child, I often heard the statement, "Sticks and stones may break my bones, but words will never hurt me!" As an adult, however, I quickly discovered that nothing is further from the truth. A thoughtless, cruel, condemning word, especially from a person you love or respect, can have a devastating, long-lasting effect.

On the other side of the coin, the proper words can inspire and encourage people to do marvelous things with their lives. When most people tell you something "for your own good," they generally proceed to tell you something bad. How much better would it be if parents told their children something good for their children's own good.

Clear Up Communication

The English language is truly fascinating and has many twists and turns, including oxymorons (phrases that combine contradictory words). For example, someone may say, "Same difference." Another person may talk about "jumbo shrimp." As you reflect on these and other word turns, you realize that some words and phrases are easily misunderstood. An old, negative expression says, "Those things which can be misunderstood will be misunderstood."

When you use words, you are communicating, but when you use phrases such as winning relationships or good leadership, you're communicating a message, one that needs to be clearly understood upline and downline in your business group. If you can't communicate effectively, few people understand what you expect of them. The individual who gets things done is an effective communicator.

Use kind and inspiring words with a helpful intent and a gentle tone of voice and you build better relationships and move up the success ladder more quickly and surely.

> An attitude can be expressed without a word being spoken. A leader's attitude is of significant importance when teaching the system of success. Our attitudes determine what we see and how we handle our feelings. These two factors greatly impact our success.

Words differ in their importance. The most important words you can say to your child or mate are, "I love you." The second most important words you can say are, "I made a mistake. Please forgive me." Those words say, "I'm wiser now and have better judgement than I had an hour earlier or yesterday." Nothing pleases a child more than to know that you are willing and sure enough in your role to say, "I made a mistake. Please forgive me." This is true also with your network partners.

Four Great Things to Say to Build Success

1. "I appreciate you."
2. "That's a great idea."
3. "What is your opinion?"
4. "Thank you."

"When my sponsor came to me one day and apologized for a remark she had made earlier I was so impressed," says Kathleen. "It was such a little thing and yet she made a specific point of finding me and taking the time to make sure our relationship was intact. I seldom was treated with the same respect at the office. I appreciated her effort and thoughtfulness."

People are people, and even the best leaders will occasionally make mistakes. You will too. When you do, admit it and move on. You will be a more effective teacher because your people will respect your honesty and integrity.

Turned On to Succeed

Every fall in Reno, Nevada, a famous car show is held. Hot August Nights draws thousands of people who come to see the spectacular display of automobiles. Many of the classic cars are a collector's dream. They are gleaming with multiple coats of polish and are showroom perfect inside and out.

My teenaged sons, intrigued by anything that moves, convinced me that we needed to make our way up to Reno for the show. We walked for miles and miles that afternoon as my sons repeated, "Sweet," and, "that car is fat!" over and over. I gawked and drooled just like the rest of the folks at these incredible automobiles while my sons dreamed of owning one someday. At the end of the day we saw several vehicles that were being offered for sale. Michael, my oldest son, pulled me towards a particular car and used his best sales technique, hoping to convince me to purchase it so we could make a "great investment."

I must admit that I secretly thought it did seem like a good deal. After finding its owner we discovered why this beautiful, shiny car was such a steal—it didn't run! While my son was obviously disappointed, even he agreed that he didn't want a car that he couldn't even turn on.

On the way home that evening I thought about the car. It looked so perfect on the outside, and yet as beautiful as it was, it was worthless to us because we couldn't drive it. I realized that the business of network marketing is much the same way—you can have a perfect business opportunity that won't take you anywhere unless you are turned on to succeed.

Change Your Opinion of Yourself

Self-image has a great deal to do with your success in network marketing and your effectiveness as a great leader and teacher. Every time you take a step forward by doing something of value, you improve your picture of yourself. Because that picture determines your performance and your performance determines your future, the daily habit of positive affirmations or mission statements is a marvelous way to improve self-esteem and ensure success in your future.

> You can have a perfect business opportunity that won't take you anywhere unless you are turned on to succeed.

Successful networkers have told me that by repeating, out loud, their mission statement or affirmations repeatedly throughout the day, they have literally become the person they affirmed themselves as. Some ideas you may want to incorporate in your own mission statement could be the following:

I am a winner…

…because I think like a winner, prepared like a winner, and perform like a winner.

…because I set high goals and work toward those goals with determination and persistence. I never stop until I reach them.

…because total commitment is my constant companion, and personal integrity is my lifetime mentor.

…because I am strong enough to say "No!" to those things that would make me less than my best, and to say "Yes!" to the challenges and opportunities that will make me grow and improve my life.

…because I have a well-earned confidence in myself, a high regard for my fellow teammates and business partners, and a deep respect for my upline leaders.

…because of my enthusiasm for life, my enjoyment of the present, and my trust in the future.

"When my sponsor first told me about mission statements and the effects of reading them everyday, I thought she was nuts," said Jamie. "I mean really—who were we kidding? Certainly not ourselves—or so I thought. But she persisted and so I did write down some personality traits that I wished I had and I began to read them out loud every morning. Eventually I memorized them and would find myself thinking about them throughout my day. I might be driving in the car or standing in line at the bank and the words would just pop into my head. 'I am a winner!'" she adds. "By repeating positive statements about myself I began to see myself differently. I started seeing myself as a winner and I soon started to act like one. By acting like a success, I did things that successful people do and eventually those actions led me to success."

> Habits are doing the right things today that will put you in the right place tomorrow.
> —BIRDIE YAGER

Jamie says it all started with a simple mission statement. She eventually became the person she described every morning. By changing the picture of herself, she changed her actions. Her actions moved her towards success. Today Jamie is a winner. Teach these success principles to your downline and just watch them grow and develop into strong leaders in your business.

Winning Habits

Birdie Yager says that winning habits are doing the right things today that will put you in the right place tomorrow. Our actions and habits will determine our lifestyle. Winning habits are the best friends you can have, particularly in the business world. Look carefully at what an anonymous writer said about habits:

"I am your constant companion. I am your greatest helper or heaviest burden. I will push you onward and upward or drag you down to failure. I am completely at your command. Ninety percent of the things you do might just as well be turned over to me, and I will be able to do them quickly and correctly. I am easily managed, show me exactly how you want something done and after a few lessons I will do them automatically. I am the servant of all great people and, alas, of all failures as well. I am not a machine, though I work with all the precision of a machine, plus the intelligence of a man. You can run me for profit or run me for ruin—it makes no difference to me. Take me, train me, be firm with me, and I will place the world at your feet. Be easy with me and I will destroy you. Who am I? I am Habit."

In the business world of network marketing, good work habits lead to progression and increased income. Being courteous and conscientious, returning phone calls promptly, and going the extra mile are all habits that lead to success. Remember, when you do more than what you are expected to do, the day will come when you're paid more for what you do.

Good habits must be grabbed firmly and with a strong commitment. Teaching good habits to your downline will be a huge step towards their success. The decision to commit to good habits will produce marvelous results in an amazingly short period of time.

The Gold Mine

Last summer my husband and I took our two youngest children to Sutter's Mill. It is a little place off Highway 49 in northern California made famous in the mid-1800s when gold was first discovered there. It is an interesting little town, rich with history. As we walked along the shaded dirt paths we talked about how it might have been to live back in those days. My son, Tyler, with all of the confidence of a ten-year-old boy, said, "I bet I would have found more gold than anyone in this whole town! I would be the richest guy around."

My husband told him about the hundreds of men who lost everything they had, even their very lives, in their pursuit of gold. Still eager to strike it rich, Tyler convinced him that we should try our hand at panning for gold. We rented a tin pan and after a brief demonstration by the local storeowner, we set out to find our golden nuggets. For several hours we bent over the river, sifting through gallons of water, dirt, and sand while the hot sun was

> "We are what we repeatedly do. Excellence, then, is not an act, but a habit."
> —Aristotle

pounding on our heads and our muscles ached from the strain of bending. After sifting and sorting through mounds of tiny particles of rock and sand, the best I found were several tiny fragments of fool's gold. Tyler ended up being the only one who actually found gold, a tiny nugget about the size of a pencil eraser.

Panning for gold was a lot of hard work. We had to go through a ton of dirt just to find one small piece of gold. Network marketing is much like panning for gold: you have to go through a lot of people before you find the golden ones—the ones who will really make it big! But when you do find those golden people, you will feel much like my son Tyler did that day at Sutter's Mill when he finally found his gold nugget. He jumped up in the air and exclaimed, "I found one. I found one. We are going to be rich!"

Teach your people to keep sifting and sorting. Don't be a fool like many of the early miners were. When they found what they thought was gold they stopped panning, only to discover later that all the gold they had collected was worthless. Don't stop sorting and sifting (sponsoring) until you have found enough gold, enough leaders to make you rich!

> Teach your people to keep sifting and sorting. Don't be a fool like many of the early miners were. When they found what they thought was gold they stopped panning, only to discover later that all the gold they had collected was worthless. Don't stop sorting and sifting (sponsoring) until you have found enough gold, enough leaders to make you rich!

No Crosslining Allowed

Crossline—it's a strange word isn't it? I'd never heard the word crossline, until I got involved in network marketing. Crosslining means to go outside of your own line of sponsorship and cross over into another one—to share business ideas with someone who is not in your direct line of sponsorship.

For example, if I personally sponsored my neighbor, my sister, and my banker, each of these business groups would be crossline from each other. My sister's business has nothing to do with my banker's business, and so on. Therefore, my sister would come to me or to my sponsor for help, advice, or support. She would go upline, not crossline (across her line of sponsorship) to my banker to ask questions as he has no interest in her business and no investment there. He should never involve himself in her group.

The biggest names in network marketing tell me that crosslining is a certain way to destroy a business. Anytime a person is crossing over into your business group and offering information, they are messing with your money and your future, as well as the individual whom they are crosslining with.

When it comes to crosslining, just say "No!"

Plug In and Power Up!

Throughout this book we have talked about utilizing one of your strongest assets, your upline. By plugging in—getting involved with them and their system of success—you will power up your business and your growth can be explosive.

A great upline leader can make a huge difference in your level of success. Your upline leaders have reached success and have great wisdom, often making up for areas where you might be challenged or while you are growing and learning.

Karen says that plugging into her upline was the key to her success. "My upline covered for me—made up for the areas where I was weak or inexperienced," she says. This great gift—the gift of service by your upline—reminds me of a story I once heard.

A little girl desperately wanted a new bike, a pink one with streamers on the handlebars. Day after day she would tell her parents how much she wanted that bike. It would have been easy for them financially to buy her a bicycle, but her father was worried that at only seven she might be too young for the bike that she wanted. So he decided to put her off for awhile. He told her, "Honey, I'll tell you what. You save all your pennies and pretty soon you'll have enough to buy the bike."

"Ok," she said and she went away. Dad was off the hook. After a few weeks he noticed his daughter doing extra chores around the house and even offering to help her mother. He asked his daughter why she was so eager to help out. Her reply, "You promised that if I saved all my pennies, pretty soon I'd have enough to get a bike. And Daddy, I've saved every single one!"

> Utilize one of your strongest assets, your upline. By plugging in—getting involved with them and their system of success—you will power up your business and your growth can be explosive.
>
> A great upline leader can make a huge difference in your level of success. Your upline leaders have reached success and have great wisdom, often making up for areas where you might be challenged or while you are growing and learning.

Well, the father hadn't actually lied to his daughter. If she continued to save all of her pennies, eventually she would have enough for a bike. But by then, she would probably want a car. In the meantime, this little girl was working hard, doing everything in her power to follow her father's instructions, but her needs were still not being met. Because of her willingness the dad took his girl to look at bikes, and sure enough, there it was, a pink bike with streamers on the handlebars.

**FIVE GREAT POINTS
TO PONDER**

1. People duplicate what they see, not what you say.
2. Attitude determines your altitude, or your level of success.
3. Excellence is not an act but rather a habit.
4. Keep sifting and sorting—sponsoring new people.
5. Plug in and power up!

The little girl rushed over to the bike. "This is it. This is the one!" she exclaimed. Then she looked at the price tag hanging from the handlebar. One hundred dollars! The smile disappeared from her face and she started to cry. "Oh Daddy," she said in despair, "I'll never have enough for a bicycle."

"How much do you have?" he inquired.

"Seventy-two cents," she answered.

Her dad said, "Let's make an arrangement. You give me everything you've got, the whole seventy-two cents, and throw in a big hug and kiss, and this bike is yours." Her father made up the difference.

Much like the parable of the bike, your upline can make up the difference for you. Where you are short, they can cover you. If you are in trouble, they can bail you out. Where you may be weak, more often than not, they are strong. I can't imagine how I would have endured some of the struggles along the path to success without my sponsor and my upline. So get plugged in and power up. Success is just around the corner for you!

Points to Ponder

Goals and dreams are as critical to success as air and water are to our survival. Success can only be reached when you determine what you are reaching for. By clearly identifying what you want, you can then develop a game plan to take you to your dreams.

People duplicate what they see, not what you say. Make sure you are plugged in and are duplicating the system of success your leaders teach. Then and only then will you be an effective teacher yourself.

Attitude determines your altitude, or your level of success. A good attitude is a key ingredient to becoming an effective leader and teacher.

Excellence is not an act but rather a habit. Develop a winning habit and you'll be a champion as well as lead your downline to victory!

Keep sifting and sorting—sponsoring new people. By your example, your people will learn that in order to build lasting financial freedom they will want to continue to put new people in their frontline, as well as in depth.

Plug in and power up! Developing a strong relationship with your upline leader will be one of the smartest things you'll do to help you, and your downline, reach the top.

CHAPTER TEN

POLISHING PEOPLE SKILLS

People Skills

Why spend an entire chapter on people skills and relationships? Because if you asked one thousand of the top moneymakers in network marketing what it takes to make the big money, they will tell you it takes lots of people in your organization. To develop a business with large numbers of people requires strong people skills. If you asked those same one thousand people what they want most in life, I can assure you that happiness would be near the top of everyone's

> Remember, you can't be happy or completely successful if you don't have good relationships, and to have good relationships you need to develop good people skills.

list. Ask those same people what they think would make them happiest of all and the overwhelming majority would say, "Having wonderful, meaningful relationships with the people I care about."

I challenge you to check your own records. You'll probably find that if you're getting along well with the most important people in your life—that is, the people you love—you are basically a happy person. This is true regardless of the status of your bank account or your position on the corporate totem pole.

On the other side of the ledger, if you're not getting along well with the people you love, it still doesn't make any difference how many bucks you've got in the bank or whether you're the CEO of a Fortune 500 company or a wealthy entrepreneur. Your life is not a happy one.

This chapter identifies the part that relationships and people skills play in your overall success in network marketing, which transitions into every other area of your life as well.

Keep in mind that you can't be happy or completely successful if you don't have good relationships, and to have good relationships you need to develop good people skills. So we are going to hear from the experts and look at some ways to polish up your people skills.

You're Number One

As you look at the part that relationships play in your life, think about yourself. What is your relationship with you? Do you like who you are? If not, what are you doing about it? One of my favorite speakers, Zig Ziglar, frequently says, "You have to *be* before you can *do*, and *do* before you can *have*." What Zig means is that your ability to get along with other people is an indication of who you are and how you feel about yourself. You have to be the kind of person with whom you and others are comfortable. The more you respect yourself, the higher the standards you set and the greater your integrity, which enables you to do the right things. When you do the right things, you're more likely to have good relationships with others and have more success in general.

> Zig Ziglar, popular motivational speaker and author, frequently says, "You have to *be* before you can *do*, and *do* before you can *have*."

Business Relationships

In the business world, relationships are an integral part of success or failure. In network marketing, relationships are the very cornerstone of a successful business. Dealing with people is probably the biggest problem you face, especially if you are in network marketing. Ok, it is also true if you are a salesperson, engineer, or brain surgeon. Research done several years ago uncovered a most important and significant fact—a fact later confirmed by studies made at the Carnegie Institute of Technology. These investigations revealed that even in such technical lines as engineering, about 15 percent of one's financial success is due to one's technical knowledge and about

85 percent is due to skill in human engineering—to personality and the ability to lead people. In Chapter 13 we will discuss leadership and how to develop the skills needed to become a great leader. For now, let's look at some ways to polish up your people skills and create a big business.

Be Available

"I knew my sponsor was busy," says Pamela. "She had another full-time job as well as a thriving network business. I was always respectful of her; grateful for time she spent with me. Even with her busy life and her other distributors, she made me feel important." Being a good leader means being available for your people, making them feel valued. This doesn't mean being at someone's constant call. But it can mean being willing to be inconvenienced from time to time.

Pamela's sponsor, Denise, said that it wasn't too difficult to manage time for her downline. "I just learned to take advantage of break time, lunchtime, and early morning hours, as well as a few minutes after work, to acquire information and cement relationships with people in my group. Sometimes just a quick phone call can be just what they need. By being available, people knew they could count on me. It helped me develop team spirit."

> **THREE TIPS TO DEVELOP GREAT BUSINESS RELATIONSHIPS**
>
> 1. Set high standards, for yourself first, and then for others to follow.
> 2. Be available—plan and schedule time for your people.
> 3. Watch your words—be mindful of the affect you have on others.

Successful networkers make it a point to be available when someone comes to them seeking information or inquiring about techniques or procedures at which they excel. They patiently and cheerfully share information and, in the process, make the team more productive. As a result, the people they teach make more progress, qualify for higher bonuses, and enjoy a better relationship with their leaders. The gratitude they feel for their benefactors bonds them to these superstars and builds team spirit. This is job security at its best! You truly can have everything in life you want if you will just help enough people get what they want.

Bite Your Tongue

When I was a little girl, my grandmother tried to teach me to choose my words carefully. If she overheard me speaking inappropriately, she would say, "watch your words." I remember the first time she said this to me. I was playing with a neighborhood friend on my swing set in Me-Me's (my grandmother) backyard. My girlfriend, Karen Belcher, wanted the swing closest to the tree. It was the one that went the highest. She had already claimed it for the better part of the afternoon and now it was my turn. She kept telling me to get off and let her have another turn. Finally she started to whine. I told her to stop whining like a crybaby. Me-Me lifted her head from the flower garden nearby and said, "Cynthia Lynn, watch your words." I had no idea what she was talking about; in fact, I upset her terribly a few days later by asking repeatedly, "How do I watch my words Me-Me?" I could not imagine how one could see one's words. In her frustration she said, "Ok, forget about watching your words young lady. Bite your tongue instead!"

> My friend, Cherry Meadows, says it this way: "You can be right, or you can be rich. I recommend rich."

Most people are not trained to handle frustration, despite the fact that frustration is a daily event for most of us. The inability to manage frustration has a greater impact on productivity and quality than intelligence, energy, vision, and creativity put together. Frustration crates a cascading or domino effect. This is called "throwing down." The leader in a successful network marketing business has learned to bite her tongue and to not dump her frustration downward. She has learned to take problems and challenges upward or upline.

The Gift of Caring

Several years ago I heard a story that touched my heart; I have never forgotten its message. My sponsor told the story about something that had happened to him one Christmas long ago.

"I was in my last year of medical school and our purse strings were so tight, air couldn't even escape!" he laughed. "Christmas season was in full swing and my three little children watched the tree hoping to find a present or two with their name on it. Day after day I saw their disappointed little faces as they ran downstairs to peer under the tree, only to find it empty once more. I was anguishing over their requests for this little dolly or that cool baseball mitt, for I knew that Christmas we would not be shopping for presents. My wife and I talked about how to make it fun for the kids anyway. We each helped the children make something special for the others. A loaf of cinnamon bread, a booklet full of coupons redeemable for hugs and kisses or taking out the trash, chocolate chip cookies, to name a few. Finally Christmas Eve was here and everyone was satisfied that they had been able to give a gift to each other and even receive one themselves. Then something mysterious happened," he said.

"I was studying at my kitchen table late one cold rainy night when I heard a noise at the front door. Who could be out this late at night on Christmas Eve? I wondered. My porch was well lit by the street light at the corner and I cracked the door open but no one was there. Just as I was about to shut the door, I noticed something shiny in the bushes at the end of my porch. I walked down the steps and saw two huge piles of something covered with dark plastic bags. When I lifted the wet bags up, the sight I saw caused me to almost fall off the porch and I ended up sitting down in a puddle of water. For there, under the plastic, were two gigantic boxes, overflowing with packages, all wrapped for Christmas!

"I hauled the boxes inside to protect them and thought that surely there had been some mistake—these must be intended for another house! I was concerned about the little kids who would be expecting these gifts under their own tree the next morning. Perhaps if I looked at the nametags I might recognize one of the neighbor children that these gifts must belong to. Then perhaps I could drop them off to the family where they belonged. As I looked inside I noticed the presents did have tags, but as I looked at them, I saw *Camille, Michelle,* and *Danielle* printed neatly on each one. *My* children's names! What on earth was going on?

"I went upstairs and woke my sleeping wife. Together we unloaded the presents and realized that they were indeed intended for us. There was a note inside that read: 'These gifts are gifts of love. Please accept them as such. Thank you for making our Christmas the greatest one ever!'

"As we placed each gift under the tree, we counted our blessings. That next morning we heard the sound of our children's laughter and squeals of delight as they found their tree full of beautiful presents—presents they weren't expecting. I explained the mysterious appearance of those gifts and the importance of giving—then we opened the gifts. If there had been used clothing in those packages I wouldn't have been any less grateful, but each of these presents held new, beautiful gifts that I could tell had cost its giver a lot of money! The generosity overwhelmed my wife and me and we held each other as tears streamed down our faces. Who could have done this for us? How could anyone have known?

"No one we knew claimed to have done this good deed. The next day, and for weeks after that, I found myself looking into the faces of my neighbors, the postman, and even strangers in line at the store. Was it him, or was it her? Because I didn't know who had given such wonderful gifts, I treated everyone like they were the ones who had. I continue to treat others like they were the ones, even today," he added. "That is the greatest gift of all!"

Why not treat everybody like someone important? Would it make a difference in your relationships with them? Would it improve your business? Would you have more friends? The answers are obvious, aren't they?

Team Building Relationships

Mark Victor Hansen, speaker and best-selling coauthor of *Chicken Soup for the Soul* series, says that team building can be a key to success for any networker.

"I've been working as an inspirational speaker for the network marketing industry for many years now, and I've had the opportunity to work with thousands and thousands of network marketers personally," says Mark Victor Hansen. "So many beginning network marketers make the same mistake over and over again. And that mistake is not forming a mastermind group right away. You need to get yourself a dream team, a group of people who are going in the same direction, for the same goal."

Developing friendships is really team building and team building is what makes strong network marketing groups skyrocket to success. People will work harder and do more for those they respect and care about. And a network marketer can create more profit and produce greater results as a team than alone.

> **FOUR GREAT WAYS TO BUILD YOUR DREAM TEAM**
>
> 1. Find leaders with a big dream and who are willing to take responsibility.
> 2. Form a mastermind group with them. Utilize each other's strengths.
> 3. Set a game plan, which would include specific individual and group goals.
> 4. Share the victory and celebrate each other's success.

I competed in track events through junior high and into high school. My favorite event was the high hurdles, but I was even better at the 440-yard relay. We were a great team and we held the record as the fastest in the region. Each of us supported the others and encouraged their success, even in events other than the 440. Susan Miles was the fastest girl I had ever seen. She broke the record in every event she ran! She was our cleanup runner in the 440 and she could sure clean up! The amazing thing was that she ran even faster in the 440—in the team event—than she ever ran alone. When our coaches asked her why, she said, "I don't want to let my teammates down. I want to do my best for them."

When you can create a team—through developing loyal friendships—you will see magic happen in your business! You will break records, grow faster, and accomplish more than you may have dreamed you could. That is what Mark Victor Hansen shared with us about building a dream team: everybody wins!

The Big Secret

What is the big secret in dealing with people? In his mega best-selling book, *How to Win Friends and Influence People*, Dale Carnegie says, "There is only one way to get anybody to do anything. Did you ever stop to think of that? Yes, just one way. And that is by getting the other person to *want* to do it!"

Always remember there is no other way.

Carnegie says you can make people do things by threatening or demands, but these crude methods will backfire, creating undesirable repercussions. The only way you can get anyone to do anything is by giving him or her what he or she wants. So, what do people want, you ask?

Freud called it the desire to be great. Others call it the desire to be important. The longing for acceptance or the craving for appreciation tops the list of most people. Your ability to create enthusism in your people could well be the greatest asset you possess, and the way to develop and bring out the best in others is by encouragement and appreciation.

> ## TWO GREAT WAYS TO BUILD SUCCESS IN OTHERS
>
> 1. Define the big *why*—the reason and benefit the other person will gain as he or she develops business with you. Unless the benefit is great enough, often the work can seem too hard.
> 2. Give hearty praise and sincere compliments to your people. Build them up and let them know you appreciate their efforts. Remember that the craving for appreciation tops the list of most people.

Day after day in offices and homes across the country people are being criticized, put down, and shoved aside. They are *hungry* for a genuine kind word and a hearty thank-you. We prepare food to feed our friends or family, but how often do we feed their self-esteem? Often those around us are going hungry for the hearty appreciation they crave, almost as much as they crave food and water.

"I was simply never good enough," said Janet. "I wasn't smart, pretty, or particularly talented. In school I was the brunt of cruel jokes. At home I was the recipient of harsh words. By the time I left home to attend college, I didn't think I was worth much. At least no one else seemed to think so." Sadly, Janet is not a minority when it comes to dishing out criticism. In fact, many women tell me that they were starving for recognition, appreciation, or just plain old kindness when they started their networking businesses.

"When one of my college classmates, Kate, invited me to a business meeting, I secretly wondered why she would ask someone like me," Janet said. "But I was flattered that she had invited me and so I agreed to join her. I really liked what I heard that night. But I didn't get in the business that night because of the company or the products. I agreed to join because of Kate.

Kate told me that she had been watching me in class and was impressed by my determination. She said she also really liked the way I always smiled at people. Kate made me feel good about myself and I was hungry for those feelings of acceptance," she adds.

I'm not suggesting tossing out flattery. Flattery is insincere, selfish, and shallow. What I am talking about is giving honest, sincere appreciation. Letting others know what they did right instead of everything they did wrong. Kate's compliments were sincere. She had seen Janet in class and knew she was a hard worker. She had also watched time after time as Janet offered a kind word or a helpful hand to others in the class. Her remarks were honest. If they hadn't been, they wouldn't have fooled Janet. They were meaningful because Janet knew they were true. She just longed to hear the words.

If you don't think that offering praise is very important, just look into the eyes of a child who's been told she has done a good job. The smallest compliment or tiny word of kindness and appreciation can light her up. Try it at work, with your friends, and at home. Watch what happens!

Win the Battle and Lose the War

You can't win an argument. You can't because if you lose it, you lose it; and if you win it, you lose it. Why? Well imagine that you compile all of your evidence against the other person and shoot his story full of holes. You proved that he is absolutely, irrevocably wrong. Then what? You may feel justified. But how does this set with the other person? How might he feel? He feels crummy, that's how! You have hurt his pride, injured his ego. He resents it—resents you.

Elizabeth James tells this story. "I had just about reached the income bracket that would allow me to work my business and leave my day job. I had sponsored several great groups of people who were each well on their way to success. A woman named Karen led my biggest group. While Karen was a smart woman, a recent college graduate, she just couldn't seem to get the paperwork straight and every week I would go over and over the same things, trying to help poor Karen get it straight. By the end of the third month I was

TWO GREAT WAYS TO HIT YOUR TARGET

1. Find the need. Ask questions then listen, really listen. By identifying people's needs, you're better prepared to help them find a way to fill them through your network marketing plan.
2. Fill their needs. Now that you know what they want, show them how they can get those things by being in business with you.

getting pretty tired of it. Then one day something happened that was the final straw!"

Elizabeth said that Karen showed up at her front door unexpectedly as she was preparing for an important meeting. "I reluctantly invited her in because I was already running a bit late," she says. " I wanted to try and be nice, be the good sponsor I was suppose to be. But when Karen accused *me* of messing up her order—that was all it took to send me over the edge! I told her in no mistaken terms who had messed up the order—it was *her*! The same person who had screwed up every order since the day she got in! I reminded her that I had been the one who had spent every Thursday afternoon for three months with her, helping her straighten out the mess she had created the week before. Hadn't I been great to offer to place her orders for her the week she had been feeling ill? Wasn't it me who held on to her check—more than once—while she figured out her ridiculous excuse for a checking account? So who is the one that had messed up her order? Certainly not me!"

While Elizabeth says that her remarks were true, they were still hurtful and unnecessary. Elizabeth says she was right, positively right about the order. Elizabeth proved her point. She won the disagreement. "As soon as I looked at Karen's face, I felt terrible about what I had said. Karen didn't know what to say. I won the argument, but I lost in the end," Elizabeth says. Karen was hurt and embarrassed. Although she knew that Elizabeth was right, she couldn't stand to face her again and ultimately ended up quitting the business. That one little episode of frustration cost Elizabeth a large business group, several months of work, and more important, her friendship with Karen. She won the battle but lost the war. Sometimes being right simply isn't worth it.

So remember what Cherry Meadows says, "Do you want to be right? Or do you want to be rich?" What is more important to you?

Hitting the Target

The first big step in getting people to do what you want them to do is to find out what will make them do it, find out what they want. This is the biggest secret of influencing or motivating people. It means hitting the target with what you say, but naturally you must know where the target is. When you know *what* will move them, you then know *how* to move them.

I trained my salespeople to do the same thing: to listen to customers, find out what they really want, then fill it for them, or hit the target. Often customers would come to our RV dealership and tell the salesperson that they were looking for a certain type of motor home. Let's say for instance a mini-home or Class C. I taught the salespeople to encourage conversation with the customer, asking them questions such as, "What type of traveling do you plan to do? Do you like camping in the mountains, or would you prefer a trip across the country? How long will you stay? Will you be using the vehicle for lots of short weekend trips, or had you planned on living in it for the summer? How many people will be traveling? Will you and your husband be primarily using it for your own pleasure, or do you have children?"

By listening, really listening, to what the customer said, often the salesperson found out that what the customer *thought* he wanted did not fit the description of what he told him he really needed. For example if the customer said he wanted a Class C motor home and then told us that only he and his wife would be using it and they planned to travel for several months at a time, possibly driving up to Canada and down through Mexico, this customer wouldn't need a mini-home that slept eight and wouldn't want to be crammed in a tiny space over the cab. What he would probably enjoy is a Class A with one large bedroom in the back and an open and airy living room and kitchen. By asking and listening, the salesperson could find out what the customer really wanted then take him to the right one. After showing him the benefits, the things he just said he wanted, getting the sale was easy— only if you knew what the customer really wanted, what really moved him.

The business of building people and building relationships is the same. Find out what others want, what they like, what they are looking for in life.

Then, and only then, can you move them by showing them how they can get what they want by doing what you do through network marketing.

Remember Marilyn's story in Chapter 1? She was a single mom raising two little boys. She said that fancy cars or diamond rings definitely did not motivate her. What she wanted more than anything in the world—what motivated her to get in business for herself and succeed—was time with her boys. She wanted to raise them, wanted to go to their class parties and baseball games. She wanted to be the one who had time at night to snuggle up and listen to the stories about their day. By helping her see exactly how network marketing could give her those precious moments with her boys, Marilyn not only joined, she worked hard to get what she wanted.

In network marketing, by helping enough other people get what they want you get what you want! If you want to win, hit the target!

Making a Difference

Imagine for a moment living the life of your dreams. Can you see it? What if every day of your life was filled with meaning, packed with purpose? How would it feel to know that you have helped change the lives of others for good? It would feel great, wouldn't it? What would it feel like to wake up every morning, rested and peaceful, eager to greet the day, excited about the possibilities of the future, knowing that because of you the world is a better place? Feels great, doesn't it?

> If you want to win in network marketing, and help enough people get what they want! you get what you want! If you want to win, hit the target!

Unfortunately, most people will never experience those feelings. They will drag themselves out of bed to the sound of the alarm, pull themselves into another day of mediocrity, and force themselves out the door to a job that has become unchallenging and unfulfilling. And they will do this over and over and over. Why? They do it because they don't know any other way. They don't know that they can change. They can make a difference.

"I wanted my life to have more meaning, more value. I wanted the time I spend on earth to count for something. I wanted to make a difference," says Michelle Dieffenbach, successful architect and networker. "I loved my career, loved designing buildings, but after a few years it just wasn't exciting any more—life seemed to have lost some meaning. I was looking for a way to do something special, something important. I found that with network marketing."

Like many women, Michelle had reached the top in her profession. She had nowhere else to go. Her days had become routine, even monotonous. She wanted some excitement, some stimulation, something fulfilling. "When I first started my network business I saw it as a new challenge, a new frontier. It was all of that and more," she adds. "Soon I found that as I helped others get their business going and they started experiencing success, I felt an incredible sense of personal satisfaction. The more people I helped, the greater I felt.

> ### MAKING A DIFFERENCE
>
> Successful networkers agree that by helping other people succeed, they felt an incredible sense of personal satisfaction. The more people you help—the greater you'll feel. The work you'll do in network marketing is lasting and often represents so much more than the money you'll bring in. From braces for children to college education to freedom from dead-end jobs—the feeling of accomplishment is incredible!

I knew I was really making a difference in these people's lives. The work I did with them was lasting and it represented so much more than the money we were all bringing in. For some it represented freedom from dead-end jobs or pounding pressure of debt. For others it meant braces on kids teeth or college educations. And for some it was that long awaited vacation or more time with their families. Everything from happier kids to healed relationships because I built this business with them. The feeling of accomplishment and personal satisfaction is worth more than all the money!"

Making a difference! I heard a story long ago that touched my heart and I have never forgotten its message. It is about an old man walking along a sandy beach. As he walks along the edge of the water, gentle waves wash up over his tanned and weathered feet. Up ahead he notices something strange, something unusual. He squints to see through the haze of the misty morning fog. Down the beach he sees someone bending, twisting and turning, doing some kind of a dance. Over and over a young girl repeats her steps; first she bends down, then twists and turns, and ends by throwing her arm out towards the sea. Maybe she is practicing for a class, or perhaps her movements have something to do with martial art, he thought. As he walked closer, he saw her once again bend down toward the sand and pick something up. As she twisted around she threw this object far out into the sea. What is she throwing, he wondered? As he got closer he saw it, a sandy beach covered with starfish.

Poor little girl, he thought. Doesn't she know that everyday the sea washes up these creatures with the rising tide and everyday as the tide goes out again these starfish lie on the sand and die? He called out to her, "Excuse me, but this happens everyday when the tide goes back out. Tomorrow the beach will be full of them again. Even if you throw them back in today, it won't make any difference."

The girl turned away from the old man and bent down once again to pick up a starfish from the sand. As she pulled her arm back and threw the creature into the ocean, she softly replied, "I made a difference to that one."

By polishing up on people skills you can build lasting and meaningful relationships. Through these strong ties you will create a team of leaders and, with your team, build a business of champions. In Chapter 11 top moneymakers talk about how team building and relationships helped them develop big businesses and how those very relationships helped them over come challenges, even during the toughest times in their lives. Through network marketing you can create an incredible lifestyle for yourself and others and leave a lasting legacy as well. And like the little girl on the beach, you will have made a difference!

SECTION THREE

Working It:
How to Make
It Work for You

CHAPTER ELEVEN

OVERCOMING OBSTACLES

The difference between winning and losing, success and failure, is often the simple ability to know how to overcome the obstacles and challenges that face those who are developing a business of their own. Obstacles come in many forms—a negative family member, lack of time, lack of finances, self-doubt, and so on. In this chapter we will discuss the issues and obstacles women face head-on and teach you how to overcome obstacles, and turn them into steppingstones to greater opportunities.

Strength Comes from Struggle

Struggle is a clever devise through which nature compels us to develop, expand, and progress. It is either a terrible ordeal or a magnificent experience depending upon one's attitude toward it. Success is impossible—unthinkable even—without it.

CHALLENGES

Strength comes from struggle. Struggle is a clever devise through which nature compels us to develop, expand, and progress. It is either a terrible ordeal or a magnificent experience depending upon one's attitude toward it. Success is impossible—unthinkable even—without it.

Life, from birth to death, is literally an unbroken chain of ever-increasing, unavoidable struggle. The education we receive from the struggles we face is cumulative—we get it a little at a time from every experience along life's journey. Someone once said, "That which does not kill us makes us strong."

A favorite poem from my youth is titled *Good Timber*. Its author is anonymous, but its message is clear. It illustrates the point I wish to make—through *surviving* struggles and trials that we can become stronger, better, more prepared to succeed.

Good Timber

The tree that does not have to fight,
For sun and sky and air and light,
But stood out in the open plain
And always got its share of rain,
Never became a forest king
But lived and died a scrubby thing.

The man who never had to toil,
To gain and farm his patch of soil,
Who never had to win his share
Of sun and sky and light and air,
Never became a manly man
But lived and died as he began.

Good timber does not grow with ease,
The stronger wind,
The stronger trees,
The further sky,
The greater length,
The more the storm,
The more the strength.
By sun and cold,
By rain and snow,
In trees and man,
Good timber grows.

Where thickest lies the forest growth,
We find the patriarchs of both.
And they hold council with the stars,
Whose broken branches show the scars
Of many winds and much of strife.
This is the common law of life.

Struggle similarly toughens the human spirit. Most people try to go through life following the path of least resistance. They often fail to understand that this philosophy is what makes rivers crooked—and sometimes does the same for humans. Much like trees, the strongest women aren't those that are most protected; the strongest women are those that have struggled against the elements—and survived. Without the strength of character that grows out of struggle, we might be sorely tempted to flow through life without plan or purpose.

Terry Gulick knows that struggles can make us stronger. "Life was going great," Terry says. "Our business was growing and we had even expanded into international markets. Australia was our biggest and fastest growing business at the time. Bert was traveling around the world helping our business partners and doing meetings. I was busy at home managing the office, taking international calls, shipping training supplies all around the world, and taking care of my two little girls. Life was good, but something happened that shook our world."

> Most people try to go through life following the path of least resistance. They often fail to understand that this philosophy is what makes rivers crooked—and sometimes does the same for humans. Much like trees, the strongest women aren't those that are most protected; the strongest women are those that have struggled against the elements—and survived.

Terry told me that she started experiencing dizzy spells that increased to the point where she would actually be walking and fall down to the ground. Her condition grew so desperate that she would sleep for twenty-four hours at a time and still feel exhausted when she woke up. "I went to so many different doctors trying to figure out what was wrong with me," Terry says. "Every doctor gave a different diagnosis and none of the treatments worked. I was desperate. My husband, Bert, was pulling more than his share of the load and my poor children—they didn't know what had happened to their mommy. I would drag myself out of bed and drive them to their volleyball games. While I sat in the bleachers watching the game, I would pass out and sleep there throughout the entire game, often several hours. Or I might take them to school and fall asleep in the school parking lot. One day as I walked to my car, I passed out and fell, tearing the skin off my knees and shoulder. Eventually I became afraid to even leave the house. It was a nightmare!"

Terry suffered like this for five years and almost died. She was bedridden for over a year, and although she had gone to several doctors, she still had no idea what was wrong. With the help of a direct in her downline, Terry finally found out what was really wrong. She had CFIDS—chronic fatigue immune dysfunction syndrome.

It has been a long, hard battle for Terry and for her family. "As I look back over the past five years, I cannot imagine where we would be financially had we not built our network business and had the support of so many great independent business partners. Most companies would not keep running when one of its key players was out of commission for five years. Traditional businesses would have shut their doors under similar circumstances. Yet our business just kept growing. Through all of the struggles I have come to the other side, and having faced my difficulties, I feel I have emerged stronger and better. Having gone through so much, I now know I can handle anything!" she adds.

As we understand the broad purpose of life, we accept the struggle for what it is—opportunity. Obstacles force us to move when we might otherwise stand still. And it leads us eventually to success that only comes through struggle. Whenever you find a successful person, you find a person who has struggled in their life, who has met difficulty, faced it, overcame it, and moved on to the next challenge.

Hitting the Wall

As any successful woman will tell you, network marketing is not always easy, but it is worth it! With this business model you can create a lifestyle that few will ever experience, other than on the movie screen or in magazines. In network marketing, you can live the life of your dreams if you face and overcome the obstacles that come your way.

In a popular movie, *A League of Their Own*, the coach, played by Tom Hanks, is talking to his star player as she is complaining about the game being so hard. He looks her square in the eyes and passionately says, "It is suppose to be hard. It is the *hard* that makes it *great*! If it were easy, everyone would do it." Embrace the struggle. Use it to help you grow—and succeed. As every successful woman I've met will tell you, "It is worth it!"

Self-Doubt

"After my divorce I felt devastated. I was raised with a belief that marriage was for life—after all my parents were still married after all these years. So, what's wrong with me?" said Jeanne. "Soon I began to look at all of my losses—all of my shortcomings. The list grew and grew until I began to wonder if I were good at anything."

All of us have failed at something—missed a deadline, lost a friend, ended a relationship. Sadly, these experiences in life can cause us to have feelings of self-doubt or inadequacy. These feelings, though often false, can have a real effect on a woman who is contemplating trying something new. "I didn't want to fail at anything again," Jeanne adds. "So eventually, I stopped trying. I resolved myself to the fact that life wasn't fair and although I was unhappy and unfulfilled, that was just the way it was going to be. I didn't want to lose again."

> "It is the 'hard' that makes it 'great!' If it were easy, everyone would do it."
> —TOM HANKS in
> *A League of Their Own.*

Just about the time Jeanne decided to throw in the towel, a phone call came from an old schoolmate. "I was so excited to hear from Sally. We had been such good friends through our school years, but attending different colleges, we just seemed to lose touch. Then after my divorce, I pulled away even more from old friends. It was just too awkward," she adds.

As you might imagine, Sally called to tell Jeanne about a great new business idea. She told Jeanne that she would come to Boston and help her get started. Jeanne agreed. "At first I was thrilled to hear from Sally—and the prospect of being in business with her. But it wasn't long after our phone conversation ended that those old feelings of self-doubt crept in."

Luckily, Sally was prepared for Jeanne. At their first meeting, Sally brought some books and other training materials for Jeanne to review. "It was exactly what I needed. As I read those books, my confidence grew. I realized that I wasn't perfect, but neither was anyone else. I began to believe in myself again. As I followed the principals in those books, took action, I began to see a small measure of success. With each small step my confidence grew. Soon I was able to help other women who faced some of the same feelings of self-doubt as I had in the beginning. The books and tapes definitely helped me not only personally grow by increasing my attitude and belief about myself, but also my bank account grew!" she adds.

Building Confidence

Cathy started her network business on shaky ground. "When I first got started in this business, my enthusiasm was off the charts," says Cathy. "But it quickly dissolved when I started calling my closest friends and associates. They were so negative! I could hardly believe my ears when I heard them say things like, "Impossible. That thing will never work. What makes you think you can be in business for yourself? You don't have any skills. I knew someone else who failed in network marketing. You better be careful."

"I began to lose some of the enthusiasm and confidence I had in the beginning. Luckily I had the sense enough to call my upline," Cathy adds. Her upline told her a few personal stories and soon both of them were laughing on the phone. "Oh, yes!" her sponsor said. "My own mother told me that she knew someone from work—someone whose husband's brother's sister from California who lived next door to someone that was once involved in network marketing—lost tons of money! Ridiculous. I quickly stopped listening to the naysayers. I looked at their lifestyles and none of them had what I wanted. My upline did. I started taking my advice from her and it has made all of the difference," she said.

We all know someone who has failed at something, whether it was a test, a diet, a relationship, or a job. Failing is a part of winning. If I wanted to lose weight—was really serious about it this time—who would I go to for advice? One of my other overweight friends who had been on the same twelve diet plans I had tried and failed or someone who had actually lost the weight, kept it off, and made it work? Seems pretty obvious, doesn't it? If you want to make network marketing work, listen to the experts, those who have really made it work, not your negative friends and family. Most of the time they don't mean to do you harm. They just don't know what they don't know.

Conquering Fear

Fear is the greatest single obstacle to success. Too often people let fear rule their decisions and actions. They hold on to a false sense of security, thinking that if they attempt to stay within the boundaries of their comfort zone that nothing bad will ever happen to them. Nothing good ever happens either!

Each of us suffers from fear of something—fear of failure, fear of success, fear of the dark, fear of being hurt or taken advantage of, fear of being rejected or abandoned. But what really is fear? It is an emotion that signals us of danger. It is intended to help save our lives. But once it has served its purpose as a warning signal, we must not permit it to enter into our reasoning when we decide upon a course of action.

Valerie Haugen knows what fear can do to stop you dead in your tracks. "I was so shy, so afraid of speaking in public, I didn't even want to go to the store alone," she says. "One day I was so hungry and our kitchen was empty. I sat in my apartment for several hours, starving, but too afraid to go out alone."

If you saw Valerie Haugen today, you might not be able to imagine that she ever had been so shy. She speaks before audiences of tens of thousands and gives compelling and powerful presentations. What's the secret to her success, you ask? "Read, read, read! I read so many positive thinking books when I first got into the business. Books helped me change my life!"

And what a life she has—a grand estate surrounded by luscious landscaping and perched on the side of a mountain. From her deck she looks out over her property, which includes a pool, guest house, an enormous garage

---

FOUR GREAT WAYS TO BUILD CONFIDENCE AND OVERCOME FEAR

1. Stop listening to negative people. Start listening to successful people in your business who tell you it can be done and you can do it.
2. Build upon your success. Use past failure as your springboard to success. With each accomplishment recognize and acknowledge your success. Give yourself a pat on the back!
3. Face your fears. Identify what challenges you the most. Get some advice from your leaders. You'll probably find they, too, faced the same fears and overcame them. You can, too!
4. Flush the guilt! Get rid of it! Get over it! Forgive yourself and others and move on. Look forward not backward! Keep your eyes on your dream.

filled with a Prevost motor home, a Rolls Royce, and a Hummer to name only a few. Valerie overcame her fears—you can, too!

"We have nothing to fear but fear itself," said Franklin Roosevelt. Those words are as true today as when he spoke them. How can you conquer your fears? By looking at them square in the face and asking yourself, "What am I really afraid of?" Often that one question will get you on the road to reason and recovery. By analyzing the situation that faces you, you are able to look at the real problem

The next step is to look at the problem from every angle. What are the risks? Is the expected reward worth taking? What are the other possible courses of action? Is there another way around this? Do I have all of the information, data, and facts? What have others done? What were their results? Once you have completed your research, take action—immediately take action! Procrastination leads only to more doubt and fear.

When Cathy met her fears in the form of rejection and criticism, she evaluated her situation. "I didn't want people to make fun of me. I hated feeling stupid or less than," says Cathy. "After talking with my upline, I began to look at the facts. I was afraid of rejection and being criticized by my peers. Another fact I had to consider was that my friends did not have the lifestyle I wanted for myself and my family—they didn't have the jobs, the homes, the money, or the freedom that I desired. My upline did. She lived the life I wanted—she was at home with her kids, taking them to dance lessons and baseball games. She even had a full-time housekeeper, so she had time to even do all of the fun things with her kids like lots of mini-vacations at the beach or mountains. It seemed like she was always doing something fun while I was at work. I wanted that kind of freedom," Cathy adds.

After really facing her fears, looking at the facts, and honestly evaluating her options, Cathy chose her dreams over her fears. "Once I made the decision to stop listening to others tell me it wouldn't work and started doing what my upline taught me, I began to quickly see success. So did others around me. It wasn't long before some of my most negative friends asked me if they could join my business group. I am so glad I chose my dreams over my fears," she said.

You can, too! Remember that fear is just *false evidence appearing real.* Face the facts, evaluate your options, and take action!

Jumping the Hurdle

Sometimes the biggest hurdle women jump over is the feeling of guilt. Remember reading in Chapter 1 about Karen Yamada Furuchi, a woman with a strong will to win? Karen faced many obstacles when building her networking business, starting with the fact that she was one of the first single women in network marketing to make it really big. "I had many other hurdles to jump along the track to success," Karen says. "None of the least was trying to raise my children alone. It was hard enough before I got involved in a network business, but afterwards I often didn't think I could manage it all."

Karen had four children to take care of and she worked full time as well. When she first saw the networking opportunity, she saw it as a way to get out of her daytime job and have more time with her kids. But in the early days of building her downline, she found the opposite was true. "I would get off of work and more often than not, I would not even go home. Traffic in the San Francisco Bay Area is brutal and often I would not have the time to get from my office to my home and make my evening meeting schedule. After working all day and doing meetings at night, I was beat! I would drag myself from the car and into the house.

> Karen Yamada Furuchi says, "Be willing to pay the price now for the reward that you will enjoy for the rest of your life. I have been able to choose what I do with everyday of my life because I buckled down and did the difficult. Freedom is worth it!"

Usually I spent a couple of hours cleaning up, checking homework, doing laundry, or just trying to catch up on bills and paperwork," she adds.

Like most working mothers, Karen was faced with a tremendous responsibility. As a single parent she was also responsible for her children. Sometimes this double duty can stop women from getting ahead in life. Sadly, most are just trying to make it through another day. "Not only was I stretched in every direction, I also carried on my shoulders a heavy burden of guilt. I felt guilty when I had to skip a parent-teacher conference or miss a ball game. I felt guilty when my daughter dropped her little chin in disappointment after telling her I would be out of town on her birthday. After awhile, I felt guilty about everything!" Karen said. "I told myself that I was doing a business on the side so I could have more time with my kids—and I saw less of them than ever before!"

Karen says that sometimes she would often do a number on herself, beating herself up emotionally for missing so much of her children's life. But she also understood one fact very clearly: if she did not do something different, even though it was difficult, she would never have time with them. "I just buckled down more than ever. I started doubling up on my meetings, delegating responsibilities to others, training people to duplicate me, and within a short time I was free!" she said. "I have been able to choose what I do with each day of my life for many years. And my kids turned out great! Some of them are even doing this business with me and my youngest son will soon get his Ph.D. I think it was because of my strong work ethic and my will to win that my kids learned to be great leaders. I am so thankful that I was willing to pay that price so I could enjoy the rest of my life with them."

Stretch Your Muscles

Any great athlete will tell you the importance of stretching your muscles before attempting to win. Sometimes in network marketing, the muscle that we need to stretch is our mind. An open mind is a free mind. If you close your mind to new ideas, concepts, people, or opportunities, you are locking a door that can imprison you. So stretch you mind to this new idea—the idea of building your own networking business—and watch what happens!

It is hard to imagine that less than a century ago people laughed at the Wright brothers' experiments in flight. Yet when people of vision were predicting that we would fly to the moon, few doubted that it could be achieved. Today it is the scoffers who are scorned.

Only with an open mind can you grasp the impact of the first rule of the science of success: Whatever the mind can conceive and believe, it can achieve. The woman with an open mind will do wonderful feats in this business, while the fool with the closed mind is still shouting, "Impossible!"

An open mind requires faith—in yourself, your upline, in your chosen business. The greatest success stories in the world come from women just like you, women who stepped out on faith, took a chance on something different, and did the impossible! The biggest leaders in network marketing are the ones who came with an open mind. They became the best students first, following a proven pattern for success, then became the best teachers. So stretch your muscle. Open your mind. Become a great student and you will be able to live the life of your dreams!

Pace Yourself

"I rushed home from work, flew through the door, threw my clothes on the bed, and quickly changed into a business suit. Then I hurriedly ran a brush through my hair, long overdue for a cut and touch up, and applied lipstick while I rummaged through the refrigerator looking for anything that didn't have green things growing on top. I grabbed an apple and headed for the door, skillfully sidestepping a pile of laundry and hurdling the boxes of training tapes that UPS had dropped at my front door," says Lori. "I hopped in the car, popped it into reverse, and slammed on my brakes! Where was I going, I wondered? I had left the address for tonight's meeting on my office desk!"

Sound familiar? Most women are running on empty, trying to do it all. And while this chapter is not about cutting back, it is about learning how to pace yourself in order to win. "In desperation I dumped a whole load on my sponsor later that evening," says Lori. "I just can't do it anymore," I exclaimed in frustration. My house is a wreck, my paperwork undone, the laundry is all over the house, and I haven't fixed a meal for my kids all week."

Lori was a go-getter. She juggled lots of balls at the same time and got a lot of things done, but she had hit the wall. Her sponsor understood what she was going through. "I know how you feel. I felt the same way, until I learned how to compartmentalize my life," her sponsor said. "I finally learned how to organize my time and pace myself by putting my life into sections. I determined first what was important to me. Then I made my list for the day.

FIVE SIMPLE STEPS TO PACE YOURSELF

1. Determine what is the most *important*, not necessarily urgent.
2. Make a daily check list.
3. Prioritize in order of *importance*.
4. Schedule each item and assign particular amount of time to it.
5. Stick to your time allowance.

Knowing I only had a certain amount of hours to finish the tasks before me, I wrote down by each one the exact amount of time I wanted to give to that project. If it was answering voice or e-mail and I decided that one hour was all I could invest in it, then that is what I gave it. If it was laundry and I gave it 30 minutes, then it got 30 minutes—but not more. Even if I could have finished folding that last load in only ten more minutes, I didn't give in."

"I stuck to my time allowances. If someone came into my office unexpectedly during my phone time, I asked him or her to wait until I was finished. Before I would have stopped everything and changed my plans. I found out that by trying to stick one more little thing in here and one more there, I wasn't getting anything finished! I can't tell you how effective this has been for me. I found out that I accomplished more in a day, balanced my workload between home, business, and family, and still managed to fit in some time for myself," she added.

Pace yourself and improve. You can do it!

Perfect Practice Makes Perfect

Summers in the Panhandle of Texas were hot and dull—at least that is how I saw them during the summer before my junior year of high school. Most of my friends had gone away for the summer on exotic vacations, and there I was stuck babysitting my younger brothers while my mother worked. Even she got to get out of town!

I spent most of that summer taking my brother, Scott, back and forth to batting practice. He was determined to improve his batting average. He spent hour after hour at the batting field or in the dusty field across from our house. He even talked me into throwing a few balls for him (or at him). I watched him for weeks, dust blowing in his eyes and sweat pouring from his brow, pick up the bat and swing hard, missing the ball over and over again. I witnessed this phenomenon with my own eyes. How could anyone practice so long and so hard and never get any better? I had to hand it to him, he was not a quitter!

Just about the time that I was sure my summer was over—all opportunity for fun blown away like the wind blowing across the plains—something marvelous happened. It started out just like any other boring day, get the kids up, fix breakfast (cereal), pick up the front room, and turn on the TV. Whoopee! That morning my brother, Scott, started bugging me really early. "Take me to the batting field. Please, take me now!" he whined. I pulled myself off the couch, dragged myself into the hot car, blasted the stereo, and headed once again to watch him swing the bat and miss the ball.

> **FOUR BENEFITS OF NETWORK MARKETING**
>
> 1. You can learn the basics from your upline leaders.
> 2. You can learn as you go. You don't have to know it all to get started towards success.
> 3. You can develop your skills while you make money!
> 4. You can keep practicing until you are perfect!

As I pulled our old Plymouth into the parking lot, I noticed something different—an unknown car. I had lived in that boring little town for three years and I knew every boy that drove a car. This was a car I didn't know and a boy I had never seen. Things were picking up already! I quickly glanced in the rearview mirror and patted my hair. "Rats," I thought. "I should have put on lipstick."

Scott was already out on the field by the time I got out of the car. Before I could even say a word, he had talked the cute stranger into throwing him a few balls. I pouted on the bleachers, working on my tan, while my little brother maintained the attention of the only hope for happiness that I had seen all summer. That is when it happened!

At first I thought I might be having sunstroke because I couldn't possibly be seeing what I thought I was seeing. I squinted against the glare of the sun and tried to get a better look. That must have been when my jaw dropped and mouth fell opened in amazement at what I was seeing. There, across the field, was my little brother, the no-hitter, slugging ball after ball out of the field. A miracle had happened and I had been there to see it! Over and over Scott smashed ball after ball out of the park. My mouth was still gaping wide open when he ran across the field towards me, grinning like an idiot from ear to ear. "Did you see that," he exclaimed, almost shouting? "Did you see me cream those balls? I bet I hit that last one all the way to Amarillo. Did you see me?"

I must have come to my senses because I kind of remember looking from my brother's goofy face into the eyes of the cutest boy in town. I shut my open mouth and tried to compose myself. "Hi," he said. "My name is Mike. Your little brother here is a quick learner."

"Mike is an assistant coach for a little league team in Dallas," Scott said. "He is here for the summer, visiting Old Man Wilson—I mean Mr. Wilson," he quickly added.

"Well, you must be some great coach! Scott hasn't hit that many balls this entire summer. His coach told him last spring that practice makes perfect. So he practices and practices for hours on end. Until today I haven't noticed much improvement. What on earth did you teach him anyway?" I asked.

"Oh, nothing much," Mike replied. "Scott is a natural athlete, he just needed a couple of pointers. Practice alone doesn't make perfect. If Scott kept doing the same thing over and over again that wasn't right, more practice won't fix it. It will only make him better at doing it wrong! Only *perfect practice* makes perfect results."

"Well, that makes sense. Maybe you could help me improve my batting too," I said as I grabbed the bat from Scott's sweaty hand. As we walked across the field to get my first lesson, I thought maybe summer break wouldn't be so bad after all. I'm not sure my batting average improved much over that summer, but I sure did learn to love baseball!

Learn the basics from your upline leaders that are teaching and practicing the principals of success. One of the benefits of network marketing is that you can learn as you go. You don't have to know everything to get started and you can develop the skills you need while you are making money. Remember that only *perfect practice makes perfect.*

Most of all—keep swinging!

Be a Superstar

Sometimes we look at the magazines or movie screens, watch the Oscars or the Emmys, and see people living an incredible lifestyle of glitter and glamour. "That looks like fun," we think. But we face reality and accept that only a few of the "lucky" ones will ever get to live the life of a star. That was true, until network marketing changed the rules.

"I didn't get involved in a network marketing business to wear party dresses or jet-set around the world," says MJ Michaels. "I got in at first to make a few hundred dollars extra a month. It took me a long time to understand that I could have anything I wanted to have if I worked hard enough—and smart enough in my business. I never dreamed that a young college cheerleader would ever make it big in business, much less be invited to the White House."

> ### YOUR GOALS
>
> Whatever your goals may be, network marketing offers you a world of opportunity—opportunity to excel and to become a superstar!

From the White House on Capitol Hill to the beaches in Bermuda, MJ has been treated like a star. "At first I had to pinch myself. I couldn't believe such a big fuss had been made just for me," MJ said. "Flying in a private jet was excitement enough, but being whisked away in a stretch limousine, ushered into a magnificent five-star property, bouquets of flowers placed in my arms and camera flashes lighting up the way, my head was spinning." MJ had learned to overcome the obstacles in her life and blazed her own successful trail. She had been invited as a special guest speaker for a large corporate convention. "It was just like being a movie star," she adds. "Many little girls dream of being Cinderella. The fairy-tale is true—but it is much better in real life!"

Perhaps your dreams don't include private jets or limousines, but what about being appreciated and recognized for a job well done? Maybe just knowing you have achieved something that others only dream of is enough for you. Whatever your goals may be, network marketing offers you a world of opportunity—opportunity to excel and to become a superstar!

CHAPTER TWELVE

THE BALANCING ACT

Trying to Juggle

As women today juggle careers, parenting, finances, outside relationships, and commitments, they feel pulled in many directions, knowing they are in trouble if they can't juggle all of their balls at once or balance all of their responsibilities. If they drop one ball the whole bunch will come crashing down around them. Eileen knows about juggling too many things in life. That is one of the main reasons she started her own network marketing business. "I took my three small children to the circus last weekend. I was at least as excited as they were, fondly remembering my early childhood—sitting under the big tents with popcorn in my lap and cotton candy in my hand—watching wide-eyed as circus clowns performed their stunts to squeals of delight of many young children," says Eileen. "As we sat in the cool semi-darkness under that huge circus tent, I watched as clowns performed for my children the same funny stunts I saw as a young girl. I watched one clown juggling several balls while riding a unicycle and blowing a catchy song on his harmonica. "That's me!" I thought to myself. I am always juggling balls and running around in circles while trying, often in vain, to sing a happy song."

> ### FOUR MORE BENEFITS
>
> 1. Learn how to climb out of debt.
> 2. Learn how to create a positive cash flow.
> 3. Learn to invest for the future.
> 4. Learn how to balance careers, family, or relationships and personal time.

In this chapter you will learn how to balance your career, family, and other delicate and important commitments in life and through it all be able to develop a successful business that will create a safety net offering a sense of comfort and peace in a topsy-turvey world. Topics such as climbing out of debt, creating a

THREE GREAT WAYS TO BRING BALANCE TO YOUR LIFE

1. Decide what is most important to you. Get a clear picture of what you really want out of life. Then make a commitment to do whatever it takes to accomplish that dream. Begin each day by writing down what you want to do that day.
2. Evaluate each item on your list. Categorize items based upon your most important priority, the thing that is most important to you. Eliminate things that aren't going to help you attain your ultimate goal.
3. Focus on your principal priority. Learn to delegate responsibilities to others and remember it's okay to say no!

positive cash flow, and investing for the future will be discussed. Women will learn skills to help them balance time, finances, careers, and families while building security for their future.

Organize or Agonize

The ability to juggle four or five high priority projects successfully is a must for every leader. A life in which *anything goes* is a life in which *nothing goes*. Steven Covey, in his bestselling book, *Seven Principles of Highly Effective People*, talks about beginning with the end in mind. Or, in other words, seeing the big picture and setting the appropriate priorities.

There is a vast difference between importance and urgency. Often women get the two mixed up. "I thought that every time the phone rang I needed to jump. Or if the kids wanted me to run them somewhere, I should stop and do it, even if I was in the middle of an important task," Eileen adds. "I spent so much time running here and there, putting out fires for other people, that I never seemed to get to finish my own projects." Like many mothers, Eileen found herself scattered in too many directions heading for no one specific destination. Once she defined her goal, set a clear plan, developed priorities, and organized her time, her productivity soared!

"I was always busy, busy getting nowhere," she adds. "After working all day I usually spent several hours working at home, either cleaning up after the kids or sitting in my office answering phone messages and cleaning up my desk. I never stopped working it seemed and yet I never could get caught up." Then Eileen learned something new, something that changed her life.

Priority Principle

"My sponsor was busy, too. She had a successful career, a large family, and a fast growing network community, yet she always seemed to be miles ahead of me," said Eileen. "One day she came to visit me and found me frustrated, as usual. As I sat on the floor, laundry piled around me and kids running in and out of the door, I asked her how she managed her busy life. She looked right at me and said, 'Priorities, Eileen, priorities.' She went on to explain how she spent her days much like mine until she learned the priority principle. She made up her daily task list, just like I did, but then she did something different. She focused on her main goal, which in her case was her family, then her second priority, her business, and then she looked at her list. She put an A by the things on her list that she knew were the most important to her main goals, a B by the items on the list that fell into the second category, and so on. Then she either delegated the rest of the list to others in her family or moved it to another day, knowing that those things were not really important in the accomplishment of her priority goals for that day. The key word here is focus; delegate and eliminate." When Eileen began to apply the same principles to her life, her business took off, the kids were happier, and her frustration lessened.

Put First Things First

Ok, you say. I make my "to do" list every morning and I am never able to get the entire list checked off by the end of the day. Each of us has looked at our desks filled with memos and papers, heard the phone ringing, and watched the door open all at the same time! Remember the feeling that came over you?

Too many priorities can overload you. Get focused on what you really want out of life. Then get a clear picture of what you need to do to get that life. Put those things at the top of your priority list and make sure those are the first things you do everyday. "I let everyone else get in the way of finishing my projects," Eileen said. "Until I learned to say no. I learned how to put first things first and say no to the rest. At first I felt a little guilty, then I realized that I was not responsible for the world. I had choices just like everyone else did. I learned to evaluate, eliminate, and estimate."

Climbing Out of Debt

"My mother always told me, 'there are two kinds of people in this world— those who have money and those who spend money.' I suppose her example taught me to be cautious. I wanted to be in the group that had money," says Jennifer Basye Sander, best-selling author and successful networker. "Make it, keep it, grow it. That is my motto."

Debt can be an awful, burdensome load to carry. Any successful businessperson will tell you that overspending is the quickest way to disaster. Our country is full of people that are living from paycheck to paycheck, robbing Peter to pay Paul. Their crushing credit card bills will consume their hard earned money for years to come, preventing them from ever really getting ahead and building up any wealth. Often they buy flashy and expensive things in order to flaunt a certain measure of status. But a smarter bet would be to invest that money into their business, into a place that will bring them a return for their investment.

In his best-selling book, *Rich Dad, Poor Dad*, Robert Kiyosaki tells us that there is a huge difference between spending money and investing money. "The main reason people struggle financially is because they have spent years in school, but learned nothing about money. The result is that people learn to work for money . . . but never learn to have money work for them."

FOUR GREAT WAYS TO CLIMB OUT OF DEBT

1. Keep a journal of your spending. For thirty days, write down every penny you spend and what you spent it for.
2. Evaluate your list at the end of the month. By looking at your spending habits you will clearly see where you could improve, cut back, and change.
3. Set up a budget and stick to it! The additional money you save by not buying that extra cup of coffee or soda can add up at the end of the month. Consider using that money to reduce interest bearing accounts.
4. Pay off higher interest bearing accounts first. By eliminating credit cards and other interest loans, you will find that you have more money in your pocket. You could use that extra money to make money with investments.

A friend of mine said that his sponsor, Dexter Yager, was one of the wealthiest men in the country yet claims to be a penny pincher! So what do these people know that we don't know?

Jennifer says, "Women need to understand that they need to wait for some of the good stuff in life, and that if they buy it too soon, they will actually delay (or even derail!) their achievement of creating wealth. It takes self-discipline to inure yourself to the seductive advertising messages and ignore their *spend, spend, spend* message. But by developing the self-discipline to resist the impulse to squander your hard-earned dollars on frivolous purchases you also will be developing self-discipline that will serve you well on your quest to become wealthy."

Sometimes we let money just slip through our fingers. If you are like most of us, you may remember a time or two when you put a certain amount of money in your wallet and later couldn't remember what you spent it on! My upline told me that if I couldn't learn how to live within my means, or to manage my money while I earned $50,000 a year, I wouldn't be able to live on $500,000 a year either. He taught me a lesson that I have carried over into other areas of my life. I followed his instruction and went straight to the stationery store that day. He told me to take a small notebook everywhere I went and to write down everything that I spent that was 50 cents or more, and what I spent it on. Then after 30 days we met again to evaluate. I could not believe how much money I spent on junk, on things I didn't really want or need.

FOUR GREAT WAYS TO GET ORGANIZED

1. Never touch a piece of paper twice! When the mail comes in or the papers from the office find their way to your home, file them immediately. Don't set them down thinking you'll put them away later. Do it now! It only takes a few minutes every day to stay organized.

2. Keep a trash can handy and throw junk away. Don't let things pile up. Magazines and news articles should be read quickly and tossed out or donated to a local school or library.

3. If you haven't used an item in the past twelve months, chances are you never will. Get rid of everything in your office, closets, and garage that you have not used in the past twelve months. It is just taking up space. Get rid of what you don't want to make room for what you do!

4. If you aren't totally successful in your attempts to organize your life, don't give up. Keep trying! Start over—you'll get better with each attempt and you definitely will benefit from the effort.

By keeping a detailed record of my spending, I could actually see where all of my hard-earned money was going. I was then able to decide if I really wanted to spend my money that in those areas or on those items. I can tell you this—it changed my life. I continue to teach this principal to others. Janet, one of my distributors, did the same. "After accounting my spending habits for 30 days, I set up a budget for myself, which included some frivolous spending, but a pre-determined amount," said Janet. "I followed that budget faithfully and after only three months, I had over $700 put away in a special savings account. I figured out that at 10 percent interest that money would turn into over $2,000 in the next ten years alone. That just made me motivated to save more!"

So come on—you can do it, too. You may even want to consider doing what my friend Janet did—have plastic surgery! She cut up all of her plastic credit cards! Perhaps you think that is too extreme, but whatever you decide, by spending less and investing in your business and future, you will not only have more money, you'll have peace of mind as well.

Clear Out the Clutter

"I am too busy to get organized," I shouted as I climbed over the boxes piled on my office floor. Ever heard that before? Oh, you say that's the way you feel too? Well, if you don't have time to put things where they belong in the first place, when will you ever have the time to go through everything and get it straight? In her book, *Organized to Be the Best*, Susan Silver says that being organized can help you be more effective. "Many women believe that they don't have the time to get organized or to stay that way. In actuality, they often spend much more time trying to find that piece of paper or remember where they put their keys. They could be much more productive if they would develop a system. Organizing is really time saving."

Ginny says that she finally hit the end of her rope and made some important changes that have streamlined her life, making it simpler and easier. "I was running so hard everyday, building my business, volunteering at the hospital, and carpooling kids, I couldn't seem to ever catch up," says Ginny. "I thought I was being efficient because I got a ton of things done in a day, but I let lots of things slip through the cracks." Ginny said that she often misplaced things like papers or an important phone number, even money! "One evening I got so tired of rummaging through my cluttered shoulder bag that I dumped the entire thing out on the bed. Sorting through the tiny pieces of paper, children's toys, gum wrappers, and cosmetics I found an envelope that I had forgotten to mail. In it was my house payment and check! When I called the lender the next day I found out that I had to pay a late charge of $65. That's when I decided to get a grip on my life," she adds.

> ### TIME AND MONEY
>
> We've all heard the phrase that time is money. It is certainly true. By spending some time to organize your life, you could actually find you have more time, and probably more money. Time *is* money, and the clock is ticking!

Ginny knew her limitations, she knew organization ranked at the top of the list. So she called Liz, her sponsor, and asked for help. "I didn't even know where to start," Ginny said. "I was embarrassed at first to have Liz see how disorganized I was, but we actually had fun that day. Liz is a great organizer and she made it seem easy. By the end of the day my office was neat, files were organized, and I felt like I had gained a huge measure of control in my life."

We've all heard the phrase that time is money. It is certainly true. By spending some time to organize your life, you could actually find you have more time, and probably more money. Ginny found out that by setting aside a few minutes every morning to get organized she still had time to do the things she was responsible for. In fact, she says that by investing that time each morning she was able to get much more accomplished by the end of the day.

So how about it? Are you ready to clear out the clutter? Set aside a portion of time each day and make it a priority. Use this time to go through your mail, file papers, make phone calls, or answer e-mail. After all, time *is* money, and the clock is ticking.

Juggling the Job

With over 75 percent of women working outside of the home today, a common concern among them is how to juggle their job and a new business. The top female networkers I have talked to all tell me the same thing: "It *is* possible!" Anyone can do it with a little planning and a big dream. The key, they say, is in priorities. While your job is certainly a priority, they say that there are many things a woman can do to squeeze more time out of a day, little things like turning off the telephone or TV. Spending that time actually talking to your partner or kids, if you have them, or even reading a motivational book, is a better investment in your future. Another tip they shared is that by planning your next day the night before you can accomplish much more the following day. "Mornings at my house were in full swing by 6:30," says Alicia. "Wake the kids, feed the cat, dress the bodies, it all takes time. Then there was the usual daily disasters, 'Sally spilt milk on my only clean dress.' or, 'Mom, I forgot to tell you that I need that notebook for school *this* morning.' or, 'Aunt Pat called last night and said her plans changed. She will be coming this week for a visit instead of next week. Oh, and her plane gets in tonight at 6. Can you pick her up?' By the time I got out the door and on the road to work, I would remember the laundry that I left on the chair, or the prescription I had intended to fill at my lunch hour, and sometimes I even forgot important paperwork I needed at the office."

SIX BALANCING TIPS

1. Prioritize your life.
2. Turn off the TV.
3. Turn on the telephone answering machine.
4. Plan your next day the night before.
5. Draw on your greatest asset: your upline and team leaders.
6. Delegate!

Alicia's life, like many working women, was busy. She said she found a way to eliminate the frustration of forgetfulness by making a list the night before. "I kept a pad of paper and a pen by my bed. Every night when I finally laid down, I'd take a minute and jot down all of the things I needed to do, or remember the next morning. It would only take two minutes to do it, but it saved me hours of headache and frustration."

The next morning it would only take her a quick glance at the list to pull together the things she needed for the day. She says that by doing this little exercise she stopped having to miss lunches to run home and grab that cleaning or prescriptions. Alicia learned how to get back some of her time.

Other working women tell me they were able to find time to build their network business by team building—through duplication. "I had a busy medical practice, a husband, and a very spoilt dog," says Sunny. "When I saw the network marketing business, I really liked the idea. I just didn't think I had the time to invest in anything outside of my practice. But the more I learned about the opportunity, the more I understood the value of duplication and the importance it could play in my financial future. The medical field is changing so quickly. HMOs, rising insurance costs, no one knows where it will end. I just didn't know how much longer I wanted to practice medicine, or how much longer I could afford to."

Like Sunny, many professionals are jumping into the network marketing arena. With rising costs and pending uncertainties in their profession, they are eager to create additional income streams, especially residual ones. But time is almost always an issue for them. Luckily, Sunny's sponsors knew just what to do.

"My sponsors, Bill and Janet, each had thriving businesses when they started out in network marketing. They both were super busy," she adds. "They figured out through trial and error how to make the best use of their time. Through them I learned how to manage my time and maximize my efforts. In the beginning I could only give eight hours a week to my new business. But by sponsoring others who had a little more discretionary time, soon many hours of work were being done in my business each week. By teaching this pattern for success to others, I quickly learned how to duplicate myself. Within a few short months I had multiplied many times the few hours I could invest in the beginning. Next year I am planning to retire from my practice," Sunny says.

The power of duplication! Why don't we look at how this can work for you? Let's assume you sponsored ten people who each had ten hours a week to invest in their new business. That totals over 100 hours of productivity in your business. Assuming they each duplicated you and sponsored ten people each who spend ten hours a week, your group activity, or work flow, would be over 1,000 hours for the week. The power of duplication! Remember J. Paul Getty, one of the richest men in history? He said there are only two ways to make money: leverage money or leverage time. The power of time leverage through duplication—it can work for you!

Do It For the Kids

Jeannie Morrone told me about her love for her kids and her struggles with the guilt that she felt as she left them each day to go to work. "As a single parent raising two kids while holding down a job can be pretty overwhelming at times," says Jeanne. "One particular time was an early morning in the winter. As usual, I was trying to get myself ready for work while at the same time, feed and dress the kids. I noticed that Tyler wasn't moving very fast and it became evident that he wasn't feeling well. This was not good timing. As a single parent my income was critical, therefore my job was critical. I could not afford to lose it. My job wasn't the only concern either. The day care center expected to be paid for everyday even if a child was out sick or the parent couldn't go to work and they themselves did not get paid for the day. I knew Tyler had heard me express these concerns to others. Perhaps that is why, when I asked him if he was sick he stuck out his chin, held up his head and bravely said, "I'm Ok Mom."

Soon after we rushed out to the car. Fighting the wind, the cold, and the kicking little legs of my baby daughter, I finally got her buckled in the car seat. I turned to Tyler just in time to notice the color leaving his face. Quickly I ran to his door and was able to help him out of the car. I stood in the driveway; cold wind blowing through my bones, holding this darling little boy's hand while he got sick on the cement. At the same time that I was patting his back to comfort him, I was thinking, "I am going to be late for work. I can't be late again," adds Jeanne.

Jeanne was able to call her mother and get some help for her sick son, and although she was late for work, she did make it. However as she sat quietly at her desk that morning, she had a turning point in her life. "When I finally did make it to work I slid in behind my desk, upset and already exhausted. As I thought about my son a thought came to me, "What am I doing? I should be home with my son." I buried my face in my hands," says Jeanne. "It hit me that the most important thing in my life, my precious family, came second to my job. That is the day I decided to make a change in my life."

Jeanne did go on to build her network business and later, with the help of her second husband, Bill Morrone, she has developed a lifestyle that allows not only her, but her husband, Bill, to both be full-time parents to their three children. "My advice to women is to do this business now. Do it for the kids," says Jeanne.

Balancing the Books

Remember MJ Michaels? When she started her business she didn't even know the difference between wholesale and retail. She even called them *hotel* and *resell*. She also admits that she didn't know how to balance a checkbook, much less keep business records straight, yet today she is one of the most successful and highly respected women in the network business world. MJ says that women don't have to be experts in business when they start. They don't have to get in knowing it all. Women can learn everything they need to know about business—from balancing the books to building a financial empire.

> ### BALANCING THE BOOKS
>
> Women don't have to be experts in business when they start. They don't have to start knowing it all. Women can learn everything they need to know about business—from balancing the books to building a financial empire.

While being able to start up your own company before having to learn all the ropes is a compelling reason to get into network marketing, it will be important to the long-term success of your new business for you to learn how to manage money and keep your records in order. Bigger companies, offer bookkeeping and income tax record supplies—complete with step-by-step instructions to set up shop and keep things straight. Other companies have similar help aids available, and all of them should have someone in the upline who is willing to offer support to the new distributor starting up a business for the first time.

In addition, there are simple software packages available in computer stores everywhere that will help you with everything from balancing checkbooks to doing accounts receivables and inventory reports. By learning to balance the books and manage your office, you will be able to feel the thrill and power from getting your first check! And as you build your business, the skills you will develop along the way will help you learn to work with numbers and feel more comfortable managing large amounts of money. As you continue to learn to run your own business, the skills you develop are transferable. Money skills are important. Remember the words of my friend, Jennifer: "Make it, keep it, and grow it!"

Invest in You

Women are so inclined to give, share, and lavish things on other people. It's the way women are raised," declares Olivia Mellan, a Washington, D.C., speaker and author who specializes in the psychology of money.

Mellan, who is also a psychotherapist and business consultant in the area of financial conflict resolution, deals with the emotional roots of money issues. She traces much of it to women's upbringing. "The message women received as we grow up is: I'm not supposed to put myself first. I'm supposed to take care of everyone else first. The feminine value is to be accommodating, not competitive."

She claims that women aren't used to being healthily self-oriented. "Think how many women put their husbands through college and their kids in private schools," she explains. "Then they end up in a financial disaster as widows or divorcees, totally unprepared."

On a smaller scale, look at everyday life. Who takes the burnt toast or the broken taco? Who is the last to get a new pair of shoes? Is it you? Even today, you probably wouldn't serve yourself the slightly larger brownie, whether you're with your father or your husband or your sister. It's not polite.

While I am not suggesting women should stop giving or caring for others, I am suggesting that it is Ok to give to yourself, to ask for your fair share. It is Ok to invest in your own future, in your own business, in you.

"My kids needed so many things," says Linda Brentwood. "There just never seemed like enough money to go around and I was usually the last in line. When I first got involved in network marketing, I saw it as a way to get some extra's for my family, for my kids. The day my first big bonus check came in the mail I was so excited! It was such a thrill to open that envelope and see my first check that represented the effort I had put in my business the months before. I rushed into the living room to share my success with my kids. They were excited too. Right away they had a long list of things they wanted me to buy with it—all for them."

While Linda's kids were just like many other kids, they didn't understand very much about money other than how to spend it. "I told them I needed to really think about it before we just went out and blew all of the money. Joe, my oldest son, had asked for money the week before to go to the water park.

I reminded him how much that day had cost him. I asked them to consider each of the things they wanted to spend the money for and how long each of those items would last. For example, Joe's portion of the money would have been spent and gone in only one day if he went to the water park again. I explained that our new business had given us this money and if we wanted it to give us more, we needed to give a portion of it back to the business. We talked about the costs of operating a business—ours compared to another type of company. I showed them some training tapes and brochures from my office and talked about the benefits that we could gain by buying more of these tools. They didn't understand it all, but they liked the idea of getting another check the next month. That night when I went to bed I felt so grateful for my new business. Because of it I was able to teach my kids the importance of delayed gratification and other important lessons of life. That night I realized that up until then, I hadn't ever taught them anything about the value of money. Those little kids had learned more in that first night about money, business, and investments than I knew when I graduated from high school. It was exciting and I was determined to teach them more!" she declared.

> **FOUR MORE WAYS TO CREATE BALANCE IN YOUR LIFE**
>
> 1. Involve your kids or partners in your plans.
> 2. Invest in yourself. Put money back into your business, your future, into you!
> 3. Teach delayed gratification and practice it personally.
> 4. Delegate some responsibilities to others or "hire it out" if possible.

Hire It Out—Delegate

All women will agree that the benefits of owning your own network marketing business are too numerous to list. However, almost all of them tell me that one of their favorite things about this business is the extra money! Many have told me that even early on in their business they earned enough extra money to afford to pay someone else to take care of a portion of their workload. "I didn't want someone else to be responsible for taking care of my children, I wanted to do it! But I sure didn't think that it was very important to include housework and laundry too!" Sheri Larsen says. "I will never forget the early days when both Scott and I were working full time, raising two kids, and just starting out in our own business. By the time we got the kids from the day care and got dinner on the table, it was time to rush out again for a meeting. I never was a perfect housekeeper, but it was getting really out of hand after a few weeks."

Like other working mothers, Sheri's workload didn't stop when she came home at night. In fact, she says it doubled. "Having two little kids was my dream and both Scott and I loved them, loved being with them. But they were a handful. Scott always said they were high maintenance!" she laughs. "When we got home at night from work we knew we only had a couple of hours before we went back out again to do some meetings. We wanted to spend some time with the kids. I didn't want to spend my only two hours of the day with my kids watching me washing dishes or running around the house. I wanted to play with them, talk to them, hold them."

But after a few weeks Sheri says that the maintenance at home was getting overwhelming. "One night as we were rushing back out the door for an appointment, I realized that I didn't have any clean pajamas to put on the kids. In fact, I couldn't even find clean play clothes for them to sleep in. The laundry was piled so high that it was about to move out of the laundry room and into the hall. Then the guilt hit! What kind of a mother was I anyway? I said I loved my children but I didn't even take the time to get their clothes clean. I told Scott that I couldn't keep doing this business with him. I needed to stay at home."

Scott talked her into going just one more time with him that night. They went to visit with a couple from Scott's office who were about fifteen years older and had three kids. After Scott gave the marketing plan both agreed to join. Then the woman looked at Sheri and said, "Oh, how I wish I had seen this business 10 years ago. I could have built it then and still had some time to spend with my kids. All I have done is work since they were little. Now they are grown up and I missed it all. You are so lucky to be doing this now. Your kids will be so much better off and so will you!" she said. Sheri was so grateful that she had agreed to go with Scott that night. On the ride home they talked about hiring someone to help with the workload at home. That next week Sheri hired a lovely woman to take care of cleaning, laundry, and shopping. She even agreed to pick the kids up from preschool and prepare three evening meals a week.

"What a difference that made in our lives," Sheri adds. "My house was spotless. I had more time with the kids and I was more focused than ever before to get this business built fast so I could quit my job and be a full-time mother." And she did.

Sometimes we need to get some help at home, but what about in the beginning when money is tight and you are reinvesting everything back into your business? Let's find out how Debi made it work for her. "There was absolutely no way that I could work all day, take care of my family, keep the house up, and do this business at night," Debi Johnstun says. "No way! I sat down with my kids one night and explained it to them. I could come home from work and clean the house, do the laundry, and cook the meals—or I could go out at night and build my business and ultimately their future, if they agreed to help me at home. It was unanimous! They voted for me to get out and build a business. They wanted me to quit my day job so I could come to their class parties and dance recitals. We all knew that day would never come unless I got this business going."

> ### THE SPIN CYCLE
>
> "Sometimes life is like a spin cycle . . . . And like the cycle of our washing machine, we've got to readjust and sometimes have to just start over. Life can be a balancing act. The better balance we have in our lives, the more productive we will be in our businesses as well as our personal lives."

Debi and her kids put together a game plan at home, much like the game plan she designed for her business. Each child agreed to a particular set of household duties. They designed a chart to track their progress and to report to their mother. Then Debi suggested they set a family goal—a reward at the end of each month for a job well done. "I had been taught in my business to set goals and determine the reward as each was achieved. I knew it was working for me. I thought it would work for the kids too," she said. And it did.

By setting a predetermined goal for the end of each month, based upon the successful completion of the goal (the household duties), Debi had a motivated group of kids. "I was so amazed! Before we started our new plan I always had to fuss at the kids to do little things to help around the house. So one of the deals we negotiated in our new plan was that I wouldn't have to even ask them about their duties. If they didn't complete their assignments, the deal was off. They wouldn't get to participate in the reward with the other children who did get their work done. From the first week we started I rarely ever had to ask if their duties were complete. They just did them all willingly and happily. It was one of the greatest things we have ever done as a family."

So whether you delegate some of your workload or hire it out, make sure that you find the time to work your business. Someday you will be free.

The Spin Cycle

Last weekend my sons were reluctantly cleaning their rooms and getting their laundry ready for the coming week. I was in my office working on a writing project when I heard a terrible banging noise coming from the hallway. It sounded like the walls were crashing in! I jumped from my desk and ran toward the sound, colliding with both of my sons. We shoved our way through the laundry room door and found the reason for the piercing sound—the spin cycle in the washing machine was off balance and the machine was literally rocking from side to side, banging against the dryer and the wall. I quickly opened the lid and stopped the racket. I began to pull out the contents of the washing machine to better balance the load. As I began to lift out the contents, I couldn't believe my eyes!

I pulled out a blanket, two towels, a sheet and pillowcase, three pairs of jeans, and several pullover shirts—probably enough laundry for three! "Who put this load of laundry in the washing machine?" I yelled down the hall.

Around the corner of his bedroom came the blonde head of my youngest son, Tyler. "I did, Mom. I was just trying to be *sufficient,*" he said. What he meant to say was *efficient*. I had given them all a little speech earlier in the week about not wasting things, like milk left out on the counter, or time, by putting things away where they belonged instead of leaving personal items laying around. We talked about being efficient, making the most of our time and efforts and resources.

So my ten year old was thinking that by jamming three loads of wash in the machine he was making good use of his time. But now he had three wet, soapy, dripping loads of wash that had to be redone, one at a time, and what he thought was efficient ended up taking even more time than if he had just done it right to begin with.

Sometimes life is like a spin cycle. We are busy, going around and around, trying to jam too much in our day and getting completely out of balance. And like the cycle of our washing machine, we've got to readjust and sometimes have to just start over. Life can be a balancing act. The better balance we have in our lives, the more productive we will be in our businesses as well as our personal lives. And like my son Tyler says, "Be more efficient."

CHAPTER THIRTEEN

LEADERS AND LOYALTY

Leadership and loyalty are critical to success in any aspect of life, whether managing a career, developing a lasting relationship, or developing a strong business. Leaders are loyal, first to their own goals and dreams, then to their commitments to others, to their product or service lines, and, most importantly, to their leaders and mentors and the system their leaders have developed. In our society today, trust and loyalty is not necessarily synonymous with success and is often an uncommon trait in traditional business. In network marketing it is a key to success.

It has often been said that a chain is as strong as its weakest link. Learning to develop a strong link between business and people—products and upline training systems—will aid you in the

> ## THE DEFINITION OF GREAT LEADERSHIP
>
> The ability to obtain followers. Being the person others will gladly follow.

development of your networking business and the financial security you seek. Let's first talk about leadership—what it means and how to develop leadership qualities in yourself.

Leadership Is Influence

In his book, *Developing the Leader Within You*, John C. Maxwell defines leadership. He says that leadership means to influence others. "Everyone talks about it; few understand it. Most people want it; few achieve it." He defines leadership as the ability to obtain followers. Most people define leadership as the ability to achieve a position, not to get followers. In network marketing you want followers. Remember, this is a volunteer army. People choose to participate. They also choose to follow, or not, depending on your ability to lead. Real leadership means being the person others will gladly and confidently follow.

Great Leaders Were First Great Students

All winners have coaches! They win more consistently than others because they are always open to listening and putting to use the new ideas that present themselves. They are always looking for a better way. The same is true with great leaders. First they were willing to learn, to be good students. Through this humble attitude great leaders are born.

To be teachable you have to want to be better! If you found the greatest coach in network marketing and you were not sincerely interested in being the best that you can be, you probably won't learn anything.

Being teachable is learning to listen differently. A lot of people can't handle this one. They have things made up in their mind—they see things in a specific way and that's it! They tend to place restrictions on what they will or won't listen to. They "already know," therefore, no one can tell them anything! How sad! It is a mistake not to look outside the rigid boundaries of our minds. It can cost you a great deal of money, too!

"I was a hotshot attorney for a big firm in Dallas," says Lynette. "My sponsor was a teacher at the local high school before joining network marketing. At first I didn't understand the extent of this great leader's knowledge, of the skills he had developed on his path to wealth and success. I mean after all, he had only been a high school teacher. What did he know about big business? What could he possibly teach me?" she adds. "When he would say to do A, B, and C, for example, I would often skip A and move along to B and C. In other words, I renegotiated much of what my sponsor was trying to teach me to do. Big mistake!"

Lynette learned that in order to move ahead quickly in her new business, it made sense to follow the leader—to walk in the steps of someone who had already reached a pinnacle of success. "When I finally understood what he had accomplished by reaching his level of success, I was so eager to listen to every detail and follow every step he laid out for me. I realized that by *asking, listening,* and *doing,* I would reach my goals much faster than if I tried to figure everything out on my own," Lynette said.

To ask for coaching or counseling can often be scary. Many people cannot bring themselves to be that courageous. It takes courage to request coaching. When you request coaching, you put yourself at risk; you make yourself vulnerable. Not fun! But it certainly is worth it! When you are courageous enough to ask for assistance, you will

> ### FOUR WAYS TO DEVELOP PERSONAL LEADERSHIP
>
> 1. Learn to listen. Don't place restrictions on what you will, or won't listen to.
> 2. Choose your coaches carefully, then trust their judgement and advice.
> 3. Be willing to ask for help.
> 4. Ask, listen, and do!

find that others will be more willing to support you and help you reach your goals. They will offer information and often go out of their way to help.

Choose your coach carefully and then surrender to her or him. A commitment to trust your leader's judgment comes with being teachable. As Lynette found out, by trusting in her upline she was able to jump over hurdles and avoid pitfalls because he showed her a better way. They taught her from experience.

When you are teachable, let your leaders know. Tell them that you are requesting counsel or help. Ask them to tell it like it is! Give them permission to assist you. Let them know it's really okay to be honest with you. Say to them, "I can take it! For me to be able to be the best I can be, I want and need your ideas, opinions, suggestions, and advice. Please say what is on your mind."

"My upline probably didn't think I really meant it at first. I finally asked for some time with him and I told him I really wanted to be better, to grow. I asked him to tell me what he thought I could do to improve," says Lynette. She says that she stopped evaluating him and became open and teachable. Her business took off from that point.

Who Is Your Leader?

Last Friday I went to my son's football game. Clinton had been working all week with his coach to improve his skills and develop some new techniques.

He was anxious to demonstrate those lessons. I watched in amazement as he bowled over the opposing team. His progress was remarkable! When we met after the game I asked him what he had done to acquire such improvement. His response, "I stopped listening to my buddies and started listening to my coach." The results spoke for themselves.

Notice in football that the quarterback only listens to the coach. That's as it should be. Once you have selected a coach, be loyal. Clinton found out that listening to his coach—and only his coach—made the difference between winning and losing. Don't be distracted by conflicting information from your well-meaning friends or other crossline distributors. They may mean well, but your loyalty is to your upline leader—the person who is investing time in you.

Often we reject quality leadership because it isn't what we want to hear. We often seek other people's advice to find agreement with our own views rather than listen to coaching that may have us stretch or be uncomfortable and yet is just the answer we were looking for on our quest for success.

Lynette says, "I didn't always like everything my upline taught me. Sometimes I needed to do things that were uncomfortable. But I always asked myself these questions, What if it works? What have I got to lose? Have they steered me wrong before? Usually I am able to forge ahead and do that task that I might have avoided before. I know that listening to my leaders and doing what I was counseled to do has been the key ingredient to my success!"

> **FOCUS**
>
> Don't be distracted by conflicting information from your well-meaning friends or other crossline distributors. They may mean well, but your loyalty is to your upline leader—the person who is investing time in you.

Loyalty Promotes Fast Growth

Sheri Sharman says that being loyal to her upline made all of the difference in her success. "I know why I was able to grow my business so fast," says Sherri. "It is because I had incredible upline leaders, Dale Koehrsen, John Alden, and Michelle McCadden."

Sherri had already achieved a large measure of success in another company before she ever heard of her network marketing opportunity. In fact, she left that company while earning a seven-figure income. She says she felt that the network marketing company she was involved with previously had incredible integrity issues. "Despite all of the money I was making in this other company, I wasn't happy inside. I wanted to find a company that shared the same values and integrity that I had," Sherri says. "When I found it, I knew it was exactly what I had been looking for. But even with my past success, I could never have accomplished what I have without the support and leadership of my upline."

Sheri was teachable. She came into a new company, after walking away from a huge income, and said, "Teach me what you know." She listened and followed their council. Being teachable will give you new opportunities for growth. It will open doors for you. As you grow and learn, you will be developing as a leader. One day others will come to you for counsel, for help and advice. Because you were a great student, you will have become a great leader. Then you will be effective in leading others.

The Law of Loyalty

The sunflower has been called the symbol of loyalty. A story is told of a ship that had been torpedoed at sea, and the crew deserted the ship for the lifeboats. Only two persons remained—the commanding officer, who had been blinded by the explosion, and his personal attendant, who had served him faithfully for many years. The captain, true to the tradition of the sea, had decided to go down with the ship, dressed in his smartest uniform and with all of the flags flying. The faithful servant had stood silently at the side of his blind master without making his presence known until all the lifeboats were filled and out to sea.

As the water gradually rose to their knees and then their waists, the captain urged his aide to save himself. The servant then told his now blind master the story of the sunflower, the symbol of loyalty. The sunflower follows the sun not only in the early hours when the day is young but also at the day's zenith when the heat is the most intense. The sunflower looks directly into the sun in the morning, is constant and steadfast throughout the long afternoon, and, as the sun declines, follows it until it finally disappears into the horizon.

The servant concluded, "That is loyalty." Then, just before the ship reared up on its end to plunge with its two occupants to the bottom of the sea, the servant added, "the sunflower follows the sun; you go down with your ship, and I go down with you."

Super people are usually people with super loyalties. Loyalty makes ours those things to which we are loyal, while disloyalty removes them from us. The law of loyalty says that we must think loyalty and put it into action. Loyalty to one's self, one's values and beliefs, is the cornerstone of one's character. Loyalty is the foundation of a person's character.

The dictionary defines loyalty as follows: "to be constant and faithful in any relationship, implying trust or confidence." If we are loyal, most people will overlook many of our errors, but if we are not loyal, nothing else we do will help much. To be disloyal is to be faithless, false, or inconstant to one's obligations.

Leaders cannot lead without the loyalty of followers. Teachers cannot teach without the student. And team building can never happen without strong bonds of loyalty. I am fiercely loyal to my upline leaders. If you want to develop a big business and learn to lead a successful organization, it will require loyalty. Loyalty begins with the heart.

Begin with the Heart

People don't care how much you know until they know how much you care. Leadership begins with the heart, not the head. It flourishes with a meaningful relationship. People will do more for someone they care about, or someone who cares about them. "When my sponsor told me she would help me every step of the way to create success, I didn't really believe it. I mean, no one had ever made my life easier in my other career. Often when someone said they would do something for me, it usually meant they wanted something in return. I always knew they would be coming around sooner or later to collect on their 'good deed.' But with my sponsor it was different. Not only did she help me get my business up and running, but every time I got myself into a corner, Amy was always there to get me out," says Cindy. "She never asked for anything in return, never expected me to pay her back. I really respect her leadership. She makes me want to be better, perform more. I would do anything for her today, anything at all," she adds.

Develop People

A leader is great, not because of his or her power, but because of his or her ability to empower others. Amy was a great leader because she created an environment where Cindy could excel and taught her by example how to do it. Cindy then became fiercely loyal to Amy. Loyalty to a leader reaches its peak when the follower has personally grown through the mentorship of the leader. Amy won Cindy's skeptical heart by helping her grow.

Edification

Leaders edify that which is worthy of praise. Edification means to build up, lift up, and offer praise and recognition. To give honor to another person would mean to edify them. In network marketing you will find edification in its purest form. I have watched time and time again as the most powerful leaders in the entire network marketing business receive recognition for achievement. More often than not, they give much of the credit to their upline. This is edification.

Edification works in network marketing much like the rest of our lives—people listen to those who are edified. If I wanted my children to listen to and respect their father, I would tell them how wise he is and what a wonderful person he is. But what if I told them that he was foolish and pointed out his

> ### LEADERSHIP BEGINS WITH THE HEART
>
> A leader is great, not because of his or her power, but because of his or her ability to empower others. Loyalty to a leader reaches its peak when the follower has personally grown through the mentorship of the leader.

silly mistakes? Would that bring confidence or trust between my children and their father? Certainly not! Would I expect that he would be helpful in raising them if I constantly criticized and put him down?

"It is surprising how much you can accomplish if you don't care who gets the credit."
—ABRAHAM LINCOLN

When I compliment my upline, offering sincere appreciation and praise, my downline organization holds them in an endearing position. They look up to the upline leaders and respect them. When my upline counsels with my people, they listen to their advice and do the things they suggest, largely because they have heard me edify these leaders many times before. Edification creates trust and loyalty and helps to build strong leadership in any organization, whether networking or in your community or at home.

Master Your Ego

The greatest addiction in the world today is not necessarily what you might think—drugs, sex, alcohol—it is the human ego. The human ego can destroy homes, marriages, and relationships faster and more efficiently than most any other addiction.

Leaders who fall victim to this addiction want to be center stage. They often are threatened by the success of others so they fail to develop and use people's talents or catch them doing something right. They want to be the best, "the fairest of them all."

Snow White Syndrome

As a young girl, I delighted in the story time I spent with my mother just before bedtime. I would cuddle up on my bed, pull the warm covers up around my neck, and listen as my mother would read from the many books aside my bed. One of my favorite fairy tales was Snow White, a fair, dark-haired young maiden under the jealous eye of an evil Queen. The Queen, with her enormous ego, was determined to be the "fairest of them all," even if she had to kill everyone in her kingdom to maintain this false pretense.

Unfortunately, there are those in leadership positions who feel much the same way as the wicked Queen—jealous, threatened, self-centered, and dangerous. This type of runaway ego can be the quickest way to kill an organization. A person with such an ego cannot tolerate anyone being better than they are. They look for opportunities to destroy the credibility of those they perceive are above them so they can maintain this false image of being the fairest of them all.

A great rule for doing business today is think more about your people and they will think more of themselves. And don't act like you are perfect. Leaders need to come from behind their curtains of infallibility, power, and control and let their very good side—their humanity—be revealed. Folks like to be around a person who is willing to admit his or her vulnerability, asks for ideas, and can let others be in the spotlight. As Norman Vincent Peale once said, "People with humility don't think less of themselves, they just think of themselves less."

Duplication versus Imitation

What is the reason for the overwhelming success of companies like McDonald's? Duplication! Duplication works. McDonald's created a simple system that is easy to teach to others. Then they did it over and over again. I have been from London to India, and the French fries at McDonald's taste the same no matter the location!

By tapping into proven successful money-making systems and utilizing the power of duplication, you will create an incredible lifestyle. Remember, duplicating your upline's pattern for success does not mean you have to imitate them. You shouldn't try to be like another person, just take their great qualities and wisdom and incorporate those things into your own personality. By duplicating their pattern for success, you win!

> "People with humility don't think less of themselves, they just think of themselves less."
> —NORMAN VINCENT PEALE

Look in the Mirror

Good leaders are committed to helping their people win. In network marketing, huge success comes only after you have helped others win big. My upline, Don and Ruth Storms, teach me by their example. Don says he always wants to "kick the newest guy out of the nest" or get them out there on their own, trying and learning and growing their way to success. By leading the way and offering encouragement and support, Don's people begin to realize that they can build a big business, they can duplicate the pattern for success that he has taught them. As they take steps on their own and accomplish success, it gives them the confidence and enthusiasm to do even more, stretch even further outside of their comfort zones. Because Don and Ruth actually *do* what they teach, it gives others hope and belief. Even the newest business owner might say, "If I follow them, do the steps they teach and duplicate this pattern in my own business, I could have the kind of lifestyle that they enjoy."

> You can't push a rope anymore than you can push someone to success. People want to follow a great leader, not be pushed and prodded.
>
> The main job of a leader is to help his or her people succeed in accomplishing their goals by setting the pace ahead of them. In other words, *do* what you teach. Then when people in your downline accomplish their goals, everyone wins.

You can't push a rope anymore than you can push someone to success. People want to follow a great leader, not be pushed and prodded. When someone fails to achieve a goal by a specific deadline, a true leader will step up to the mirror and take a peek. In most cases, the biggest cause of the problem is looking you in the eyes.

The main job of a leader is to help his or her people succeed in accomplishing their goals by setting the pace ahead of them. In other words, *do* what you teach. Then when people in your downline accomplish their goals, everyone wins.

Motivating Others

Motivation can be a difficult concept for many leaders. Many assume that money, prizes, or special vacations are high-grade motivators. In reality, what motivates one person may not motivate another. "I got in this business not for the cars and jewelry, but to win at something. After feeling like a failure in my marriage, I wanted to feel like a success at something," says Jean Parker.

Suppose you have two excellent people. You would like to reward one with an incentive trip, but travel, it turns out, is not an issue with this person since her previous job was as a flight attendant. She may see increased responsibility as an appropriate reward. On the other hand, you would like to reward the second person with more responsibility, but her spouse's unexpected illness has kept her juggling too many balls. For this person, travel is a greater motivator than increased responsibility.

Know Your Players

In her book, *Personality Plus*, Florence Littauer says that by knowing your players you know not only what will motivate or inspire them, but how to lead them based on their personality style. In her book Littauer says, "Understanding other people's personality traits can be extremely helpful in developing a strong network marketing business. When you understand how another person thinks, what really makes them tick, then and only then will you know how to motivate or lead them."

Knowing how to identify and work with different personality types will be a tremendous aid in developing strong leaders and securing a financially sound business structure. Of course, you can't know everything about every person in your business, but knowing what makes your key leaders tick can often mean the difference between average business growth and sky rocket explosion!

Do It Over and Over and Over

Leaders should recognize that good performance, both their own and others, is a journey, not a destination. Everyone learns by doing. It takes time and practice to achieve specific goals. You can be too hard on yourself and that is often very counterproductive. Don't expect perfection from yourself, your downline, or your upline. While self-criticism is healthy when evaluating past performance and resetting future goals, it should not be destructive. It's unfair to be hard on yourself the first—or the second or third—time you attempt something new. It is also unfair to expect such an unrealistic standard from others. It's not necessary to do everything exactly right the first time.

"As an attorney I was always concerned with getting it right," said Barbara. "When I started this business I quickly saw that it was different from any business I had ever known. I immersed myself in training material. I felt I had to know every detail before I presented the marketing plan. One day my sponsor suggested I try and 'practice' my presentation on her. Thank goodness she got me *up and doing*, or I might have stayed in my office, pouring over the books forever!"

> Activity is the only way to truly grow, develop, and improve. The greatest lessons come from experience. Leaders learn by doing. Always do your best and remember, if at first you don't succeed, try, try again.

Activity is the only way to truly grow, develop, and improve. The greatest lessons come from experience. Leaders learn to do. Always do your best and remember, if at first you don't succeed, try, try again.

We learn best by doing. A favorite statement in a popular George Lucas film is made by a little creature called Yoda. When attempting to teach Luke Skywalker how to tap into the power within him, Yoda says, "Try not. Do or do not—there is no try." To reach success in network marketing perhaps we should say, "There is only do or do not."

Perhaps we shouldn't be so concerned about our performance if it is paralyzing our progress. I once heard the master of network marketing, Dexter Yager, say, "This business is very forgiving." If you make a mistake or don't get it just right, it is all right. You will! Just keep doing!

If at first you don't succeed, try, try again.

Don't Reinvent the Wheel

If it ain't broke, don't fix it. Have you ever heard that before? This phrase refers to someone who, not being able to leave well enough alone, is determined to take apart a perfectly functioning object with the intent of improving it then wastes time trying to get it back together again. Sometimes networkers will get to a certain level of success and think they should find a *better* way. This dangerous kind of thinking is referred to as the "idea of the month" and it is a certain way to fail in this industry. For example, sometimes would-be-leaders will attend a large group convention and listen intently to many of the industry's top leaders share their secrets of success. Thinking that they have just found the key to open the doors to success, they run back into their group and create a new game plan, changing the already successful training system. They try to reinvent the wheel.

It is counterproductive and often highly destructive. Your upline leaders want your success—sometimes more than you want it for yourself. If there is a faster way to get to the top, they are sure to let you in on it! For now, if it isn't broken, don't try to fix it!

Developing Leaders

If you are not sure how much direction people need to do a task, it's always better to oversupervise than undersupervise in the beginning. Why? Because if you find your people are better than you thought and you loosen up, they will like you and respond in a positive way. It also helps as you seek to communicate your growing respect for the quality of leadership your people are producing.

On the other hand, if you undersupervise your people and later discover their skills are not as good as you anticipated, you then have a sticky situation. Even when it is appropriate to correct or redirect their work you may find they perceive your efforts as undue criticism, micromanaging, or even perse-cution. After all, they aren't doing anything differ-ently, so why are you suddenly bent on changing things? Resentment grows.

YOUR UPLINE LEADER

Your upline leaders want your success—sometimes more than you want it for your-self. If there is a faster way to get to the top, they are sure to let you in on it! For now, if it isn't broken, don't try to fix it!

It is easier to start off leading the way and then release them as they take more and more of the responsibility. It is easier to loosen up than tighten up.

Don't Work Harder—Work Smarter

This saying is common sense but not common practice. Most people still think there is a direct relationship between the amount of work they do and success—the more time you put in, the more successful you will be. One successful entrepreneur, when asked to speak to a group of college students about what it took to be successful, said, "This will be the shortest speech in history because it is easy to be successful. All you have to do is work half a day. You can work the first twelve hours or the second."

While successful people do work hard, they think before they act. They are proactive, not just reactive. Most people mentally have a sign on their desk that reads: don't just sit there, do something! The best advice I ever received was to redo the sign to read: don't just do something, sit there—sit there and think. Planning and preparation makes for efficient effort and pays in the long-term scheme of things. But remember, don't use planning as an excuse for inactivity. Planning should move you to action.

If you don't take time out to think, strategize, and prioritize, you will work a whole lot harder, without enjoying the benefits of a job smartly done.

The Door Opener

Commitment opens the door to achievement. As a leader, you will face plenty of obstacles and opposition, if you don't already. And there will be times when commitment is the only thing that carries you forward. Decide what kind of person you are and what kind of person you want to become. We all know people who fall in one of the following categories:

> a cop-out—a person who has no goals and does not commit;
> a holdout—a person who doesn't know if they can reach their goals so they're afraid to commit;
> a dropout—a person who gets started toward a goal but quits when the going gets tough;
> an all-out—a person who sets goals, commits to them, and pays the price to reach them.

Commitment is the enemy of resistance for it is the serious promise to press on, to get up no matter how many times you are knocked down. If you want to get anywhere worthwhile, you must be committed.

Performance Pays

People who produce good results feel good about themselves. It is in the doing that we feel successful, long before the goal is attained. When people produce good results, they feel good about themselves because they know they have done a good job and they have something to show for their effort. A good leader will make sure her people know what their objectives are.

Make sure people know what their goals are. Do everything possible to support, encourage, and coach them to accomplish those goals. Promote your upline's training system and teaching tools. Your role as a leader is even more important than you might imagine. You have the power to help people become winners.

> **FOUR WAYS TO GET PEAK PERFORMANCE FROM OTHERS**
>
> 1. Look for what is right in people and praise them for it.
> 2. Give sincere praise for specific performance.
> 3. Give honest praise immediately.
> 4. Encourage people to keep it up!

Praise the Praiseworthy

"Growing up wasn't easy. I was always being put down, told I wasn't good enough," says Jane. "What drew me into network marketing in the beginning was the feelings I came away with after meeting with my sponsor. She encouraged me—told me I could do this business. What a contrast that was to the messages I was hearing at home!"

People crave recognition and appreciation—acknowledgement of a job done well. Too often in offices across the country the opposite is taking place. Employees, stifled by a power-driven management, are being acknowledged only when they are seen making the smallest mistakes. From work rooms to courtrooms, from offices to classrooms around the world, people are crying out for an honest compliment—a pat on the back for their effort and accomplishments. Leaders understand that. Good leaders will recognize their people often, sometimes looking for the good things they do and choosing to overlook their shortcomings. "My sponsor told me over and over again, you can do it, Jane! She said it so many times that eventually even I believed her," she adds.

Look for what is right in your people, both up and downline, and praise them for it. Give sincere praise for specific performance. In other words, saying thanks for everything is meaningless. If you say "great job" to a poor performer and "great job" to a good performer, you sound ridiculous to the poor performer and you demotivate the good one.

Give honest and sincere praise immediately. Make it specific. Encourage people to keep it up and they will have their dreams. It is a marvelous way to interact with and affirm the people in your life.

Try it at home with your kids, your friends, and your parents. Watch what happens.

Mission Statements

Knowing where you're going is the first step in getting there. Creating your own personal mission statement is an important exercise that has helped others define who they are, identify priorities, and keep a perspective on target. It involves identifying your passions.

Develop your own personal mission statement. It should be filled with positive affirmations of who you are, what you are becoming, accomplishing, and achieving. Once you have it written down, read it out loud at least three times a day until you memorize it. Then keep it up. You will find, as many great leaders have found, that repeating positive statements about yourself moves you in the direction to actually become that person.

Great Leaders Are Great Servers

The flock is not there for the sake of the shepherd. The shepherd is there for the sake of the flock. The greatest leaders I have personally known were the greatest servers. By serving others we become humble. In our humility we are more teachable. By being teachable we are open to learning, to expanding our knowledge and understanding. As we continue to learn and grow, we evolve into the very leaders we serve. We now have become the example, the one to follow. We hold the mantle, and by our example others will learn to serve, follow, and develop into leaders themselves. Thus we continue to create strength in our business as well as our world.

Positive Thinking Pays!

"A positive attitude can make you rich!" says Rebecca Smith. "People are drawn to a positive person. It's kind of a magnet of sorts. I can tell immediately what a person's attitude is. A great attitude is reflected in everything they do, everything they touch. You can see it in the expression on their face, the look in their eyes. It is in their body language, the way they stand or the spring in their walk. We speak a strong language that the human ear can't hear. People want to be with others that make them feel good."

Rebecca says that a positive attitude will not only attract others to you, but will help you do things you never imagined you would be able to do. "I started riding horses when I was 5 and by the time I was 12, I was working as a trainer. I later ran a huge operation with horses that sold in excess of $150,000. As a successful horse trainer for many years, I imagined that would be what I'd do for the rest of my life. But when the owners of the land decided to sell, my lease was up!" she adds. "I went to visit my brother in Florida to sort of re-group and while I was there I went to the Cypress Gardens in Orlando. As I watched those magnificent ski shows, I knew right then that was what I wanted to do as a career. Only one problem—I didn't live in Orlando and I didn't know how to ski!" laughs Rebecca. She began to learn the importance of a positive mental attitude and as she approached the manager of the show, she told him that performing in Cypress Gardens was her dream in life. "He told me to come back when I learned to ski," says Rebecca. "He probably thought he'd never hear from me again."

POSITIVE PEOPLE

People with a great attitude get things done. They just naturally see the best in others—the best in any situation. A positive person will focus on the goal and not the obstacle—they want to win!

When Rebecca went back home, she made a deal with her father. "I'll help you on the fishing boats," she said, "And at the end of the day, you pull me behind the boat while I learn to ski." Rebecca says that she bummed rides off of lots of her father's friends that summer and did in fact learn to ski. She landed that job in Cypress Gardens and attributes it all to a positive mental attitude. So when she saw the network marketing opportunity, she applied the same principles of success and today she is making waves as one of the top performers in the industry.

> ### INTEGRITY
>
> Trust is an essential element in any relationship, particularly when you are trying to develop a strong and binding link between yourself and your leaders. Integrity in network marketing is everything. People will do anything for those they trust and nothing for those they don't.

People with a great attitude get things done. They just naturally see the best in others—the best in any situation. You've heard the expression, turn lemons into lemonade? Surely a positive person coined that phrase. They look for what is right, for solutions. A positive person will focus on the goal and not the obstacle—they want to win!

Many years ago a popular shoe manufacturing company sent its two best salesmen to Africa. It was a new territory for the company. Both were given shoe samples and sent on their way. Each man was to report back to the main office in two weeks. The company was surprised when after only one week both men called.

The first salesman's report was dismal. "No one wears shoes in Africa. We can't sell shoes here," he reported.

The second salesman had a much different experience. "No one wears shoes in Africa. This is the greatest place in the world to sell shoes. Everyone is buying!" he exclaimed.

Success or failure was determined by each man's outlook of the situation. Where one man saw defeat, another saw victory. Our own success is a product of our attitude. Your altitude is determined by your attitude. How high you climb up the ladder of success is in relationship to how high your attitude is. In network marketing yours needs to be up!

Get Real

Be honest with yourself. There is no pillow as soft as a clear conscience. In today's competitive environment, some leaders are tempted to abandon ethical considerations. Somehow they think that playing by the rule of "anything goes" will win for them.

These leaders are jeopardizing far more than they imagine. First of all, they stand to lose respect. The number one characteristic people say they are looking for in a leader is integrity. They also risk losing competent people. You can make a quick financial gain by taking advantage of people in traditional business, but not so in network marketing. Trust is an essential element in any relationship, particularly when you are trying to develop a strong and binding link between yourself and your leaders. Integrity in network marketing is everything. People will do anything for those they trust and nothing for those they don't.

Everything my own upline, Don Storms, has ever told me has been right. I always knew I could trust him—count on him. His integrity is what really drew me to him. Because of my trust in him, I was able to open up, reach higher, stretch further. I once questioned Don's conservative manner and teaching habits. He told me, "Cynthia, if there are ever any surprises, I want all of yours to be up!"

Thank you, Don. They always have been.

Mentors

The biggest moneymakers in network marketing tell me that they would not have made it to the level that they did if it hadn't been for their mentors. What is a mentor? A mentor is a person who has wisdom and knowledge, who has already reached the level of success you desire and is willing to help you do the same. A mentor is a guide and helps you along your path to success.

"All of the big changes in my life can be attributed to the counsel of my mentors," says Jennifer Basye Sander. "I used to work for someone else and now I work for myself. One of my mentors is Mark Victor Hansen, himself a best-selling author of the *Chicken Soup for the Soul* series and a successful network marketer. He encouraged me to succeed."

As an editor for a big publishing house, Jennifer often attended various book conferences across the country. But this one was different she tells us. "When my boss asked me to sit in on a Mark Victor Hansen and Jack Canfield seminar, *How to Build a Speaking and Writing Empire*, I thought it would be kind of hokey. I mean after all, I was a big-city girl, a sophisticated opera lover. What could I possibly get from a Mark Victor Hansen seminar? After all, didn't they write those namby-pamby books?" Jennifer wondered.

What she found out changed her life. Jennifer was pulling in a salary of $45,000 because she was great at coming up with good ideas for books—so great in fact that her ideas have generated over 15 million dollars worth of retail sales! "What's wrong with this picture?" Jennifer asks. "While at this conference I began to think. Shouldn't I be doing this on my own?" Mark's seminar gave me the nerve to do for myself what I had been doing for my company—to take a chance on me!"

Today Jennifer enjoys being a mentor for others as well. "The mentors in my life have given me a light, a torch to pass on to others. By sharing what I have learned with another person that light is being passed around. I see it as a way to bring light and beauty to the world," she says. Jennifer is a mentor for many women across the country. She has inspired others to succeed and has touched their hearts with her kindness and generosity, as she has mine.

Who are the mentors in your life? Are you seeking their counsel and following their advice? Perhaps your mentor will inspire and guide you to make choices and changes in your life that will enable you to reach the pinnacle of success. Then you can share that gift with others. Sometimes the greatest rewards in life come by helping others succeed.

SECTION FOUR

Women of Influence:
Success Stories of
Women at the Top

CHAPTER FOURTEEN

WOMEN OF INFLUENCE

Carol Waugh

As a top executive with Xerox, I thought I had it pretty good, but that all changed when my boss retired and I got the new boss from hell. After being the "princess" for the past eight years and then having this new guy come in who could find nothing right about my work, my performance, or me, I began to hate my job. I was demoralized in the corporate structure and I think that was when I started paying more attention to my good friend, Rita Davenport.

Rita was excited. She loved what she was doing with her life and her new company. She often talked to me about how great she felt about having her own business and leaving a legacy for her family—my personal hot button. After my new boss arrived at Xerox, I started listening a little better to the messages Rita was sending me, but the final straw was one morning in the spring of 1991. I walked out to the mailbox and among the huge armful of mail, I found a magazine. Right there on the cover was my good friend Rita's picture. She was in a beautiful sequined gown standing next to a grand piano. The caption read, "In perfect harmony." Rita had just hit the big time.

It was at that moment that it occurred to me, "I need to pay attention!" I knew that Xerox did not plan for me to grow old gracefully. I also knew that many women were leaving corporate America to start their own businesses, in fact over 450,000 women in 1991 alone. It was in March that I made the decision to get out of the corporate rat race and run my own race—to win!

Let me paint a picture of my life at the time. I was in a new marriage, had three kids in college and an ex-wife on the payroll, and we were in deep financial debt. I had just quit my job with Xerox and started my new enterprise. In the first 10 days I had sold over $1,500 worth of products, all from my kitchen table! I knew it was going to work.

Although the "party plan" did not appeal to me, I knew that if I was going to teach it I first had to learn it, so I went from one lady at the kitchen table to several in the living room. I started holding meetings in my living room every Monday night. My first meeting was with only one lady! We both agreed to each bring another one the following Monday and we upped our meeting to four ladies. We continued to challenge each other and grow. Soon it was like a snowball—once you get a little momentum, get the enthusiasm going— it keeps getting bigger and bigger!

By December of 1991, the company my husband worked for closed. He was a CPA and a national sales manager. Suddenly we were both working our own businesses from home. Money was really tight. We even paid some alimony payments on credit cards! Month after month we watched our debts pile higher and higher.

Around this time I read a great book, *The Power of Your Subconscious Mind*. I began to understand that what I put into my mind, I could create. I got serious about improving myself, about becoming the kind of person that attracts others. It wasn't always easy. I faced challenges just like everyone else does. I remember a particular day when I'd made my first attempt at a distance group. I drove by myself to Woodbury, Tennessee, a two-hour drive— each way. I went into the home of my new lady who had five other women there. I didn't know that she taught pre-school. There were little kids yelling and running around. And all six of these women smoked cigarettes. I had allergies and I thought I was going to die!

After a very difficult day I faced the long drive home alone. My total sales had been only $50—a small sum for over a four-hours drive and a near death experience! I started to think poor me. That's when I decided—I was building the Waugh foundation, not Xerox. I was willing to pay the price. I changed my attitude right then and there. I decided that although I only had sold $50, I had six new customers that I would be able to share more products with later. Remember—there is no one person who can make or break your business—only you!

I buckled down and got serious. I worked my business *everyday*. I used to go to work at Xerox everyday. Why wouldn't I be willing to work as hard for myself as I had for my employer? I got more and more customers and I told each one, "My job's available. In the meantime, I'd love you to be my customer."

We worked our way over that mountain of debt. It takes paying your dues. In the first few years you may seem to only be putting money back into your business, but if you will stick with it the money will come. After three years we were really bringing in substantial money and after five years we were out of debt. In fact, our beautiful home is almost paid for. We will own the title to it in four months! Then we will start building the home of our dreams in a gated community where we own land. Early on the business was difficult, but God blessed my business, my efforts. I kept on going even through the down times.

I have a great team of power women. These women and the milestones they have accomplished let me know that I've really made a difference and that feels good. Today I have over 5,000 in my team and I didn't find the majority of them. While no one person will make or break your business, find that person that will grow a big business. Every minnow knows a whale!

I learned to see people in their highest possibility. By encouraging and motivating others to do more, they begin to believe in themselves. My greatest reward is that my family, who is most important to me, is proud of me. That has always been my hot button, my reason. Timing is everything! When people are ready and the opportunity is presented—great things happen. One of my new leaders is a manicurist. Sharon is really dreaming big! She is making it happen. So is Diane Davis, a former kindergarten teacher. Women from all walks of life can be living the life they dream about if they will just get serious. Some success is luck but most of it is grit and determination. If you don't get serious, it probably won't happen for you. As I often say, "If you want to run with the big dogs, you've got to get off of the porch!"

Ruth Storms

The sound of ringing doorbells and telephones sent shudders up my back and caused my hands to shake, for I always knew it was bad news—either a bill collector on the phone or a policeman at the door. We were in financial trouble and had just moved to a new town to try to "start over." I didn't know how much more I could handle. Much to my relief, the person at the door was Dexter Yager.

Don Storms and I were married some years before in Massachusetts. Every girl dreams about that moment—her wedding day. They talk of it, plan it, and rehearse it over and over again in their minds—thinking words like pretty and perfect. But my hopes were dashed as we woke that morning to a terrible storm. In fact, this was the worst hurricane to ever hit Massachusetts. I thought there was some irony to that. Don's father was the Reverend Storms and he was to marry his son, Don Storms, and me during the worst storm we'd experienced. I thought to myself, "Well, we are certainly off to a "stormy start!" But as we managed through that day, a wonderful rainbow appeared in the sky. "Happy is the bride that is rained on," someone behind me said. This was indeed my lucky day. In our honeymoon suite, lit only by the soft glow of lanterns, Don and I dreamed of our future together. We talked of many things that first wonderful night together. I don't remember any mention of doorbells and bill collectors.

When Dexter rang the doorbell that night and came into our home, I did not see that he offered an answer to our financial woes, but Don did. We had never had much financial success in our lives. Don traveled, often for weeks at a time, singing at different churches across the East. Back home I canned vegetables from the garden, stored frozen food, and learned how to stretch a soup bone into three meals. Often we would go several weeks without any money. Dinner was often soup, but somehow Don always managed to make things work. So although I did not want to have anything to do with this business at first, I trusted Don. He saw the benefit of this business, and he was not afraid of hard work. If it was hard work that would make success for us, I believed Don Storms could do it. I supported him, and so we began.

I was a terribly shy person then. I still am shy today. I did, however, believe in supporting my husband. When I realized that by doing little things in this business I was pleasing Don, it made me feel very happy. But it took a lot for me to do some things. One particular day Don had asked me to call some of the ladies in our business. Oh, how I dreaded it. I was terrified and I did not want to do it. I felt my hands shaking as I reached for the phone. I hurriedly dialed the number and as the woman on the other end of the line said hello, I tried to calm my heart and talk. Out of the corner of my eye, I saw Don standing in the doorway. The look of love in his eyes was priceless. I began to notice at other times the way he looked at me when I would reach out of my comfort zone to help him or someone in our business. This was worth every ounce of my effort.

It is so interesting to me now as I look back on it. Most of the things I feared doing in the beginning I now love. At first, I could never have imagined standing before an audience of women and sharing my feelings with them. Yet now, some of the most rewarding moments have been as I have shared my own learning experiences with other women and seen the look in their eyes as they began to believe in themselves, perhaps for the first time. There was a time that I didn't even want to go to parties. I didn't think I had anything to say to anyone. Now, when I began to give from my heart to others, I find I am able to affect other people's hearts in a positive way. I have learned that you are able to do things you never imagined you could do—and love it!

In the beginning, I kept finding excuses not to build this business. I had children to care for, church meetings to go to, and vegetable gardens to tend. This would keep me so busy that everyone would understand I simply did not have time to build the business. We did not get off to a fast start in the business, but when we finally did get going, we doubled Don's income. For our family, that meant so much. The feeling of security for me was indescribable. Every month the bills were paid. On time! We were able to provide music lessons for the children and have some fun adult toys, like a motor home, for Don and I to enjoy with our family. No more did I fear the ringing of the telephone. Now when the doorbell rang, it meant that a friend was calling on us. The feeling of dread was gone! The sense of satisfaction of accomplishing this flowed over into our lives and into everything we did. Eventually we were enjoying a lifestyle beyond our expectations.

This is not to say that we did not have struggles. Some of the most challenging and difficult times were yet to come. The hardest struggle of my life started with a phone call from our oldest son, Wesley. He was away at college at the time. When the phone rang that afternoon, the voice on the other end was not the usual one of our sweet boy but a sad one. "Mom, Dad, I am sick." Later, when Wesley was diagnosed as terminally ill, we were devastated with the knowledge that we would soon lose him. Your children are not supposed to die before you. How does one prepare for this? I felt such pain in my heart I thought it would break in half. I felt as if I were suffocating. I wondered how I could go on breathing. Through all of this heartache and the loss of my sweet son, I held tight to Don and to my other three children, Lee, Gail, and Brenda.

In our society today, many people, especially women, feel so alone, helpless, and abandoned. They often find themselves searching for associations and relationships that are meaningful, lasting, REAL. When you lose someone that you love, it can shake your world right down to the very core. Because I had reached out of myself to others, in my time of great need, I had many others who reached back to me, circling me in their love, holding me up while things around me fell apart. I was not alone. Perhaps because of the love and support of these wonderful friends, I decided that I could either let my broken world fall apart or I could pick up the pieces and build something beautiful. And we did.

Last month Don and I stood on the very college campus where we had fallen in love. We held hands once again and walked under the cool shade of the elm trees, up those same steps where we had walked so many times before. Life was so much different for us now. We were invited to the college that day as guests of honor for a groundbreaking ceremony to celebrate the building of a new library. As the primary financial donors to this multimillion dollar project, Don and I were honored guest speakers and were ushered through row after row of students, faculty, and dignitaries, all in attendance for this special event. I told those bright young students to follow their hearts and not listen to those who would tell them, "It can't be done." Anything is possible to those who believe.

Today when the doorbell rings, I welcome it. The mere sound of it creates a feeling of expectation, for I know it is a friend, a family member, or often a bouquet of flowers. And if you are willing to follow your heart, in every storm there is a rainbow.

Sheri Sharman

I believe that all of my blessings—my health, my abilities, and my enthusiasm—are gifts from God, and therefore are things I must share. To that end, I am willing to work tirelessly, and many times anonymously, to help others achieve their goals of success. I travel constantly to help others set up their goals of success. I also travel to help others set up meetings and to conduct real life interactive marketing seminars, because I know from experience how the right training can dramatically improve someone's life.

And I am rarely more than a phone call away from helping someone, because it wasn't that long ago that I was the one in need. After a tough divorce, I found myself a single mom with mounting debt and little resources. I worked as a pre-school teacher, a job that I loved, but one that left me in fear of not being able to survive financially. I knew I had better change something in my life if my life was ever going to change for the better. So I explored network marketing. With hard work and incredible perseverance, I achieved my first real taste of financial freedom.

Unfortunately, it turned out to be somewhat bitter. I found that despite all the external trappings of success, I wasn't happy inside. I felt the company I was with at the time had incredible integrity issues. So I did what those who are only interested in material success would consider unthinkable—I walked away from a seven-figure income in search of a company that believed in the moral priorities of God, family, and then career.

I finally found what I was looking for—a network marketing company with integrity. I think network marketing is a gift from God. And since the day I finally found the answer to my prayers, network marketing, my work ethic and commitment to help others succeed has propelled me through some hard times and into the top income brackets at a near record pace. I give credit for my fast results to my upline leaders. They helped, trained, and inspired me every step of the way.

My newfound success has afforded me some time to spend on the things that matter most to me. Some include quiet talks with God, a day at the lake skateboarding with my son, Eric. Lunches with my mother and best friend, Imo, and candlelit dinners with my boyfriend, Rob. Rollerblading along the

San Diego beaches with my friend, Stephanie, and conversations with the friends and family in my business that I believe in and hold so dear. It's a lifestyle that may not interest someone purely focused on achieving the outward glitter of worldly success, but in the heart of these remarkable network marketing women, they are the most valuable things on earth.

Deborah Jones

The last thing I was looking for in January of 1995 was another business. At the time I ran a fairly large sales and marketing business for the mortgage industry, as well as a large direct mail order business associated with that field. My very humble beginnings grew into a significant and thriving enterprise and my husband, Doug, and I feel very blessed. Success did not come without a price however. I was on the road for almost 200 days of the year. The year before I left the industry I made 2.6 million dollars, but I was a prisoner of income. I created a life where my business owned me. If earning a living is costing you your life—what's the point?

Having spent the better part of the last 20 years working in the mortgage business, if someone had told me in 1994 that the next year, 1995, I would become a strong advocate for natural health, I would not have believed it. But if they told me I would be doing this in the network marketing arena, I would have told them they were crazy! But that was before I experienced a miracle with my youngest child.

I have two wonderful children. My oldest is my daughter, Joy. My youngest is my son, Andrew, and he's the one who's had health challenges. From the time Andrew was born until he was 6½ years old, he had a chronic intestinal and colon disorder. I won't bore you with all the technical details of his situation, but the long and short of it was that ever since Andrew was born his body didn't give another part of his body the message that he should have a bowel movement. Consequently, he would go for extended periods of time without having a solid waste elimination from his body. The longest amount of time he went was 21 days. You might imagine the health challenges a situation like that can present. A chain of health problems are created.

During Andrew's first four years of life, my husband, Doug, and I took Andrew to the doctors repeatedly about his situation. As his parents, we just knew something wasn't right. Over and over again we kept hearing the same uninformed answers. "Well, you know everyone's body is a little bit different and that's probably just normal for Andrew," the doctors would say. And we would be sent home again and again, trying to care for this very sick little boy.

When Andrew was 4 years old, his condition worsened and he finally captured the attention of the medical community. This began a year of Andrew being under medical care with numerous tests being conducted. At the end of a year, our doctor still wasn't real sure what was causing Andrew's problem.

That brings us up to the end of 1994. In November of '94 a friend of mine that I've known for over 10 years, Mark Victor Hansen, was speaking at a conference for me in Mexico. You may have heard of Mark. He is the *New York Times* best-selling co-author of the *Chicken Soup for the Soul* series. Doug and I were talking to Mark about Andrew's condition and we hoped he might know something we could try.

And he did! Since that day in November of 1994, our lives have never been the same. The first week I put Andrew on a fiber and herbal combination, within 24 hours of taking this, Andrew's body started to work and he had a normal bowel movement.

After spending years, and thousands of dollars, trying to get medical treatment for my son to relieve his problem, thirty-five dollars worth of what some would call home remedies fixed his problem. It also put me on a crusade!

No one should have to suffer what my little boy suffered. I've committed myself to informing as many people as I possibly can about the benefits of natural approaches to health and well-being. I know there are a lot of people out there in the general public, just like I used to be, that are completely ignorant as to what medicinal herbs can do for them or someone they love. No one should have to go through what Andrew did as long as there are options—and there are options!

As you might imagine, my husband, Doug, and I learned everything we could about the products and the company that had helped my son back to health, but when I found out that they came from a network marketing company, I almost blew up! I am glad I listened to the entire business plan because listening has changed my life.

Well, that's how it all began for us—first with Andrew—then with understanding the benefits of network marketing to us. In these past short years, I have found that everything Mark told me that first day was 100 percent true. Think about it for a moment . . . How many times during the course of the week do you hear people say things like, "My job is killing me. I can't believe all the stress I'm under." Or people might say, "I'm so tired. There doesn't seem like enough hours in the day to get everything done." Ever hear things like that? Sure you have. All the time!

Not everyone has a little boy at home with a health challenge like I did. Their issue may be time poverty, a stress-laden work environment, not getting paid what they are worth, corporate downsizing, under-employment, no quality of life, being a prisoner of income—the list could go on and on. Network marketing has answers for all of these challenges.

From ground zero, never having been involved in network marketing before, my husband and I reached a level of success that most professionals dream of, and in a field we'd never even worked in before. And we did it without a major capital investment or expensive overhead.

For the first time in more than a decade we found ourselves free from the prison of income. Our income was no longer based solely on our performance. Network marketing is the best business model there is. It's based on cooperation, no competition and that totally changes your world of work and the way that your revenue comes to you. Although the monetary rewards are wonderful, that's not the best part. The best part is that we found ourselves having fun again. In our other business, which was stress laden, the money was so good that it was hard to imagine anything else being able to be as lucrative so we kept saying to ourselves, "Hang in there. Next year will be better. We'll have more time for ourselves, more time for our kids, more time to just relax." Well guess what? Things don't just get better unless you make a change and network marketing has afforded us the opportunity to make that change. If you have ever wished that there was a way that you could have both time and money freedom, I would urge you to seriously look at network marketing. Over 90 percent of people in network marketing are female. The opportunities are endless for women.

As a successful networker, Ken Pontious, once said, "A year from now you'll be saying one of two things. Either you'll be saying you're glad you did, or you wish you had." Don't let this be one of those golden opportunities that you let slip through your fingers. The time has never been better for you to join and if you pick a great company and work their system diligently, you won't be sorry.

Gloria Mayfield

I was born in Detroit, Michigan, the third of four daughters. My parents worked hard and expected us to do the same. They worked so we could attend college and we all did. I went to Howard University and then on to Harvard for graduate school. With an MBA from Harvard, I went right into a corporate job with IBM. In my first three years with IBM, I was top sales person. I was ambitious and hardworking. I earned everything I got. Then I got pregnant with twins. I had a high-risk pregnancy and took a leave from work. I lost the twins at five months. I was heartbroken. That was in August. By October I was expecting again, but lost that baby only four months later.

IBM had taken my territory, which I understood, because I had been gone for three months with the last baby. But when I returned, they had moved me to finance—which I had no training, experience, or ambition for. That was a tough one. As a black female I had always known what it meant to work hard and I wasn't afraid of work. But I really had to fight to get a territory in the sales department. I eventually did get my own territory, but things were never the same and I was unhappy and unsure of my future.

I took a job with Stratus Computers. I was a top manager in the company, mainly because of my education at Harvard and my success with IBM, but I still felt the struggle of my gender and my race. I had done everything they told me to do. I got the best education and I had some of the best jobs in corporate America that you could have—but I was miserable. The reality is that corporate America can be a mean, unhappy place. It's filled with a lot of lonely people having to pretend they like each other when they really don't. I loved sales. I was great in sales, but I wanted to get out of the corporate rat race and I didn't know how. I certainly never dreamed it would be with direct sales and network marketing.

It all began when my girlfriend who lived two doors down from me invited me to come over to her house for a skin care class. I agreed to join her and I really had a good time. I also liked the products. She invited me to get involved in the business with her. Let me paint a picture for you of my life at that time—I worked 60-70 hours a week with a one-hour commute every day—each way. By this time I had two small kids at home. I hired live-in help as I left my home each morning at 6:30 and returned 13 hours later around 7:30 at night, exhausted and stressed out. And if that weren't enough to break superwoman, I was in the middle of a very nasty divorce. My husband, a Harvard graduate himself, was being difficult through the divorce and my life was truly more stressful than most people could have imagined or survived.

I did agree to get involved—first for the extra money. But what really drew me in and what really kept me in was the recognition, acceptance, and the opportunity to impact women's lives. I knew that there were a lot of hurting women out there, women just like me who had children to raise and mortgages to meet who needed the money that they could have in this industry, as well as a safe environment that was uplifting and positive. Money, success, and positive relationships—who could beat that combination?

I changed jobs about that time and went to work for Harvard Business School, becoming the Assistant Director of Admissions. While working full time at Harvard and raising two kids as a single parent, I still built a half million dollar network marketing business that year.

I just buckled down and focused. I worked hard, but I also chose sharp women to work with. These women were like-minded—they all wanted the same things I did—to be a role model for our kids and other people and to empower women to create financial independence for themselves. I quit my job at Harvard and I have been in pursuit of excellence and helping other women to achieve it.

Many women are realizing that corporate America is not all it's cracked up to be. Many are tired of inflexible hours that make raising children a stressful, guilt-ridden challenge; many are fed up with corporate ethics and yearn for work that is more value-based and fulfilling. With network marketing women can achieve what they really want—which for most of us is a higher income base, financial security, more flexible work hours, and more time with our families. And maybe equally important—to be really recognized and rewarded for the hard work we do. The opportunities with this industry have done that for me. The same opportunity awaits each of you. Dreams really do come true.

Marion Culhane

Because of my 20 years of professional growth and experience as a seminar leader of the subject of "Letting Go of Limited Beliefs," I have never doubted for a moment that my partner and I would be successful in network marketing. I was committed from the very beginning. I was ready to allow it to happen. In fact, I didn't find my business—it found me!

Let me tell you how it all began. My background is in the nursing field. As a nurse I was committed to help people and was concerned with their well-being. My life has always been devoted to helping others improve the quality of their lives. I had been teaching personal growth seminars for several years and in fact was on a retreat in Oregon with a good friend of mine. My friend had been suffering through menopause and was raving about a new product that had relieved her of the terrible hot flashes common to many women. She gave me a tape about these products and I listened to it on my drive back home from the retreat.

I also started taking the products that my friend recommended. Within three days after I started on the products, my own menopause symptoms, including the terrible hot flashes, went away! It was simply amazing. When you have these kinds of incredible results, you can't help but get excited about it! Needless to say I was sold!

I became a serious student of network marketing. I read a book every week on the industry and listened to an audiocassette every time I was in my car—about 6 tapes a week. I listened to these tapes over and over again until they really sunk in and I felt confident that I knew how to approach and teach others.

Then I developed a list of names, over 200 names of friends and acquaintances who I wanted to share the business with, and I called about four new people everyday as well. I told them that I was involved with a new business and that people were having great success in improving their health with the company's products. I told them I would like to send them some information about the business opportunity and products. Then I would send them the stuff and follow up within a few days to check on their interest level and either sign them up or get them on the products.

I always tried to meet people on their level, but I dedicate my time to working with sincere business builders. I found out that by talking to 10 people a day for 10 days in a row a snowball effect will start. If you have ever built a snowman you know what I mean. You may start out in the beginning with only a small handful of snow. You grab it tight, packing it into a tight ball, then you drop it into a pile of fresh snow and start rolling it around, picking up more snow with each turn. The more times you turn the snowball over, the bigger it gets. The bigger it gets, the more snow it picks up with each turn. Soon that tiny handful of snow is a huge snowman.

Network marketing is the same way. The quicker you talk to people and the more "turns" or contacts you make, the bigger and faster your business will grow. Soon just one more call creates an enormous growth cycle for you.

Within seven months of starting our business, my partner, Louis (who had his Ph.D.), and I were making a five-figure income. At the end of our first year, I was pulling in a strong six-figure income. We have an amazing group of people—a great team! Today we are enjoying an incredible lifestyle. Everything you do in this business is a win/win opportunity. Enjoy the journey and have fun! The payoff for helping people is fantastic. It is great friendships, fun, and financial freedom. I have never been involved in any endeavor that's been as deeply satisfying as network marketing.

Laura McClure

I think my story is a bit different from the majority of other women who start their own network marketing business. It has been my experience that most women, who get involved, do it for the money. Either they want out of a job, or they don't want to get one outside of the home. When I got involved with network marketing I did not need the money. I was a stay-at-home mom, wife of a very successful dentist, who lived a comfortable lifestyle. So, you may be wondering, "Why did you get involved?" Well, it's a good story and I'll start at the beginning.

I met my husband when I was only 18 years old. He was already in his dental practice and 8 years my senior. When we married I continued to help him build up his practice and for over 10 years I ran everything in his office, without pay. I didn't take a salary because I wanted to help him and I felt I was helping to create our future. Plus, I had plenty of money for the necessities of life anyway.

Mark, my husband, was a great dentist, but I was the one that made it all work. From scheduling appointments, to paying bills, to hiring and firing of employees—I did it all. Mark got the credit! I mean to say that I did everything behind the scenes. I was quiet and efficient. He showed up and did the dental work and got the recognition, appreciation, and credit for a successful dental practice. I got nothing—except the personal satisfaction of a job well done. But again, that was Ok with me. I wanted to help Mark and I believed in his dream.

When we decided to start a family I wanted to be at home to raise my kids. We have two wonderful children that we dearly love. So I became a great at-home mom. Running an efficient household and taking care of my kids. I knew I did a good job as a parent, but I just never really gave myself credit for anything. I didn't see myself as of much value. My job was to make my husband's dream come true—not mine! I didn't even know what mine was.

So there I was, an at-home mom, overweight and under appreciated. I had gained an extra 15 pounds that I never could seem to get off and I am sure this contributed to my lack of self-esteem. I had thyroid problems and had been up and down. I began to notice the weight changes of my neighbor,

Stephanie, but hers were down not up! Stephanie seemed to be thinner every time I saw her. In fact, she lost over 140 pounds! I wanted to know how. She told me she had been taking these great weight loss products and after being very overweight for much of her life, she had shed those pounds and created a successful business at the same time. I quickly agreed to try her products and in November I started. It was hard to lose those 15 pounds but I kept thinking about Stephanie's 140-pound loss! By January I had dropped them all and in the meantime had gone to several nutritional classes and was taking lots of vitamins that Stephanie suggested.

People were noticing my new look too. Many of my friends were asking me how I had dropped those extra pounds and telling me how great I looked. I sent eight people down to Stephanie's house to buy products before I realized that I was giving away money. It isn't that I needed the money, but I understood the business world and I knew that I could make a business of my own with these great products. So I began! I got customers and followed up with them on a regular basis. I truly cared about them, their health and success, and they knew it. Soon I was able to teach them the advantages of becoming a distributor. Then they started making money of their own. It was great!

I loved helping other people. Because I didn't really need the money, I wasn't afraid to give it away to help others. It has come back to me tenfold because I didn't look at myself first, my wants and needs, but looked instead at how I could make a difference in someone else's life. One of the best rewards was that finally I was doing something for myself—by myself. This was my own business and I was good at it! This business was just for me. I got recognition for it—even if it was just the customers loving me because I had helped them improve their health. It was a wonderful feeling to be appreciated and respected by others.

If I can build a successful network marketing business, anyone can. Sure, I was great at running Mark's office—but I didn't have to talk to people either. I was a pretty shy and quiet person. I've never been outgoing or outwardly friendly and I don't meet strangers well, but I did it anyway and you can too. One of the best things I did was hire help. I did this early on because

I knew that I'd need some help if I was going to make this business work and still maintain my values as a wife and mother. I didn't want to sacrifice my kids for the money because I didn't need the money. I understand that is not the case for many women. I hired help so that I could have time to do what I did best—take care of my kids and talk to people about the products and business. Someone else could do the paperwork, housework, and answer the phones. It really freed me up.

After about one year in business something happened. It was a real turning point for me that day. Mark came home one day and said that he wanted to open up another practice. He wanted me to come and run it, from the ground up. I knew what that meant—I'd have to quit my networking company to do it. That happened to be on a weekend when I had a big conference to attend. I went to this meeting and listened to the stories of successful people. It seemed they were speaking just to me. I came back from that weekend knowing I needed to solve my problem. I had to decide whether to stick with my dream, or drop it to build Mark's. I chose to stick with my dream and yet still encourage my husband to pursue his. I chose to not give up on my own business—not give up on my dreams. I am so glad I did.

Now, four years later, Mark's new practice is still not paying for itself—mine is earning a whopping five-figure income month after month! Women are good in this industry. They are natural networkers—now they get paid for it. While women lead the numbers in network marketing, they still aren't at the top of the pay scale. One reason is that when they get in, get focused and get going, they make money. When the money starts piling up their previously uninterested husbands wake up and decide that this is a pretty great little business after all. By this time the women, who have worked hard—and often alone—to reach the pinnacle of success, are grateful for any amount of help their husbands are willing to offer. Then what started as their wives' business, soon becomes their own. But most of these successful companies were started and built by very enterprising, dedicated women.

Network marketing offers a world of opportunity for everyone—especially women. While I am certainly not at the top of the income-earning bracket, I still earn a big five-figure income and it just keeps growing! Many women earn in a year what I bring in every month. The income opportunity is definitely here, but perhaps there are others, like me, who will find network marketing a much more rewarding business that just the paycheck. They will find, like myself, a rich reward in helping others, in giving and sharing and they will also enjoy the "benefit package" offered through this type of business of recognition and appreciation. Whatever women are looking for, they probably will find it through network marketing.

Saana Benzakour

I am twenty-six years old, but I started in network marketing when I was only twenty. I guess I have always been an entrepreneur of sorts. I think I follow my father's example. My parents were born in Morocco and immigrated to Canada in the '70s. My father was always in a business of his own, usually the clothing industry. Both of my parents taught me by example to work hard. I was the oldest of four daughters. We spent our summers in Morocco visiting our grandparents and other family members. Our parents wanted to keep our culture alive, our language and our relationships fresh.

In school I studied only French. At home we spoke Arabic. I grew up in the suburbs. All of my neighbors were business owners and all were from different countries. We had Greeks, Italians, and Jewish friends. All of the children of these families spoke their native language of course, but all of them also spoke English. I was the only kid that didn't speak English. I wanted to know what my friends were saying so I taught myself English—by watching the *Cosby Show* and *Family Ties*.

My parents worked hard to provide a good life for us. We weren't spoiled, but we didn't lack for anything either. We wore very nice clothes, enjoyed a good life, and vacationed. I worked from the age of 13 part-time, at first in my father's store and later in other retail clothing stores. I went to the University and studied political science. This is where I met Patrice, my husband. He was 3 years older and much different from me. We soon became best friends.

I despised the subway and so every morning I would catch a ride to the University with my mother as she made her way to work. One particularly cold winter morning as we drove through the early morning traffic, I was struck by a thought that made such an impression on me as to change the way I looked at life. There we were, driving along, listening to the radio. I was looking out the window at the other cars and drivers. The air outside was so cold that the exhaust from the cars made billowing clouds against the chill of the winter air. As I looked at those people I thought, "Everyday these same people drive along these same roads. They all breathe the same dirty air. They fight their way through this traffic to the same jobs. They are probably all even listening to the same radio station! And they do this for 40 years. Not me! This is not the life that I want for myself."

So when my younger sister told me about a new business she was involved in, I listened. She invited me to a meeting and I went along and even took a friend. Both my friend and I signed up that very night. Although I was very young, I knew that network marketing offered a much better lifestyle than anything I had available to me. My friend didn't really do much with the business, but I did. That first year was an important growing experience for me. In fact I can honestly say that I learned more about business and success that first year of network marketing than I learned in my entire schooling years.

Because I was young and still a college student, I didn't have the confidence to approach successful people yet, so most of my recruits were young college students like myself. After that first year I gained the confidence to talk to Patrice about my business. He was my "hottest" prospect you might say. He got involved with me and we began to learn to work together. We married and continued to work towards our dream of building a big network company and having financial success.

However, as newly married couples often find, their money doesn't always last for the entire month. Patrice and I were broke. Now remember, I had lived with my parents until I married. They provided very well for us and I always had everything I needed and much of what I wanted. One of the things that every girl enjoys is nice clothes, and at home I had a lot of them. After I married, I was on a strict budget and it was very painful! I wore the same clothes for two years. We both worked odd jobs to get us through because we knew in our hearts that network marketing was the career path we wanted to follow. We made many sacrifices for our business. We invested in training material and seminars. Once we even slept in our car so we could go to a conference. We couldn't afford the ticket to the conference and a hotel room. We did without other things too because we believed in our dreams.

Patrice began to investigate other networking plans to see if we could perhaps find one that was better suited to our goals and personalities. We wanted something that was new, something that was high tech. We were so excited when we finally found the answer to our dreams. We began to talk to our friends and associates and everywhere we went we had our antennas out, listening to people and collecting business cards. We brought a few hundred people to that first big conference and now, only a few months later, we have over 2,000 people in our network. It is so exciting! I have never had so much fun in my life. And we've only just begun!

We are not techies. We don't know that much about computers, but we know enough to know that we are going to be using them more and more. The Internet makes everything possible by streamlining and quickening the pace and the way we do business. We have been able to save a lot of time by using the phones, fax, and e-mail to communicate with our people. We use conference calls and Web broadcasts for training. Recently we had a huge conference in Florida. Many people couldn't have made that trip from Canada to Florida. The company brought the conference to them. By simulcast event through satellite technology people in Canada could be part of the Florida conference. And for those who couldn't attend the satellite broadcast, they could view it online at their own computers. It's a great, new world out there and for people with a dream, who have vision, it's going to be a great life ahead for them.

As for Patrice and I, we are very happy. Our business is growing so fast and the momentum is picking up everyday. We are in a position to start thinking about a family. I wanted children but didn't want to do what I had seen other mothers forced to do—drag sleeping babies from their warm beds. Pour cereal down their mouths and shove them into their little snowsuits before packing them into the car for the morning commute to the day care. Then coming home at night exhausted, hurry and cook supper, wash clothes, do homework, and fall into bed only to pull yourself back out again to repeat the frustration of the previous day.

Network marketing brings families back together. Business builders can create a lifestyle where they can spend more time with the kids. They have the money to meet their financial needs—and then some. Their quality of life is improved. To women everywhere I say, "Stop the insanity!" Get out of the rat race and get back to your dreams.

Dreams really do come true. When I told my parents that I was choosing network marketing as a career and would not be continuing my education, I knew they were disappointed. My father never said no, or tried to get me to do anything different, but I felt he wanted me to get my masters or Ph.D. When I would come home to visit, we would sit around the table at dinner, my younger sisters talking on and on about school, about their report cards and my parents would praise them. Part of me wanted that praise too. One day I went to see my father. I brought with me several magazine articles that had been published recently about me and about my success with network marketing. I handed them to my father and said, "Here father are my report cards." As he read each one a big smile came on his face and I knew he was proud of me. That meant more to me than anything.

I thank God everyday for my blessings, for my family, especially my husband, Patrice, and for this great business of network marketing that allows me to live my dreams.

Laura Kall

I graduated from college in 1992. I was 22 years old when my dad began to give me the "wake up call." He would come into my bedroom at 5 a.m. and shout, "You've got to get up and get the train!" I am definitely *NOT* a morning person and this was absolute torture for me. But my father wanted me to understand that unless I made some better choices for my future, this is the life I would get every morning for the rest of my life. I had already begun the interview process for a number of companies, trying to find one that would offer me the most advantages.

I was 22, but looked like I was 17. I had a magna cum laude business degree from the State University of New York at Binghamton, but I had no business experience. I wished I were someone else—older and male—so that people would take me seriously. After going to several interviews and seeing the reality of most starting companies, I decided that working for someone else was never going to pay me what I was worth.

I decided to investigate the company my parents were involved with. I started a couple of weeks after graduating from college. Now someone might imagine that because my parents were already successful in network marketing, my road to success would be easy—not so! By the time I joined them in business, my parents had already retired with a downline organization of hundreds of thousands of people. They had already talked with every person that I had ever known in my life. I had to start from scratch! Plus, I didn't have the business expertise or the credibility that my parents had. I knew network marketing worked, my parents were living examples of success, but would it work for me? I decided that instead of focusing on all of the things I didn't have, or on my weaknesses, I'd focus on my strengths. I made an inventory of them—friendly, outgoing, not afraid to talk to people.

Then I started doing what my father had already taught me. I'd get up at 5 a.m. and take the train to Manhattan. I'd stop people right on the street. I knew I'd find some who were open-minded enough to listen to me, and I did! I didn't get many no's. I think it is because I wasn't threatening. I'd walk up to a complete stranger and tap him on the shoulder and say, "Excuse me, can

I ask you a quick question?" some would say "Yes" and some of them would walk right past me.

To those who said "Yes" I'd explain: "I know this is totally crazy but I'm expanding a business in this area, and if it didn't jeopardize what you're doing now, and had tremendous income potential—would you give me your business card, so I could send you some information?" I found that if I said that over and over again, I'd get plenty of cards. I used to be able to collect 20 cards in one hour. I literally couldn't have gotten a better response if I'd have placed a full-page ad in *USA Today*. I was determined to win and I didn't care what price I had to pay for success. I worked hard but unlike many traditional businesses, I never had to compromise my values to reach the top.

As a top leader, I had the opportunity to be very much involved in a new company, a sister company based around technology and the Internet. I immediately knew I wanted to be involved. First of all, I knew anything these successful entrepreneurs would start would turn to gold, and second I knew that more wealth will be created on the Internet than any other industry in my lifetime.

Experts predict there will be 327 million people on the Internet by the year 2000 and that ultimately *TRILLIONS* of dollars will be spent online as people change their buying habits from shopping in traditional retail stores to shopping on-line in stores. I see this business as a 10 billion dollar company in the not so distant future, so you can bet I'm out there working! My family continues to earn an outrageous amount of money each month based on a sales organization that was started 14 years ago. This is the same future I see for the leaders-to-be in the e-commerce arena.

Network marketing has changed substantially thanks to the technology now available to help us make better use of our time. For example, thanks to live teleconference calls, I don't have to be out on the road every night doing meetings like I used to do. I can now be in hundreds of cities at once. This also makes it easier for new reps, who may not have the confidence in the beginning, to get started by using the credibility of their leaders through this technology.

When people ask me how I created a business group of over 10,000 people, I tell them, "One person at a time." I make more money in one month than most people make in a year. I am not saying that to brag, only to illustrate the power of network marketing and the potential it offers women. I love being at home with the kids and my husband. The fact that I am building a multimillion dollar business without having to get dressed up every morning and fight that commute to the office and work in a stressful environment is great! Instead I get to work in a relaxed environment and work around the schedule I set. I love not having a boss. I love the flexibility of working from home. I don't understand why more people don't work from home. It's great, especially for parents.

My day usually starts around 9 AM. I wake up "naturally." I play with my 2 and 4 year old and then take my 4 year old to pre-school. When I get home I get on the phones for about 4 hours a day. That's what I love about this business. Most of what I do is convenient and is done over the phone in a casual and friendly manner. Later in the afternoon I go to the gym, play golf or play with my 2 year old, then pick up my 4 year old from school. In the evening I have dinner with my husband and kids, spend quality time with the family until the kids go to bed, and then spend some time talking with my group leaders or new prospects for a couple of hours. Network marketing has allowed me to have the freedom I wanted and live the lifestyle I dreamed about. And the greatest thing is—anyone can do it!

Shelleen Vallenty

As I look out across my yard, I see the leaves on the trees swaying against the gentle breeze and feel the warmth of the sun on my face. The laughter of my children floats through the air like the sweet smell of summer flowers in my garden. As I turn my face towards their squeals of delight I smile thinking, "Life is wonderful." But it wasn't always that way for me. In fact, it wasn't very long ago when I thought happiness might elude me forever.

Several years ago while working for a property management company, I was feeling overworked and underpaid. As the health insurance administrator I was in charge of the company's health insurance, 401K program, and all of the associated human resources responsibilities. I managed 300 employees and then my boss piled on more. He tripled my workload to 1,100 employees without any additional support or compensation! I worked a ton of hours and missed precious time with my friends and family—all for a whopping 25 thousand dollars a year!

When I found out that I was expecting my first child, I decided that something had to change. I wanted to be able to be home with my child, to raise and care for him. I dreaded the thought of dumping him off at day care, not being able to hold him when he was sick, laugh with him as he took his first step, or hear him say his first words. It was me I wanted him to call Mommy, not the day care attendant. My heart ached with the desire to be able to stay at home and be the mother I dreamed of being.

I knew there were other women who were working at home and had heard of home-based businesses before. In fact, my parents had been involved in network marketing when I was growing up. I decided I would build my own business from my home, while spending those precious moments with my newborn son.

I worked with three different companies in the next three years and experienced a moderate amount of success. Then disaster struck—my marriage was in turmoil and I was in the middle of a divorce. I knew I really had to get serious about getting my businesses off the ground as I needed now more than ever to be financially independent to meet the needs of my family and support my son, Zachary. My friends urged me to get a "real" job and place Zach in day care. "Everyone else does it, Shelleen. You can too," well-meaning friends would say. I couldn't do it. I just couldn't leave him all day long. I had been home with him long enough to know the true joy a mother feels in her heart while sharing those once in a lifetime experiences with her child.

I worked off my kitchen table and used a laundry basket for a filing cabinet. My dining room table housed my computer, fax machine, and two place mats—one for me and one for Zach. I reminded little Zachary everyday not to spill anything because I was afraid it might get into the wiring of my "office."

Zach and I lived off a $200 a month grocery budget that I eventually had to reduce to allow for marketing materials for the business. I thought if I ever saw another plate of macaroni and cheese or bowl of Top Ramen, I might die! But these times taught me many important lessons, none the least of which was that a person has to have a very compelling reason, sometimes known as the dream, for doing a business, or they probably won't ever reach the level of success they desire. When I talked to people about my company and what it could afford them, they knew I meant business. They heard the conviction in my voice, saw it in my eyes, and felt it from my heart. If people do not have a burning desire and a true conviction in what they are doing—despite their best intentions—they will fail. Others won't want to join in business with a person who does not believe in what they are doing and is not willing to sacrifice whatever it takes to make it to success.

For me, my why, my reason was rock solid. I wanted to be home with my son, Zachary. That is why I built my business so aggressively—so I didn't have to leave my little boy everyday in day care. Some people try to use their kids as the excuse for not building a business. Humbug! Your kids should be your *reason* for doing it! My son was my inspiration. I told myself that Zachary would always remember the example I set for him. I couldn't let him down.

As I continued to grow in my business, my business grew. I learned that this business of network marketing is not about selling products or services, but more importantly about relationships with people. As I built a rapport with my business partners, I increased my circle of influence and leadership. I learned about communication and the importance it plays in successful business relationships, as well as personal ones. Making new friends becomes easy when you are involved in something you truly believe in and want to share with others, for their benefit. Once I became involved in close relationships with others, my products practically sold themselves.

In the beginning I approached other mothers. I related with them, understood their needs and concerns. I wanted to help them. I even developed a script that I could teach new people so they could begin to see success of their own. It went something like this:

"Hi! My name is Shelleen. I was wondering if you might be able to help me? I represent a company that is looking for some additional home-based representatives in this area to help me launch a new product line. Do you know anyone that might be interested in earning a good part-time, or even full-time income while working from home?"

When I started looking for potential business leaders, I wanted to find people who needed a change in their lives. I was looking for people who were burnt out in their careers, people who were as frustrated as I was with corporate politics and not being paid what they were worth. I looked for moms who wanted to be home with their kids. I knew that to have a secure financial future for Zach and myself, I needed to develop a strong business base with committed team leaders. If I had to rely solely on consumer loyalty, my income would never be secured. Genuine residual income comes from finding other people who want to build a secure business income of their own. Residual income is like being paid for a song every time it plays on the radio. I wanted go-getters, people who would be leaders. You get what you ask for—so I asked for business builders—and that is what I got!

I spent lots of time working from home with a three year old as an assistant! There were days that this was my greatest challenge! I learned to be very creative to find a way to work and achieve my goals without sticking Zach in front of the electronic baby-sitter (the TV) all day. But it definitely was worth it and you really can develop a huge business in network marketing while raising a family. I did it—you can too!

It wasn't all peaches and cream, but I am a successful stay at home mom and I have managed to earn over a half a million dollars a year for the past three years in a row. And I even managed to find the man of my dreams, my husband John and a father for Zachary. Together we are building our dreams and sharing hope with others around the world.

Beverly Savula

Ask the average woman how she starts her workday, and you'll get an earful—the snarl of rush hour traffic, the stale coffee in the break room, the confines of that cubicle on the 44th floor. I begin my day on the lake. I work from home on the shores of a gorgeous, secluded lake that is nestled among hardwood forests and surrounded by the northern Georgia mountains. My husband, Dave, and I have secured a way of life that make most people's vacations look like work.

Dave and I love our life. He tells people, "If you could build a resort in miniature, this would be it." Every morning I watch the sun rise as I gaze out of the vast expanse of glass that forms the entire rear wall of our home, with its 22 vertical feet of breathtaking view opening onto the forest, the lake, and the lighted footpath leading down to our dock. That's where Dave trawls for big bass every morning.

Not far from the foot of the Appalachian Trail, Lake Lanier covers some 38,000 acres and is bounded by more than 500 miles of serpentine shoreline. When the U.S. Army Corps of Engineers dammed the Chattahoochee River and flooded the surrounding valley, hilltops became islands, slopes became shoreline, and the entire region transformed into some of the most spectacularly desirable real estate in the entire South. It's like we found a little piece of heaven.

Our first experience with network marketing was as a customer. Within a few years, we were attracted by the idea of a home-based business and became associates (distributors). I think one of the greatest benefits of network marketing is to have the flexibility to work from your home. Your home is certainly the most comfortable place from which you can operate a business, and it stands to reason that where you're most comfortable is where you're going to do your best work. Dave and I set about to create the ideal expression of that concept—and produced a masterpiece. The "workplace" doesn't get any more comfortable than our house. I tell you this not to brag, but to prove that you can climb out of the corporate office and create an environment that you look forward to working in everyday.

Growing up, I used to pore through magazines to look at all of these big, beautiful places; I knew that was the kind of place I wanted for our family. I found the house I'd dreamed of just a few minutes' boat ride from our vacation cottage. We moved in about a year ago. Today, what was once an occasional vacation escape is now our family's everyday life.

Entertaining guests is very important to Dave and me and to our business. We bring in a lot of our associates to spend the weekend with us to relax and have fun. We treat our visitors to lunchtime barbecues on the 60-foot deck in back. Afterwards, there's swimming, fishing, or water skiing. Typically, we end the day by taking visitors on a sunset cruise out to one of the little coves or islands for a light evening picnic.

Both of us agree that the key to making a guest feel comfortable lies in striking a balance between accessibility and privacy. The house's 6,000 square feet of living space allows visitors plenty of room to move about the house, while a separate guest apartment in the finished basement—with its own family room, pool room, bedroom, bath, and kitchenette—gives them a place of their own.

Hosts and their guests need to be able to spend time together, but they also need time and space apart from each other. Many of our guests come here on business and the privacy of the downstairs guest quarters gives them a place where they can get work done if they want to. For even more privacy, visitors can stay in our original vacation cottage across the water if they choose. It's a rustic, three-bedroom cabin with a family room, fireplace, and a screened porch overlooking the lake and a private dock. It's the kind of place that makes you feel as if you've stepped into a little mountain lodge in Canada.

Dave travels frequently, giving presentations around the country, while I hold down the fort, communicating with our associates, answering questions, and coordinating Dave's business travel. We're not in the business of impressing people. It's for us and for the people who come to stay with us.

Collette Van Russen

When someone shares an intimate, private, or personal experience with others they open up a part of themselves, revealing their feelings, their heart. When that happens, they put themselves at risk—to be judged, misunderstood, perhaps rejected, or even hurt again. I have a personal experience to share with you. I tell you these things not for your pity, or to paint a picture of despair, but for hope. It is my desire that in learning about challenges women might find strength and belief that they too can overcome whatever obstacles they currently face and create a wonderful life for themselves. My life was not always so wonderful. In fact, it was a desperately dark afternoon when my husband walked out on me after twenty-one years of marriage.

I had done what many other faithful and supportive wives do—work hard for many years to put my husband through college. It seemed worth it at the time—the opportunity to build a future together, create a family, and ultimately live the lives of our dreams with our children. After my husband completed his education and started in business, I was eventually able to stay home from work. And in the years to come, we had five wonderful children and I was a stay-at-home-mother. Life was not without challenges, however. Our last two children, both girls, were born with a critical disease, Cystic Fibrosis. Cystic Fibrosis is a serious, life-shortening genetic disorder. As of yet, there are no cures or controls, though there is encouraging progress in the war against this disease.

As a mother with two young children who were terminally ill, my life was difficult at best. My husband chose the week that our youngest child, Lexi, had been taken to the hospital and put on oxygen full time, to walk out on us. It was particularly tragic time for us all. Suddenly I found myself with five children to raise alone, two who were critically ill. I had been a stay-at-home mom for so many years. My career choices were extremely limited as I had no marketable skills, and with the five children at home, particularly with two who required medical assistance, it was impossible for me to work outside of my home. After a difficult legal battle and situations too horrible to describe, my husband ended up paying me $200 a month in child support. That is, $200 a month *total*—not $200 for each child!

Certainly these were low points in my life, but I had so much to concern myself with in caring for the children, I couldn't let these circumstances stop me, no matter how bleak my life seemed. I had to go on. After a while, Lexi's condition deteriorated and she underwent a pioneering procedure, a double lung transplant. This was in August of 1993, just a few weeks after her thirteenth birthday. The transplant went beautifully, but just nine days after surgery, Lexi's body rejected the new lungs. In an attempt to save her life, she was put into a medically induced coma and remained on life support in intensive care for nearly three months.

Lexi had lost so much weight during her ordeal and she was down to only 50 pounds. Her little body was devastated by the ordeal she had been through. My other daughter, Sharlie, had lung function tests that had reached the point that our doctors were discussing the possibility of putting her on the transplant list as well. I was desperate. During this time, my brother had been telling me about these great health products. He really believed they might help the girls. So when Lexi was finally discharged from the hospital, I started both the girls on these products.

I began to see a marked improvement in both Lexi and in Sharlie after about five months. When Lexi first came home from the hospital, she couldn't walk because of the drugs administered to her had left her legs and feet paralyzed. The nerves in Lexi's legs and feet started to regenerate. Lexi blossomed—she gained weight, her hair grew back shiny and healthy, and her coloring improved. The next 18 months were wonderful as we enjoyed life with each other. We lost Lexi to the disease at fourteen years old, but she lived out her dreams of being able to participate in everyday activities—skiing, running, dancing, riding a bike—the things she had never been able to do before became a reality for her. And although I know that Cystic Fibrosis is a degenerative disease, I can't deny that for the first time in her entire life, Sharlie seems to be holding her own.

Due to my divorce and Lexi's medical expenses, our family faced a very serious financial situation. I was looking into filling for bankruptcy when I began to consider doing Network Marketing as a business. I desperately needed income—and fast! Lexi's physical therapy expenses were massive and

I still had a large family to support. However badly I needed to make money, I needed to be at home with these children even more. Network Marketing seemed like the perfect business. That was about six years ago. Today I am the top income earner in my company and my business spans the globe. While may people dream of luxury cars and new homes, I dream of helping find a cure for Cystic Fibrosis and bringing hope to those around the world who might need help. Network Marketing has given me this opportunity—to be at home with my children, and to expand my business around the world, changing lives, one person at a time. It is a wonderful opportunity. I highly recommend it!

And while money isn't everything—it couldn't fix my broken marriage, or bring back my precious child—it can offer opportunities that will enrich one's life and give meaning and personal fulfillment to anyone with a dream and the determination to make their dreams come true. If a divorced mother of five can do it, you can do it too!

Carolyn Wightman

After I graduated from Stanford University, I went to work on Capitol Hill in Washington, and then to the Peace Corps. When I came back from the Peace Corps, I was at a turning point in my life. My first husband and I had been living in seclusion in the Polynesian islands. The only way you could get there was by flying to a grass landing strip, and only three planes flew in per week. We got from one island to another by boat.

We were literally still living out of boxes when I went up to spend Thanksgiving weekend with my parents and saw my mother using these new cleaning products. I was attracted to the environmental philosophy behind them and I asked her how I could get them. She'd bought them as a retail customer, and told me they were sold door-to-door.

I had a negative mental picture of door-to-door salespeople, so I called the company. They asked me for my zip code and put me in touch with someone who lived near me. I called and asked to buy the products, and she said, "Why don't you meet me over at my supervisor's place of business?" I agreed, and she gave me a Beverly Hills address. I showed up at a lovely home and found that these "door-to-door" salespeople happened to be professional stockbrokers.

This was my introduction to Network Marketing. It was the combination of the company's philosophy and the professionalism of the people I met that made me take a closer look at the business. I looked at my alternatives as a young woman in the early '70s, when there was virtually never equality in income for women. Even with my expensive college degree, I didn't have any marketable skills. I saw that if you produced, this business would pay, and that they didn't care who they made the check out to.

By the time my first marriage ended, I'd made the decision that I was never going to be financially dependent on anybody else—and in just a few years, having my own business made that possible.

Back then, network marketing was businesses completely different from anything people experience today. When people would ask us how we did the business, we really did not know. We just said, "You just talk to a lot of people. You just show them what you've got." We didn't have training available, such as cassettes, videos, direct mail, or even voice mail. We didn't have any of that technology that makes our business much easier today. Our only choice was to build the business by classic word-of-mouth.

Now, we've accelerated the ability to reach people, and that's allowed networkers to be much more effective much more quickly. That's great, and yet I don't think there is any substitute for the hands-on, high-touch part of this business.

In the beginning, I wasn't motivated so much by wealth as by poverty. I think it was sheer persistence and willingness to keep on doing something until I found what worked for me that made me successful. Now, I'm operating from a powerful vision—of where I see my company, where I see my personal business, where I see the industry, and where I see the whole world.

A wonderful Peace Corps expression is, "If you're not part of the solution, you're part of the problem." I'm devoted to being a big part of the solution—not just building a business and having a big income, but offering a service to people, helping to improve their education, giving people hope, making a difference in their lives. That has always been a powerful motivation for me.

After 28 years, I'm not bored! I am not doing the same thing I've done every year. Something is always a little bit different and I am always learning and adding to my skills. The best thing about Network Marketing for me is the freedom to rise above the need to focus on survival. By being able to accept those benefits, we can take the freedom of time and the potentials of financial independence, and use them for whatever contribution we want to make to ourselves, our families, our communities, and the world.

Betty Miles

As the wife of a Senator, I had to be cautious about making business choices. Whatever I did, ultimately reflected on my husband's political career. When I told him I wanted to get involved in network marketing, he said Ok—but with some exclusions. I had to agree not to contact any of our friends, family members, neighbors, church members, or anyone in politics or government! Well, that just about wrapped up most of my warm contacts, but I was already successful in my own insurance business and I had developed an extensive clientele over the years, so at least I had somewhere to start.

But the dream of success started for me many years before I ever heard about network marketing. All my life I have been chasing the American Dream—the dream of financial prosperity, personal happiness, and a safe, secure retirement. And as a young girl, growing up in Charleston, South Carolina, it seemed as certain as the coming dawn.

I grew up in an average, all-American town, part of an average, all-American family, believing, like most of the kids around me, that I was entitled to—and would one day be able to live—the "American Dream." I was the oldest of five children and we all felt the same way. Our parents taught us that success was ours to achieve. All it would take is hard work, a good education, a little tenacity, and we would be on our way.

But something has changed in the past 30 years. For millions of us, the dream of financial freedom and security is nothing more than that—just a dream.

My folks taught me that a key to success is to get a good education. My husband and I have five sons—four of them between the ages of 23 and 28. Between 1989 and 1995, each one of them graduated from a prominent university, all with good grades. And not one of them received a single corporate job offer. Not one! And for most college graduates today, they will change their careers at least 8 times during their lifetime. It is difficult to not feel sorry for these college graduates—and the parents who paid their bills. In our world today, a good education isn't the key to success anymore.

I was also taught that getting a good job would secure my financial security. Not so! Believe me, I have had some GREAT jobs in my lifetime. The problem word in that sentence is "had." The notion of "lifetime employment" is part of history, not the future. Jobs with large corporations are disappearing. I recently saw a chilling cartoon in the newspaper featuring a politician at an after-dinner speech announcing, "This administration has created 7.8 million jobs!" Behind him is the waiter, thinking, "Yeah, and I have THREE of them!"

The very definition of what makes a good job—a high salary, lots of benefits, job security, etc.—is beginning to change. More and more of us are making compromises, scaling back our own American dream. And if you are a baby boomer, you've got a lot to worry about. In 1996, the first "official" baby boomers began turning 50, and teenagers who grew up with long hair and the Beatles are moving on to Grecian Formula and Geritol. Many people have the idea that when you turn 65, you stop working, and you live the high life in Hilton Head or West Palm Beach. But those of us thinking about our financial futures know that it is not that simple. Nobody is going to hand us an easy retirement, and for many of us, the question is whether we will ever be able to afford to retire. For our financial futures to be secure, we must act now. If we rely on the government, we may be in serious trouble when we try to enjoy our "golden years."

The American dream was what I pursued, chased tirelessly, began to live, and then seemed to lose. That was the bad news. The good news is that through network marketing, you can find your path to financial freedom and personal wealth—not climbing that corporate ladder, but riding a new wave of business opportunity—network marketing!

After only four months of developing my own network marketing business, I exceeded my income from my insurance business—after 20 years of work! I had the opportunity to re-think my life, my future. Network marketing has given me the opportunity not only to believe in the American dream—but to live it everyday of my life. And you can too!

Jan Ruhe

Can you imagine your life today without access to cell-phones, answering machines, and computers? How about fax machines, e-mail or the Internet? And let's not leave out those other little necessities in life like self-cleaning ovens, self-sticking stamps, cassette and videotapes? Our day-to-day lives, much less our businesses, would be almost unmanageable without the conveniences we have grown accustomed to. Yet, I built my own network marketing business without any of these wonderful tools. At the time, we had nothing but raw enthusiasm and our big mouths!

It was twenty years ago when it all started. I had two little children: Sarah, a 4-year-old and Clayton, a 2-year-old and was expecting our third baby soon and I was very unhappy in my marriage due to some serious religious differences. I was looking for a home-based business—something that would allow me to make extra money and still manage to be at home with my kids. I found it in a most unusual way.

It was a quiet evening when I walked over to my girlfriend's house. I had been invited to Jane's house for a home party, a company that was selling products through small gatherings at people's homes. I went because I didn't want to disappoint Jane and I thought it would be fun to get away and visit some friends. The lady who was presenting these great products grabbed me from the beginning. As soon as she started demonstrating her products and explaining the benefits from using them, I was completely sold! "This is it!" I thought. "This is the answer to my situation. I can have my own Network Marketing business, create financial independence from my husband, and still be at home with my children. Perfect!" And so I got to work.

Meanwhile, the tragedy and abuse in my home life continued to escalate until it was unbearable and I filed for divorce. Unable to "change" me into the type of religious zealot he had become, my husband thought he would be better suited to raise our children. He filed for custody and began a brutal and costly custody battle that went to jury. It was awful, ugly, and long. I went into debt for over $100,000 before it was over. I was finally granted custody of my three kids.

Those days were bleak and hard. I kept borrowing more and more money to pay my divorce attorney and I didn't think it would ever end. I hired Child Psychologists for the children and counseling for myself. We all went to counseling every week for many months. I needed an income to support my family as I was not getting any child support during this long ordeal. I began to really work hard at my networking marketing business, even charging a wardrobe that would be suitable and representative of success. My good friend, Diane Folsom Miller heard of my dilemma and showed up with her Mercedes trunk full of clothes that she "just couldn't wear anymore." It was during my darkest times that others would reach out a helping hand to me and keep me from drowning.

With my new wardrobe and a new attitude of determination, I set out to make it big in network marketing. My new wardrobe certainly gave me the outside image that I wanted to convey, but inside I was a wreck! I was sort of like a duck on water, looking calm and controlled, but paddling like hell under the water. I sold my wedding gifts, all of my furniture, old clothes and every wall hanging that I had to make my house payment. I had no financial support other than the money I was earning in my network company, so I went to work and hit it hard—I had no other choice.

After all I had been through my self image was rather low. I knew that if I were to succeed, I needed to improve my image and quickly. But how, I wondered? I started at the library, checking out every book I could on self-image and attitude and began my own personal growth and development program. It was by far the smartest decision I ever made. I thank God today for books by Og Mandino, Robert Schuller, John Milton Fogg, and others. The books I read changed me and changed my life. My car became my classroom as I listened to tape after tape of successful, positive thinking men and women. I became a student of success. And it worked!

I started out scared half to death, not knowing how I would financially survive from week to week. As I thought about my future, I imagined that my possibilities for happiness or even a relationship with another man were next to none. I figured that no man on earth would want a woman who was broke, had an enormous debt, and three little kids to boot! Yet through all of the discouragement and despair, I kept on working toward a pin-prick of hope that I would someday have a comfortable life and happy family.

There were disappointments for sure along the way, however, there were angels that crossed my path as well. In the midst of great loss and disappointment came some of the most wonderful people I have ever known, people with whom I continue to strengthen my relationships with today. Great friends and mentors.

So today, after twenty years involved with network marketing I can tell you that life is great! It was all worth it! In my company today, I have the number one organization in the world. I work with some of the best women leaders in my company. I have written two books on network marketing, *Fire Up!* and *MLM Nuts $ Bolts* and co-authored *True Leadership.* I travel around the world, speaking and teaching others the way to success in network marketing. Ten years ago I married the most wonderful man in the world, Bill Ruhe, who ironically was one of the attorneys that helped me in my divorce case. My oldest daughter, Sarah, is a college graduate and went on to Semester at Sea. While she was in Africa, we went on a mother-daughter safari. My son, Clayton, is a student in Alabama where my daughter Ashley also attends the University.

Today I thank God for the critics, the tough times, the fear, the pain, the climb, and the journey. I said good-bye to the young woman I once was, sacred, depressed, and exhausted. Because of what I went through, I became the woman who I am today, a role model for other women, a "Hope Coach." The personal growth has been worth it all, but the financial rewards aren't bad either! In the mid-90's I became a U.S. Millionaire. The bills are paid, I am educating two children with no financial pressures, and I have great friends all across the world. I enjoy an incredible lifestyle, live in the home of my dreams, drive neat cars, but mostly, I am happy, contented, fulfilled, and thrilled! The future has never looked brighter and yours can too!

"Dream big. Your dreams are going to see you through," (lyrics from the *Fire Up* CD.) Believe in yourself, you don't have to fake it until you make it— you are already a wonderful human being. Expect miracles, don't be surprised by them. There truly are angels among us. Open your mind and heart to what you can be. Focus on your dreams for you really can have them. If a broke, divorced mother of three can do it—so can you!

Ponder what you read in this wonderful book and spread the word about this book to everyone you know. We believe in you, big time. Be the best you can be. Go for greatness. Dream big and fire up!

CONCLUSION

Like the other women in this book, I too have my own story. It started several years ago. It was the middle of a cold winter night as I quietly slipped out of bed. Not wanting to wake my sleeping husband, I gently closed the bedroom door behind me and softly tiptoed down the stairs to the kitchen. As I flipped the switch on the wall, I squinted through the bright glare of the kitchen lights. There, lying on my kitchen table was the reason for my sleepless night. Before me was my table, generally a joyful place of gathering for my family, but tonight it was barely visible under the stacks of bills, most of them overdue. I sat down before this overwhelming mound of debt, dropped my heavy head in my arms, and with tears streaming down my cheeks I thought, "How could this have happened to me?"

My husband and I had spent fifteen years together working hard to build our business, a recreational vehicle sales and service center, one of the largest in northern California. We had invested not only all of our money, time, and effort, but our hopes and dreams. Never having been afraid of hard work, we had given so much of our lives to the accomplishment of our goal, building a successful business that would provide us with a nice lifestyle, education for the kids, and a comfortable retirement.

Sitting alone on that cold winter night I began to face the reality of our situation. We had lost our business, our personal finances, even our family home, but even more important, our dreams. I felt a sense of desperation as I contemplated the options for my future. Little did I know the most difficult times were yet to come.

We struggled through many losses that year, but we learned important lessons of life and through the struggles we somehow became stronger, wiser.

As we pulled together we found a surprisingly unexpected excitement about the prospect of starting over. Yes, we had lost everything, but we had each other and we began to dream again. The losses that I had experienced the previous year would be infinitesimal in comparison to the loss I would soon experience and was not prepared for. That next year our precious daughter, Rebecca, was born. Two months later my husband died. A grieving widow, with four children to raise—one of them an infant—I was on the threshold of a journey I felt ill prepared to undertake.

As I evaluated my assets and liabilities, I knew that the small amount of social security money would not be enough. I mentally reviewed the jobs I could apply for—yet how could I leave my children now, in a time of such great need? I could not bear it. Then I remembered! I received a check every month from a small, part-time network marketing business that Cal and I had started sometime before. At the time we started this little business, we were both working 60+ hours a week at our dealership and yet even with such committed effort, we found our RV business seemed somewhat controlled by the economy, rising interest rates, or gas prices, rather than by the effort we put in. We were searching for additional ways to diversify our income, yet again and again we found that to develop additional income sources we needed either money or time to leverage. We did not have either.

It was during this time that we met a young couple who talked to us about network marketing. My first reaction was one of repugnance. My image of network marketing was that of door-to-door salespeople, home parties, or overbearing people in desperate circumstances that were relentless in their attempts to recruit others into some kind of illegal pyramid scheme. I learned through this successful young couple that my image was not only tarnished, it was wrong! We found that with a minimal investment, limited time, and very little risk, we could begin to build up a "nest egg." And we did.

Who could have imagined that it would be this part-time business that would help to sustain me during this devastating time? With limited help, I was able to stay at home with my children, and for several years the checks kept rolling in. It was hard to believe that we had invested millions of dollars and fifteen years of our life into our RV dealership and had nothing to show for it except a pile of bills and nasty calls from creditors. Yet after part-time effort in a small business, I received money every month for several years. I later married again. Together with my husband, Floris, we continue to build the network marketing business that has given me the freedom to make choices for myself and for my family. That is what this type of business can offer you—choices and freedom.

Network Marketing is a powerful method of doing business and is one of the best business opportunities on planet earth. You might suspect I am biased in my opinions, but after hearing part of my story you would expect me to be, wouldn't you? I have a great passion for helping women and I have written this book to help those of you who are searching for another way to develop financial independence and security, a better choice for your life and your future. With network marketing you can meet the financial needs of your family and live a lifestyle that others only dream about.

Dream Big does not promote any one particular network marketing business, rather it envelopes many to help enhance your understanding of multi-level marketing and teaches you how to start a business of your own, offering simple techniques and addressing head-on the issues and challenges women face today. You have read stories of other women—women just like you—who have made it to the top with their own network marketing businesses, you get a glimpse into the opportunities that lie ahead for you. Their success stories, combined with the know-how, the motivation, and the belief you will need, will enable you to reach the top in your own business. Dream big, dear reader! Your future is waiting.

—Cynthia Stewart-Copier

COMPENSATION PLANS

The compensation plan, or marketing plan, is the method by which a network marketing company divides commissions among its distributors. The compensation plan largely determines how much money you'll make, and how quickly, for a given amount of work. There are many ways to make a plan appear more lucrative on paper but in reality have it pay no more than any other plan. When choosing a company, pay close attention to the compensation plan.

Some distributors will claim their compensation plan is superior, using phrases such as Infinite depth! Massive spillover potential! 75 percent payout! More upfront money! Which do you choose? Who should you believe? What does it all mean? Choosing a compensation plan can be a daunting experience. Pay attention to details and listen closely, and you'll be able to decide which plan is best for you. If you are planning to develop a long-term network business, you won't be taken in by any "get rich quick" schemes.

Remember—if it sounds too good to be true, it probably is!

AUSTRALIAN.
Unlimited first-level width, infinite depth, linear commissions. This is usually referred to in the United States as a "two-up" plan. The commissions earned by the first two distributors on your first level are passed up to your sponsor. Likewise, the commission from the first two distributors recruited by your third recruit (and on) are passed up to you.

BINARY.
First-level width always limited to two, infinite depth, generational commissions. Sometimes referred to as a Binary Lateral. This plan determines commission payments based on the accumulated sales volume in each of the two legs (group volume under each of the two first-level distributors), usually on a weekly basis. Little consideration is given to actual levels, only the total volume in each leg. The more volume that occurs during the week, the higher the commission payment. Most binary plans pay based on the leg with the least volume, and the excess volume in the strong leg is either carried

over to the following week or "flushed" (forfeited). Binary plans generally allow multiple positions by a single distributor.

BREAKAWAY.

Unlimited first-level width, infinite depth, generational commissions.

An unlimited number of distributors can be placed on any level. However, when a certain stage of advancement has been reached, based on various qualifications usually involving monthly wholesale personal and group volumes, the distributor and his or her group (downline) "breaks away" from their upline sponsor. This process usually involves eliminating the breakaway group's volume as a source of volume in meeting the upline sponsor's monthly qualifications. Commissions (usually called overrides) can still be earned on this breakaway group once the upline sponsor has reached an equivalent or higher stage of advancement. A distributor can earn overrides on an unlimited number of legs or business groups.

Advantages of the Breakaway

Unlimited earning potential. Of all comp plans, the breakaway or stairstep provides the best opportunity for people to make it big. That's because the breakaway allows you to build a larger organization and to draw commissions from a greater number of levels than is possible with other types of plans.

Deeper pay range. Let's say your plan pays out commissions only to the sixth level. In a unilevel or matrix, that would mean you are forbidden to draw income from your seventh level or lower. But in a stairstep or breakaway, a distributor on your sixth level can break away, after which you collect an override or commission on that distributor's group volume. If that distributor has a six-level organiza-

tion, that means you're drawing commission from sales occurring on your twelfth level. Some breakaway plans let you draw income from as deep as twenty levels down, a depth unattainable in other types of plans.

Bigger downline. The breakaway offers unlimited width. You can recruit as many people as you like into your frontline, and they in turn can recruit as many as they like. The depth may be limited to six levels or so, but you can go as wide as you like, building a huge downline potentially tens of thousands strong.

Company stability. Companies with breakaway plans tend to have a higher survival rate than others, perhaps due to higher corporate profits. Most of the larger established companies, such as Amway, Shaklee, Nu Skin, Quorum, and others, use the breakaway. Approximately 90 percent of all MLM companies that are at least seven years old use the breakaway compensation plan.

Disadvantages of the Breakaway

Delayed gratification. Stairstep/breakaway plans tend to be the hardest to work. Most of the money comes from the "back end"—from the deeper levels that only become available to you after you've had a number of breakaways. That means you have to work long, hard, and successfully before you start seeing any significant money. Delayed gratification is the name of the game in breakaway plans.

Complexity. Breakaway plans tend to be complex and often difficult to explain to new recruits.

Top-heavy distribution of commissions. Some network marketers call the breakaway the "Republican" plan because it tends to channel more money to the top achievers and to the corporation. This is often perceived as a disadvantage. But is it? "Socialist" plans do indeed distribute commissions more evenly through the ranks, but they also have a statistically lower survival rate. The problem with socialism, in network marketing as in nations, is that an equal share of the pie isn't worth much if there's not enough pie to carve up.

For all of the above reasons, breakaway plans work best for serious, dedicated network marketers who are willing to sacrifice, work hard, and delay their gratification. For those who stay the course, this plan offers the best chance to build a substantial residual income.

DOWNLINE.

All of those distributors who are within your personal organization. They all branch off from you and are in depth from you.

GENERATIONAL COMMISSIONS.

Commissions are based on the group volume of the distributor on that level. For example, if a breakaway plan paid 5 percent on level six, this would include the entire group volume of the level six distributor, not just the volume that occurs on the sixth level. This group volume rarely, if ever, includes the volume of other breakaway groups.

LINEAR COMMISSIONS.

Commissions are based on the actual volume that occurs on that specific level.

MATRIX.

Limited first-level width (usually two to seven positions), finite depth (usually five to twelve levels), and linear commissions. Usually all volume that falls within the pay levels counts toward monthly qualifications. Matrix plans are described by the first-level width limit and the number of levels, for example, a 2x12 (no more than two distributors may be placed on your first level, and the plan pays twelve levels deep). All distributors enrolled beyond the first level width limit are placed in deeper levels. This is commonly referred to as "spillover."

Advantages of the Matrix

Spillover. Any recruits you bring into a matrix over and above the number allotted for your frontline will "spill over" into your lower levels. For example, if you have a 2x12 matrix and you recruit six people, four of them will spill over into your second level. Theoretically, this means that a person can just sit in a matrix organization and do nothing, waiting for some high achiever in his upline to build a downline for him through spillover.

Easy to manage. In breakaways and unilevel plans, you can theoretically have up to 100 or more people in your frontline, people you are directly responsible for training and sponsoring. In a matrix you only have to sponsor the two to three people in your frontline.

Simplicity. Matrix plans are very simple to explain to new recruits.

Disadvantages of the Matrix

Lazy downlines. Matrix plans tend to attract people who don't want to work; they want their upline to build an organization for them through spillover.

The leech effect. Matrix plans tend to be "socialist" in their distribution of commissions, rewarding top achievers less and nonachievers more. Top achievers get less return on their investment of time and energy because a greater share of commissions is sucked up, leeched, by downlines full of lazy spillover junkies.

Limits to growth. Matrix plans limit the size of your organization. In a 2x4 matrix, for example, you can never have more than 120 people in your downline. A stairstep/breakaway or unilevel plan allows you to have that many people in your frontline alone.

Government scrutiny. Because of the spillover effect, matrix plans can be "played" almost like a lottery. Government regulators tend to scrutinize these plans more than others because of their excessive reliance on luck.

STAIRSTEP.

Any type of plan that has multiple stages or ranks of advancement. For example: Bronze, Gold, and Diamond; or Member, Leader, and Director, and so on. Although any of these plan types can be designated a stairstep, this term rarely precedes any type of plan other than breakaway. All breakaways are "stairstep" breakaways.

UNILEVEL.

Unlimited first-level width, finite depth (usually five to nine levels), linear commissions. No breakaway occurs and an unlimited number of distributors can be placed on any level. This plan usually pays out on a small number of levels as opposed to the breakaway plan. The term was originally used to describe any type of plan that had only one (uni-) stage (level) of advancement (compared with a stairstep of ranks that could be achieved). Today it is commonly used to describe any nonmatrix, nonbreakaway type of plan regardless of the number of ranks or stages of advancement.

Advantages of the Unilevel

Simplicity. Because it lacks breakaways, the unilevel is very simple to explain to new recruits.

Unlimited width. As in stairstep/breakaway plans, the unilevel allows you to recruit an unlimited number of people into your frontline.

Spillover. Unilevel plans often stack their highest commission percentages on the third level. For example, the first two levels may pay out 1 percent each and the third level 50 percent. Distributors will thus put as many new recruits as possible on their third level. Since every distributor's third level corresponds to someone else's first level, that means that each distributor with three or more levels in his or her organization is helping to build someone else's frontline.

Easy qualifications. Because there are no breakaways and no concept of encumbered and unencumbered volume in a unilevel plan, all the sales volume of your organization counts toward your monthly quotas all the time, no matter what. You don't lose volume every time someone breaks away. You don't have to rush madly each month to make up for lost volume when someone breaks away, as you so often do in breakaway plans.

Disadvantages of the Unilevel

Limits to growth. Because it lacks breakaways, the unilevel only pays out on a small number of levels. Theoretically, you can make up for this by recruiting wide—putting a huge number of people into your frontline. But although unilevel plans place no limits on the number of people you can personally sponsor, there are physical limits to the number you can sponsor effectively. All other factors being equal, a unilevel organization will tend to be smaller than a stairstep/breakaway organization.

Laziness. Because unilevel plans limit growth, they tend to attract a less ambitious breed of distributor, the type more interested in being a wholesale buyer than in building a large downline.

upline. The direct line of distributors who are above you. For example, your sponsor and their sponsor and so on.

NETWORK MARKETING TERMS

Achievement Level. A position in a network marketing organization that a distributor obtains usually by purchasing a certain amount of product at wholesale in a given month. The more products you purchase, the higher your position, the deeper your discounts for purchasing product at wholesale. In a stair step/breakaway plan, achievement levels are also called stair steps.

Back end. The later, more advanced stages that a distributor reaches after progressing through a compensation plan. For example, you might say that a breakaway plan pays more on the back end because you get higher commissions after you break away. In other plans, back end corresponds to the lower or deeper levels of a comp plan, as when a plan pays 5 percent on the first level, but 20 percent on the third level, thus paying a larger percentage on the back end.

Benefits. Any form of payment or compensation a distributor derives from working a network marketing business. Can include bonuses, overrides, retail and wholesale commissions, or special perks and premiums.

Breakaway. A distributor who has "broken away" from his sponsor's personal group by meeting certain monthly volume qualifications. Usually, the breakaway's monthly volume no longer counts as part of the monthly group volume of the breakaway's sponsor. However, the sponsor will continue collecting a royalty or override from the breakaway, which is a small percentage of that breakaway's organizational volume.

Bonus. Money that a distributor receives as a commission for volume he or she has created in personal product purchases, retail sales, or wholesale purchasing by downline distributors.

Counseling. A time distributors spend with their active upline discussing personal challenges, business successes and organizational planning.

Crossline. This term refers to distributors who are not in your group or in your direct upline/downline line of sponsorship. For example, when you personally sponsor two distributors, they are "crossline" from each other.

Crosslining. "Crossline" distributors sometimes seek or attempt to acquire business-building information from each other. This practice can be detrimental and in some companies, is forbidden.

Depth. Anyone in your group is considered 'downline" or in "depth." Building depth is the key to longevity in most network marketing plans. The process by which you assist those whom you have sponsored to sponsor others is referred to as "building depth." When you sponsor someone, they are "one is depth" from you, and your organization is one level "deep." As you help personally sponsored distributors get someone sponsored, the newest person is "two deep" from you or "two in depth.

Distributor. An independent sales representative of a network marketing company.

Downline. All the distributors below you in the chain of recruitment and sponsorship of a given network marketing company—that is, the people recruited by your recruits, and so on. Refer to depth.

Dream. In the context of building your network marketing business, the "dream" refers to your vision of the future for yourself and those you love. It is sometimes referred to as the why. What are your hopes and aspirations for the years to come? In Chapter Four you are given a roadmap for defining, clarifying and reaching your goals. Your dreams give you the energy and the drive to reach your goals.

Edification. Network marketing is build upon relationships, which are founded on trust and mutual respect with both the upline and downline distributor. The most effective way to bring out the best in people is to concentrate and build on their strengths as opposed to pointing toward weaknesses. When you identify the positive qualities in your upline or downline associates, you nurture them through "edification" and help them become stronger.

Follow Through. Refers to a meeting or appointment that is arranged after you have shared your particular marketing plan with the new prospect. Sometimes is referred to as the "second look".

Frontline. Those distributors on the first level beneath you, whom you directly sponsor.

Function. Anytime a group of distributors gets together for training and motivation, it may be called a function.

Generation. All the distributors in a particular let or organization; it is headed by a distributor who has broken away or achieved some other set qualification.

Generational Income. An income that is paid from generation to generation, or from the income creating distributor to their children.

Ground Floor. The start-up phase of a network marketing company. Ground-floor opportunities care considered attractive because they give distributors a chance to position themselves high up in the company's chain of sponsorship before the company reaches the momentum phase. However, the vast majority of ground-floor opportunities never reach momentum and do not survive.

Infinite Depth. Infinite depth is receiving commissions from an infinite number of levels, generally decreasing in percentage of profit with each level down.

Leg. The organization of one distributor in your organization, especially one in your frontline. For example, if you sponsor Joe, everyone from Joe down would be considered as "Joe's leg."

Level. The measure of how far down a distributor is in an organization in relation to another distributor. For instance, if Distributor A recruits Distributor B, that means Distributor B is in Distributor A's first level. If Distributor B then recruits Distributor C, that means Distributor C is in Distributor B's first level but in distributor A;s second level. Levels re critical in understanding compensation plans because all plans specify a certain number of levels on which they "pay out." A six-level plan, for example, pays a commission only on those distributors who are six levels or less below you.

Matrix. A type of compensation plan that sets a limit on the number of people you can recruit not your frontline. (See Compensation Plans.)

MLM/Multilevel marketing. An older term for "network marketing." Many network marketers consider the terms "MLM" and Multilevel Marketing" to be obsolete.

Momentum. The most rapid growth phase of a network marketing company. In momentum, sales and recruitment takes of exponentially.

Network Marketing. Any form of selling that allows independent distributors to recruit other independent distributors and to draw a commission from the sales of those recruits.

One-on-one. Rather than inviting a prospect to join a group of people to present the marketing plan or the opportunity, a distributor may decide to meet with a prospect for a more informal meeting. Most distributors usually sign up as a result of this type of meeting.

Opportunity. When a distributor "sells the opportunity" rather than the product, that means he or she is recruiting new distributors, or selling the idea of the business, rather than retailing a product.

Opportunity Meeting. A meeting held by distributors to present and sell the opportunity to potential recruits.

Organization. Distributors in your downline who fall within your pay range—that is who fall within those levels from which your compensation plan allows you to draw commissions.

Overrides. The small percentage a distributor receives from the monthly group volume of his or her breakaway legs. Also known as royalty.

Payout. The total percentage of revenue a network marketing company "pays out" to its distributors in commissions, overrides, and bonuses. Theoretically, the payout corresponds to the percentage of profit each distributor receives from his or her network marketing business. Percentage of payout if often used as a selling point for recruits, as in, "Company X has an 85% payout!" In practice, it would be hard for any company to pay out more than about 60% without cutting its profit margins dangerously thin. Most companies that offer higher percentages usually have hidden catches or qualifiers that make it extremely difficult for any distributor to achieve the full payout. This is frustrating for distributors, but necessary for company survival.

Personal Group. Distributors in your downline organization who have not yet broken away. Or your downline group.

Plug In. The term "plug in" refers to when distributor taps into a proven empowerment process of books, tapes, meetings, and especially their upline leader.

Prospect. A person you are trying to recruit into your downline.

Qualify. As in to "qualify a prospect", means to ask questions to determine whether or not a prospect is looking for a better lifestyle and a way to make more money. This process of qualifying can save a distributor time and energy.

Qualify. As in to "qualify for a particular commission", means to reach a certain level of productivity, whether in volume of product, or overall sponsoring.

Qualifications. Achievement quotas that distributors must obtain to qualify for higher commission levels. Qualifications can take the form of monthly group or personal volume quotas or even recruiting quotas, such as recruiting a certain number of people into your frontline.

Recruiting. The act of signing up, or registering people to join your business.

Renewal Fee. A small yearly membership fee that some companies require from their distributors. Network marketing companies are forbidden by law from making a profit from "selling" distributorships. But small annual fees are acceptable for clearing out inactive distributors and keeping records of active ones.

Retail Profit. Money earned from selling product directly to customers.

Royalty. Another term for overrides.

Saturation. An imaginary point at which a network marketing company exhausts the market for potential recruits and growth stops. True saturation is virtually impossible to achieve, and is usually just a pejorative term used by competitors to discourage potential recruits from joining a competing company, as in, "Don't join company X. It's already saturated!"

Sponsor. A person who recruits another person into a network marketing company, then acts as the mentor to that recruit, training him or her to sell, recruit, sponsor, and train others to dot he same. Can also be used as a verb, as in "to sponsor" someone.

Stairstep. See Commission Plans.

Stockpiling. The practice of purchasing and storing more product inventory than a distributor is realistically capable of selling. Stockpiling is the natural result of front-loading.

System. This terms refers to an organized, time-tested and proven success program of books, tapes, and training meetings which have been carefully designed to help distributors become informed and inspired and reach the upper levels of success.

Three-Way Call. A recruiting and training strategy whereby a new, inexperienced distributor invites a prospect to participate in a phone call with the distributor and his or her sponsor. The inexperienced recruiter listens quietly and learns while the sponsor gives the opportunity to the prospect.

Upline. People who are above you in the line of sponsorship. For example, your sponsor's sponsor and their sponsor, and so on.

Unilevel. See Compensation Plans.

Wholesale Buyer. A person who signs up as a distributor for the sole purpose of personally consuming product at the wholesale price and who does not sell the product to others. Wholesale buyers are a boon to any downline because they form a committed and dependable customer base.

Width. The number of people a distributor is allowed to recruit into his or her frontline. Stairstep/breakaway and unilevel plans generally allow infinite width. Matrix plans limit width, usually to two or three people.

INDEX